50 Ways to Mutual Fund Profits

ALAN LAVINE

IRWIN
Professional Publishing
Chicago • London • Singapore

Irwin Professional Book Team

Publisher: *Wayne McGuirt*
Executive editor: *Kevin Commins*
Marketing manager: *Tiffany Chenevert Dykes*
Managing editor: *Kevin Thornton*
Project editor: *Lynne Basler*
Production supervisor: *Diana L. Treadway/Carol Klein*
Assistant manager, desktop services: *Jon Christopher*
Compositor: *The Publishing Services Group*
Typeface: *10/13 Palatino*
Printer: *Quebecor Printing/Book Press*

Times Mirror
Higher Education Group

Library of Congress Cataloging-in-Publication Data

Lavine, Alan.,
    50 Ways to mutual fund profits / Alan Lavine.
       p.   cm.
    Includes index.
    ISBN 1-55738-886-5
    1. Mutual funds.   I. Title.
    HG4530.L357   1996
    332.63'27—dc20   95–36330

To Ruthie, my terrific sister

Foreword

At last there is an easy-to-read book that shows people how to manage their mutual fund investments. Whether you are investing in mutual funds through your IRA, company pension plan, a variable annuity life insurance policy, or in a taxable account, Alan Lavine's *50 Ways to Mutual Fund Profits* shows you a multitude of ways to manage your hard-earned money.

Over the last decade, money has poured into mutual funds. Unfortunately, no one really tells you what to do once you own the funds. This book shows safety-minded investors how to maximize the return on their investment without the risk of losing their life savings. Families can learn about tried-and-true ways to build wealth through the use of dollar cost averaging, diversification, and portfolio rebalancing. There are strategies that show you how to invest, when to buy, and when to sell. This book also highlights some little-known tactics that are used by conservative pension fund portfolio managers. You can use them just one-half hour a year to boost the return on your investments and gradually build your wealth.

Bond fund investors lost their shirts in 1994 when interest rates rose over 2 percent and bond prices plunged. Some bond funds lost more than 10 percent. But had you used certain low-risk bond fund investment strategies discussed in this book, you most likely would have avoided large losses and come out smelling like a rose.

There are many ways to invest in mutual funds. Venturesome and aggressive investors comfortable with risk can read about mutual fund trend-following and fund-switching strategies. Market timing certainly isn't for all people. But those who like to switch between stock funds and money funds as investment conditions change will learn several ways to go about it.

There also are important sections on how to manage your money when you retire. Alan Lavine's book shows you how to make systematic withdrawals from your mutual fund and retirement savings accounts. You learn the best ways to set up a portfolio of mutual funds to give you the most income with the least risk during your golden years.

You'll also learn how to use variable, fixed and immediate annuities and how to protect your money from the ravages of inflation and rising interest rates.

50 Ways to Mutual Fund Profits looks at managing your variable annuities and variable life insurance polices. Few books cover this subject. Policyholders will learn how reducing insurance expenses and charges can help boost returns over the years. They will learn how they can borrow against the cash value of their life insurance if they need to and how to take money out of an annuity or insurance policy during retirement years.

Alan Lavine's book is a shining light that will help you invest wisely. It should be enjoyed for it will help you build your wealth to reach your financial goals. This book belongs on everyone's bookshelf.

John Wasik
Senior Editor, *Consumer Digest*
Author of *The Investment Club Book*

Acknowledgments

The author would like to thank Kevin Commins, Irwin book editor, for making this book possible. Special thanks to Dr. Avner Arbel, finance professor at Cornell University and Charles DeRose, host of the syndicated radio financial talk show *Your Financial Advisor,* for their encouragement. Thanks to my wonderful wife, Gail Liberman, editor of Bank Rate Monitor, for reviewing and commenting on the manuscript. You have the patience of a saint.

I would also like to thank my editors: Mary Hellen Gelespie, business editor, *Boston Herald;* Robert Powell, editor-in-chief, *Variable Annuity Market News;* Susan Postelwaite, managing editor, *Miami Daily Business Review;* Evan Simonoff, editor, *Financial Planning;* Tom Sidell, managing editor, *Your Money;* John Wasik, senior editor, *Consumer's Digest;* and Peter Maloney, editor, *Nest Egg.*

I also would like to extend special thanks to all those individuals and investment companies who contributed their investment strategy research for this book.

Contents

Part I: Back to Basics

Part II: Selecting Funds that Are Right for You

Part III: Mutual Fund Investment Strategies

Contents

PART I

Back to Basics

Chapter 1
Introduction

As of this writing (mid-1995), there were more than 70 million mutual fund shareholder accounts on record in this country, with total assets of more than $2 trillion. Over the last four years, net sales of mutual funds totaled over $750 billion. One of four families invests in mutual funds, according to the Investment Company Institute (ICI), a Washington, D.C. trade organization. Most households own two funds—a stock fund and a bond or money market fund. The average mutual fund investor is a 45 year-old male or female who earns $45,000 to $53,000 a year, according to ICI data. The average household has $43,000 invested in mutual funds. That amount is about 38 percent of the average household's total of $113,000 invested financial assets. Most people use mutual funds as a way to save for retirement, the ICI also reports. Retirement dollars accounted for 21 percent of all mutual fund assets. Mutual funds are $211 billion of the $725 billion IRA market, or 29 percent of total IRA assets. Total net mutual fund assets held in pension and profit sharing accounts had increased to $75 billion by year-end 1993 from $28 billion in 1987. *Money* magazine reported that 35 percent of the publication's readers own at least one long-term equity fund as part of their company's 401(k) plan.

Why Invest in Mutual Funds?

Many of us have some understanding about the ins and outs of mutual fund investing. Nevertheless, the fundamentals bear repeating. On the positive side, mutual funds are:

- Safe: investment companies are highly regulated by federal and state governments.
- Liquid: the money is never more than a telephone call away from your checking account. The investments are never subject to substantial interest penalties, compared with bank CDs.
- Professionally managed.
- High-yielding: you typically can earn more than bank CDs and money market accounts.
- Low cost: you can invest for as little as $200 to $1,000 and make subsequent investments of just $50.

Many funds that don't carry up-front sales charges or loads are called "no-load" mutual funds.

If you invest in a fund through a stockbroker or financial planner, you typically will pay a commission, also known as a "load." Front-end loads can range from as little as 2 percent to as much as 8.5 percent. Some funds have back-end sales charges that decline annually from 6 percent to 1 percent, based on when shares are redeemed. Other funds charge a flat 1 percent annual fee, but carry no front- or back-end charge.

Besides the "loads," both load and no-load funds also charge portfolio mangement fees which run .5 percent or less. Some funds may also charge you 12b-1, or sales distribution fees, that range from .25 percent to 1 percent annually.

Today there are more than 6,000 mutual funds on the market—more funds than there are stocks traded on the New York Stock Exchange. The reasons for this growth are:

- Investors are comfortable investing in professionally managed mutual funds.
- Banks and insurance companies have jumped on the mutual fund bandwagon. As of this writing there were more than 1,000 bank mutual funds available. Because you can invest in stock, bond and money funds at your local bank, traditional bank savers have joined the move toward mutual funds.

- In addition, over the past three years, $40 billion to $60 billion annually has been flowing into insurance company variable annuities and life insurance.

A variable annuity is an insurance contract that lets you invest in stock and bond mutual funds. The insurance part of the annuity is the death benefit guarantee. If you die, you are guaranteed that your beneficiaries receive the money you contributed or the current value of the annuity, whichever is greater. These variable annuity death benefit guarantees have added appeal to risk-averse investors.

Variable annuities also are popular because of the tax breaks. With annuities, your money grows tax-deferred until withdrawn. That makes them hot products. Who wants to pay higher taxes? With a variable annuity, your money can grow tax-free until age 85, the age at which most insurance companies require withdrawals.

Adding to the attractiveness of mutual funds is the fact that many brokerage firms have reduced their front-end loads. Some charge as little as 4.5 percent. Brokerage firms also have "wrap accounts" in which a stockholder hires a professional to mange your individual stock and bond portfolio or fund investments. You pay a 2 percent annual fee for the manager, but no load for the fund.

Among the latest developments are no transaction fee mutual fund accounts. You can consolidate all of your no-load funds in one account. Charles Schwab, the San Francisco-based discount brokerage firm, pioneered the concept of No Transaction Fee (NTF) mutual fund accounts a couple of years ago. Now others have jumped on the bandwagon. Jack White & Company and Fidelity Investment's discount brokerage firm have NTF programs.

There are a number of advantages with NTF accounts:

- You can invest in funds with a single phone call.

- You get one monthly statement.

- Liquidity: if you need cash, you can write a check on your mutual fund.

- Venturesome investors can buy funds on margin.

- You can have your dividends and capital gains automatically reinvested.

- Your trades are automatically swept into your money fund.

- You have access to a representative 24 hours a day.

Manage Your Mutual Funds like a Pro

Despite the popularity of mutual funds, there is nowhere for an investor to learn how and when to choose from among the 6,000 mutual funds available, short of paying a stockbroker or financial planner. The cost can be as much as 1 percent of the investment!

If you are among the increasing number of mutual fund investors, you probably lack expertise, time and money, and desperately need mutual fund management advice from someone you can trust.

You need to know what to do once money is invested, how to reduce the risk of losses, when to buy and when to sell, how to speculate, how to minimize taxes, how to avoid excessive charges and what to do if the stock or bond market tumbles.

This book explains in plain English mutual fund investment strategies you can use to protect what you have and to see your profits rise. Consider this a guide book of mutual fund money management methods.

It is a compendium of many different easy-to-understand investment tactics. You can thumb through and read about a specific strategy. You can review an analysis of each tactic, its strengths and weaknesses, and get a feel for the risks and rewards you might experience if you applied the method to the real world.

The book presents a wide array of investment strategies and suggests ways to select the best ones that meet your needs.

Conservative investors will learn ways to boost returns and reduce risk through such strategies as dollar cost averaging, value averaging, constant dollar, constant ratio and portfolio rebalancing methods of managing mutual fund money. These are easy-to-use methods that can be used as infrequently as once a year.

More sophisticated investors can use one of the market timing strategies highlighted here to profit from short or longer-term trends in the stock and bond markets. Using moving averages on investment cycles to switch between stock funds and money funds can be rewarding. You can learn how to bottom fish for underperforming stock funds that may bounce back with a vengeance. Or how to spot fund managers who have hot hands.

Even if you have an IRA, 401(k), variable life insurance policy, or variable annuity, you can apply pension fund investment strategies to enhance the return on your investments. Since your money is invested in one of these tax-sheltered accounts, you won't pay taxes on your mutual fund trades. Over the long haul that may save you money, provided that you've gained from investing.

Each chapter is a two-to-four page explanation of a specific mutual fund investment strategy. You will learn how each tactic works and how to apply the information to manage your investments. Learn the advantages and disadvantages of each investment approach, as well as the criteria for selecting each kind of strategy to fit a specific investment objective. Sources of information on each strategy also are included in the chapter, as well as an example of how the strategy performed over the short and long-term.

Even if you don't necessarily apply a strategy from this book directly, you will learn research and market trends that are sure to assist you in the course of any investment tactic you undertake.

Go No-Load and Save

Unfortunately the majority of mutual fund investors pay dearly for their investments. Sixty percent of all mutual fund investors pay commissions to stockbrokers, financial planners or other registered representatives for the privilege of investing in mutual funds. Only 40 percent of all fund investors buy no-loads.

Paying a sales charge to buy a fund costs us dearly. The average load fund hits you with a 5 percent sales charge. In 1992, net mutual fund sales totaled $200 billion. That means brokers, financial planners and others collected a hefty $10 billion in commissions. If we had invested that $10 billion we paid stockbrokers at a 10 percent annual rate of growth, we would be $20 billion dollars richer by the turn of the decade.

Personal hand-holding by a stockbroker isn't worth the fat commissions you pay. I believe investing in no-load mutual funds, funds that don't charge commissions or hidden fees, are the investments for the 1990s. That's why millions of savvy investors put their savings in no-load funds.

Professional Management

Today, there are more than 6,000 mutual funds on the market with over $2 trillion in assets. The reasons why many invest are simple. You get professional management. You get diversification. You don't need much money to invest. You have liquidity. You can diversify your investments. They are low cost. You can set up automatic investment plans.

Diversification

When you invest in a mutual fund, you invest in a portfolio of securities—either stocks, bonds or both. The pool of securities is managed by a professional money manager who has a staff of research analysts working for him or her. Most mutual fund portfolios own at least 25 to 50 different securities. By federal law, no more than 5 percent of fund assets can be invested in any one issuer or 20 percent invested in any one industry (unless you invest in a fund that specializes in a specific sector of the economy).

Diversification reduces the risk that you'll lose money if one or two stocks in the portfolio plunge in price. You own 20 or 30 other stocks that may be up in price. So gains in the rest of your portfolio will offset the declines in just a couple of stocks.

Here is how diversification reduces what they call in the halls of finance nonmarket risk, or the risk that you will lose money due to bad news about a company.

Say you are a shareholder in the Go For Growth Stock Fund. The fund, with assets of $10 million, has a 2 percent stake in a hypothetical stock, Front Page Inc. The fund also invests in 100 other issuers because the portfolio manager prefers to be well diversified.

A fire breaks out at Front Page's production facility. Losses are estimated in the millions, and the stock's price drops from $10 per share to $8 per share. That day, the fund's position in Front Page Inc. dropped 20 percent. What was worth $200,000 yesterday is now $160,000 today.

An investor who just owned Front Page would be pretty upset with such a loss. I would be. Who would want to lose 20 percent of his money in one day? Here's how diversification saves the day!

The Go For Growth Stock Fund owns 99 other stocks in a wide variety of industries. The day the Front Page's stock fell, the overall stock market rallied. The Dow and S&P 500 gained 1 percent in value that day. Since our stock fund's holdings are highly correlated with the performance of the overall market, and our portfolio manager is a pretty good stock picker, the value of the fund gained a total 1.2 percent the same day that Front Page's stock nosedived.

The value of the fund increased to $10,120,000, less a $40,000 decline in one stock, resulting in a net gain in the portfolio of $10,080,000.

Even though we took a big hit on one stock, our fund gained .8 percent for the day. We didn't outperform the market averages, but diversification saved the day!

A Family of Funds through Thick and Thin

Most mutual funds are also part of a mutual fund family. You can invest in the U.S. and overseas stock or bond funds, as well as different kinds of bond funds. So you can get another layer of diversification. Split up the old investment pie among U.S. and international stock funds, U.S. and international bond funds and money funds and you also reduce your risks of losing money.

If your U.S. stock fund is down, there's a good chance your overseas fund may be up, especially today.

Lower Your Risk

If you own a bond fund or a money fund along with stock funds, you reduce the volatility of your investment. Stocks, bonds and cash don't perform in tandem. So you've got yet another extra layer of diversification.

Remember the stock market crash in October of 1987? I'll never forget it. The market was up substantially. Some hot growth stock funds were up 50 percent and the year wasn't half over.

The average stock fund lost 20.4 percent in the last quarter of 1987. But world bond funds and U.S bond funds gained 10.8 percent and 3.3 percent respectively. Most investors took a hit. Fortunately, those who were well-diversified both at home and overseas lost half as much as the average stock fund.

Liquidity

You've also got lots of liquidity when you invest in mutual funds. You can redeem shares over the phone by calling the fund's toll-free number. You also may switch among the stable of funds as your needs and investment conditions change.

Automatic Investing

You can arrange to make automatic investments in your funds. Your fund can electronically withdraw money from your checking account.

You have a wide variety of funds to pick from based on your tolerance for risk. Read on.

What I Like Best about Mutual Funds: Good Performance

Invest for the long term. Even though stock prices have fluctuated over past decades, equities have a great track record. Of course, we can improve on the buy and hold performance by picking the best-managed mutual funds. Over the past six decades, financial assets have experienced the largest net gains. The S&P 500 stock index earned an annually compounded 10 percent rate of return, according to data published by Ibbotson Associates, Chicago.

Long-term corporate bonds averaged 4.8 percent, long-term government bonds averaged 4.1 percent and U.S. Treasury bills averaged 3.4 percent.

The mutual fund track record is something to crow about. According to Lipper Analytical Services, Summit, NJ, the average stock fund gained 11.6 percent annually over the past 30 years ending in June 1993. By contrast, the S&P 500 gained 10.6 percent during the same period.

At 11.6 percent, your money doubles in a little over 6 years.

Past performance is no indication of future results. But at least we know what to expect from the stock market: short-term volatility in return for long-term growth. If we can improve on an already good formula, we'll all be better off.

They're Cheap Too

Mutual funds also are a low-cost way to invest in the financial markets. You can invest for as little as $200 to $1,000 and make subsequent investments of just $50 into your favorite mutual fund. Many funds don't carry upfront sales charges or loads. If you do pay a load, it can range from as little as 2 percent to as much as 8.5 percent. The management fees for running the portfolio are usually .5 percent or less, depending on the total assets in the fund. There are also several fund groups that have deferred sales charges ranging from 6 percent to 1 percent, depending on when shares are redeemed. Some funds may also charge you 12b-1, or sales distribution fees, that range from .25 percent to 1 percent annually. (See Exhibit 1–1.)

Exhibit 1–1

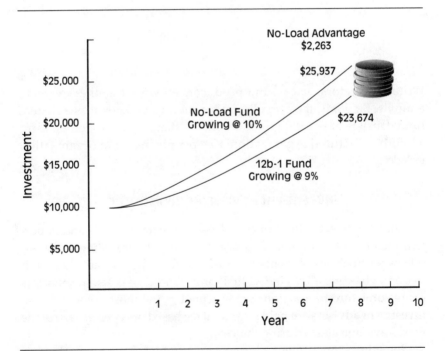

Source: American Association of Individual Investors

Chapter 2

How Mutual Funds Are Organized

Writers, directors, actors, and producers all work together to create a movie. Similarly, the carefully crafted production known as a mutual fund consists of several key components that, woven together, form a tightly structured organization. Key people in a fund organization include:

Investment Adviser/Administrator

For shareholders, the investment adviser is the most visible and important member of a mutual fund organization. The investment adviser selects portfolio investments according to the fund's established policies and objectives. This individual (or individuals) is also responsible for making sure transactions are executed at the most favorable cost. Investment advisers are paid an annual fee based on a percentage of the fund's average assets during the year.

Sometimes, investment advisers also administer the fund. This role may include duties such as providing accounting services, overseeing internal procedures and controls, and preparing and filing SEC, tax, shareholder, and other relevant reports.

Directors/Trustees

Fund directors and trustees serve as watchdogs for shareholders by monitoring the adviser and other key individuals and organizations closely affiliated with the fund. To help ensure objectivity, a certain percentage of the board of directors must be entirely independent of the fund's investment adviser or principal underwriter.

Directors and trustees are supposed to view their roles as if they were overseeing their own business. They keep tabs on investment performance, as well as on investment advisers and others who work for the fund.

Shareholders

The rights of mutual fund shareholders are similar to shareholders of any company. All mutual fund shares are voting stock. Shareholders may elect individuals to the board of directors, ratify the board's choice of independent public accountant at an annual meeting, and have a role in approving investment advisory contracts.

The fund is legally required to send shareholders relevant literature, including proxy materials and annual reports.

The Great Mutual Fund Bazaar: How Shares Are Bought and Sold

Most people are familiar with frenetic scenes of mayhem on the floors of the New York Stock Exchange and other major trading arenas. Although mutual funds do not have the equivalent of a fast-paced centralized trading floor, the process of buying and selling shares can be equally exciting.

Funds typically distribute shares through a principal underwriter. Some underwriters employ their own sales forces, while others distribute shares through a network of broker-dealers. In either case, a sales charge, typically ranging from 3.0 percent to 8.5 percent, usually is included in the offering price. Sometimes, the sales force is paid through a back-ended exit fee that kicks in if an investor sells shares before a specified period of time.

Investors also may purchase fund shares from the underwriter or fund with little or no sales charge. These "no-load" funds may incur heavy advertising expenses, which they hope to make up through advisory fees. Some funds allocate a small portion of their assets toward advertising and distribution expenses.

Mutual fund ads are closely regulated by the SEC. So-called "tombstone ads" may contain limited information about the fund. "Omitting prospectuses" ads can contain more information, as long as inquiries are followed up by prospectus. But shareholders cannot buy a mutual fund through an ad. They must read the prospectus first. In addition, all sales literature must be approved by the National Association of Securities Dealers (NASD) before it can be distributed to shareholders.

Upon request, mutual funds legally are required to redeem outstanding shares at their net asset value, a figure derived by dividing the fund's total net assets by the number of shares outstanding.

Custodians and Transfer Agents

The millions of mutual fund transactions executed each year require a gargantuan behind-the-scenes record keeping effort. The securities a mutual fund invests in are kept under lock and key by an appointed bank custodian, which segregates mutual fund assets from other bank assets. The custodian may only respond to transactions requested by appropriate fund officers.

Fund transfer agents maintain shareholder account records, including purchases, redemptions, and account balances. They also calculate dividends and authorize payment by the custodian. Plus they prepare and mail periodic account statements, providing federal income tax information, shareholder notices and confirmation statements, and maintain a customer service department to respond to account inquiries.

Laws that Protect Investors

Companies establishing a mutual fund are required to comply with a myriad of regulations geared to protecting shareholder interests. Starting a mutual fund is a costly, complex process designed to turn away con-artists looking for a quick buck.

First, they must contend with the United States Securities and Exchange Commission (SEC). The bible of mutual fund regulation is the SEC's Investment Company Act of 1940. It requires mutual funds to have independent director oversight. It also prohibits conflicts of interests between funds and affiliated individuals such as directors, officers, or investment advisors. Mutual funds that offer shares to the public are required to register them in accordance with federal law and state "Blue Sky" regulation. And anyone selling shares to the public must be a registered broker-dealer.

Although mutual funds are set up under state law as corporations or business trusts, they differ from other companies. First, they usually have external management and have no employees of their own. All operations are conducted by a third party such as an independent investment adviser, a bank, or a broker-dealer. Generally, they continuously offer new shares to the public. And they are legally required to buy back outstanding shares at the shareholder's request.

Setting up a mutual fund can easily run $100,000 or more. There are legal fees for contracts, corporate documents, registration statements, state filings, and education of new fund sponsors. Mutual fund companies also must pay state registration fees. To register a fund in every state can easily run $25,000. Printing adds another $25,000 or so to the tab. Tack on another $25,000 or so for more exotic funds with unusual features that require special provisions.

That's just the beginning. Once a mutual fund begins operating, it must pay management fees and costs associated with transfer agents, custodians, accountants, and other business expenses. By one estimate, a mutual fund needs to have $50 million to $100 million in assets to remain viable.

Obviously, there are easier ways for financial hucksters to make a living. The laws summarized below, which govern all mutual funds, clearly point to a tightly regulated industry which closely guards shareholder interests.

The Investment Company Act of 1940:

This act, the heart of mutual fund industry regulation, is one of the most comprehensive and stringent sets of securities laws on the books. It goes well beyond most state and federal anti-fraud and disclosure rules to encompass a gamut of protective restrictions on mutual funds, investment advisers, directors, officers, employees and principal underwriters.

The 1940 Act prohibits self-dealing and conflicts of interest between affiliated individuals, such as investment advisers, and the fund. These individuals may not knowingly sell to or purchase from a fund securities or other property, nor may they borrow money from it. The 1940 Act also limits commissions that brokers receive for selling a mutual fund.

Mutual funds must also maintain detailed records of securities they own. They must file detailed reports with the SEC, and have financial statements in the annual report to shareholders certified by independent public accountants.

Because they continuously offer new shares to the public, mutual funds are subject to special SEC registration rules that allow them to register an indefinite number of shares.

The Securities Act of 1933

The 1933 Act requires that all potential shareholders receive the latest prospectus before they invest, and places significant restrictions on advertising content. The 1933 Act provides for registration of all public securities, including those offered by mutual funds.

The Securities Exchange Act of 1934

This Act regulates practices by broker-dealers, including principal underwriters who sell mutual funds. It provides that all broker-dealers must register with the SEC and become a member of a national securities exchange or the National Association of Securities Dealers (NASD). Registered broker-dealers must maintain detailed records on their financial positions and customer transactions, segregate customer securities in custodial accounts, and file reports on an annual basis with the SEC.

The Investment Advisers Act of 1940

Under the Investment Advisers Act, all investment advisers to mutual funds must be registered. They must also meet record keeping, reporting, and other requirements.

The Internal Revenue Code of 1954

The 1954 Internal Revenue Code helps ensure that the tax burden placed on mutual fund shareholders remains similar to those who invest in individual stocks. It accomplishes this by essentially treating the fund as an investment conduit, or "regulated investment company." The mutual fund structure allows it to deduct from federal taxes any distributions of net income to shareholders. The funds currently distribute profits and net income to shareholders, who in turn report these distributions on their tax returns. To qualify as a regulated investment company a fund must meet a number of requirements, including prescribed diversification standards.

Blue Sky Laws

In addition to federal law, most states have in place regulations regarding securities offerings to their residents and requirements for broker-dealers doing business in their jurisdictions. These "Blue Sky" laws outline the procedure for registration of shares, which is often accomplished automatically when the mutual fund files with the SEC. State statutes may also impose limits on mutual fund expenses or restrict speculative investment activity

Chapter 3

Types of Mutual Funds

Mutual funds come in different varieties based on risk and investment objectives. With more than 4,000 mutual funds on the market, some say there's a mutual fund for all seasons. So, individuals can match their level of risk and investment goals with their mutual fund objectives. While no two mutual funds are exactly alike, they fall into several broad-based categories.

Growth Funds. When you invest in a growth stock fund, you invest for capital appreciation. You want to see the value of your investment grow by leaps and bounds. You don't want income. There are two different types of growth funds. The differences between them are slim.

- **Long-term growth funds** buy good quality companies whose earnings should outpace their competitors, the economy, and inflation. The fund manager tries to buy at attractive prices, and often holds onto the stock as the company's earnings and profits grow. Typically, growth funds are best suited to the needs of younger investors willing to assume greater short-term risk in return for growth over the longer term.

18

- **Aggressive Growth Funds.** Aggressive growth funds are a second cousin to growth funds. In the 1960s these funds were called "go-go" funds. In the bull market of the 1980s, they were called "hot funds." Aggressive growth funds typically are characterized by high portfolio turnover. The fund managers trade stocks a lot. On average, an aggressive growth fund turns its portfolio over almost every six months.

Aggressive funds are a speculative investment. These funds often buy small company stocks, or emerging growth stocks. They may own large company growth stocks, if they think they can make a big profit. Some funds borrow money to buy stock. That means they leverage their investments for big gains.

When you invest in an aggressive growth stock fund, you can expect to lose as much as 20 percent in one year. You also can make as much as 30 percent in another year. You may be in for a wild ride, but over the long term, your investment should grow.

Aggressive funds, however, aren't for the faint of heart. You have to be willing to take risks. You have to accept losses in bad years. For that reason, like growth funds, they are ideal investments for younger investors.

Growth and Income Funds. Growth and income funds invest for both capital appreciation and income. They typically invest in large company stocks traded on the New York Stock Exchange. The majority of growth and income funds own S&P 500 stocks. The stocks pay dividends of 3 percent to 5 percent. So you get income, which you can reinvest in new fund shares, plus share price appreciation.

Dividend income is important. About 40 percent of the return on the S&P 500 over the past 10 years is due to dividend income. You buy new shares. When the market goes up, your profits multiply.

Dividend income also serves to cushion losses in a stock market decline. At the time of this writing, you would breakeven on a growth and income fund despite a 3 percent to 4 percent drop in share prices.

Balanced Funds. A balanced fund invests in both stocks and bonds. The average balanced fund invests 60 percent in stocks and 40 percent in bonds. When you invest in a balanced fund, you own an all-weather investment. Because you own two different assets, you get protection if one asset performs poorly. Typically, you will earn about 60 to 80 percent of the return on the S&P 500 with half the risk when you invest in a balanced fund.

I frequently refer to the stock market crash of 1987, probably the worst period in recent investment history.

Based on Lipper data, all diversified equity funds lost a whopping 22 percent in the third quarter of 1987. Ouch!

But balanced funds only dropped 10.9 percent. Whew!

There is a big trade-off for safety over the short-term. Growth funds gained a total of 334.2 percent for 10 years ended in 1987. By contrast, balanced funds gained just 268.01 percent during the same time period.

You see what kind of long-term growth you sacrifice for safety: 66 percent, even with the bad quarter in 1987.

Equity Income Funds. Here's another safe haven for conservative investors. Equity income funds are second cousins to growth and income funds. They invest in even higher-yielding stocks than growth and income funds. But you also get capital appreciation as a kicker. Equity income funds own a lot of utility stocks, preferred stocks, as well as some growth stocks. They own all kinds of utilities including telephone companies, oil and gas and natural gas stocks. Equity income funds also own bonds.

Equity income funds are lower-risk investments compared with the other types of growth stock funds. But they have done exceeding well over the past 10 years because interest rates have declined. Equity income funds grew at an annual rate of 13 percent over the past 10 years ending in August of 1993. By contrast, the average diversified equity fund grew at a 12 percent annual rate, while the S&P 500 gained 14.95 percent annually over this period.

How did equity income funds do in the third quarter of 1987? They lost 14.1 percent, compared with the 20.4 percent decline in the average equity fund and a 23.2 percent decline in the S&P 500 with dividends reinvested.

Global/International. These funds come in two forms. Global funds can invest in both the U.S. and overseas stock markets. International funds exclude U.S. stocks and bonds from their portfolios. These funds are attractive because they offer an extra layer of diversification to mutual fund holdings. Many of the world's stock markets lead or lag the U.S. market. As a result, losses in U.S. holdings may be offset by gains overseas.

You can also invest in overseas bond funds. Foreign mutual funds, however, carry additional risks. Changes in the value of the dollar in relation to other currencies can affect the market value of overseas holdings. Investors also face political risks and must contend with volatility of a particular country's markets.

Sector Funds. Sector funds are specialized mutual funds. They invest in a specific industrial sector, such as health care, banking, technology, precious metals, chemicals and drugs.

Fidelity Investments, Vanguard and Financial Programs are three mutual fund groups that have a stable of sector funds.

Sector funds are risky. Your fortunes rise and fall with the financial condition of one industry. For that reason, sector funds are volatile. Look at the health care sector. Fidelity Select Heath Care is down 10 percent this year-to-date, at the time of this writing. But over ten years, the fund grew at an annual rate of 15 percent.

Other sector funds that are widely owned by investors include precious metals funds and utility stock funds. Precious metals funds are extremely volatile. The sector has grown at a measly rate of 2 percent annually over the past five years. It was in negative territory until last year. This year-to-date, however, the funds are up 61 percent due to fears about inflation.

Other types of sector funds can be used judiciously. For example, during bear markets and economic recessions, sectors in which business is characterized by a stable demand for goods are considered safe harbors. Traditionally, utilities, defense, food, soaps, tobacco and beverage are defensive investment sectors.

Fixed Income Funds. Bond funds have several investment objectives. Some invest in long-term bonds, others in intermediate- and short-term notes. In addition, there are bond funds that invest in a wide variety of bonds. You have U.S. Treasury bond funds, government agency funds, investment grade corporate bond funds, junk bond funds, and foreign bond funds.

You face credit risk when you invest in corporate bond funds. When you lend money to a business, you face the risk that the business could default on its interest and principal payments. The most credit worthy issuers carry triple A ratings by Standard & Poor's and Moody's. Investment-grade–rated issuers carry single A to triple A ratings. Lower-rated issuers pay higher yields because there is a greater risk of default during economic recessions. Bonds rated double-B (BB) or lower are called junk bonds. Junk bond at this writing yield around 9 percent.

There also bond funds that invest in government securities. Funds that invest solely in U.S. Treasury securities carry no credit risk or default risk because the bonds are backed by the "full faith and credit" of Uncle Sam. Government securities funds also invest in U.S. government agency debt obligations. These funds invest primarily in bonds issued by the Federal Home Loan Bank Board, the Government National Mortgage Association, the Federal National Mortgage Association, and the Federal Home Loan Mortgage Corporation.

Bond funds are not without risk. Although there is a low correlation between bond and equity returns, bond funds can be just as volatile as stocks. Bond prices move in opposite directions to interest rates. When interest rates rise, bond prices fall. In addition, the longer the maturity of the bond the greater the price volatility.

The exhibit below illustrates how volatile bonds can be when interest rates change. Based on a rate of 6.5 percent, at this writing, a rate rise of 1 percent would cause a 30-year bond to lose 11.9 percent in value. By contrast, if rates fell 1 percent, the bond would gain 14.6 percent in value.

Here is what you could gain or lose when you invest in bond funds.

Exhibit 3–1 Change In Value of Bonds with Change in Interest Rate

Years to Maturity	1% Decline	1% Rise
1	.96%	–.95%
5	4.32	–4.11
10	7.6	–6.95
30	14.61	–11.87

Money Market Funds. Money funds invest in short-term money market instruments.

They invest in T-bills, CDs, commercial paper, and repurchase agreements, which are over 100 percent collateralized. Since the funds are required to carry an average maturity of less than 90 days, they can maintain an unchanging net asset value of $1. The net asset value is the price per share less expenses to operate the fund. There is no price volatility with money funds, but you earn lower yields.

Money funds have check writing privileges. The safest money funds invest in Treasury bills and notes and other U.S. government agency obligations. The funds that pay the highest yields invest in money center bank CDs and commercial paper—IOUs of top credit rated corporations.

Municipal Bonds for Tax-Free Income

Municipal bond funds are more attractive than ever now that we must live with higher income tax rates.

The new tax law enacted as part of President Clinton's budget package raises the top tax rate to 39.6 percent from 31 percent for couples filing jointly with taxable incomes over $140,000 and individuals with taxable income of over $115,000 (see Chapter 11). Those with taxable annual incomes of over $250,000 would pay a 10 percent surtax, making their tax brackets a whopping 39.6 percent.

Someone in the new 39.6 percent tax bracket who invested in a well-managed tax-free fund that yields 5.4 percent would earn a taxable equivalent yield of 8.9 percent. By contrast, the pre-tax yield on long-term Treasury bonds is just 6.4 percent today. That's a whopping 2.5 percentage-point yield spread.

Municipal bond funds invest in bonds issued by state and local governments and government agencies. The bonds are issued to raise money for public projects and services like road building, water and waste treatment facilities, airports and toll roads.

Municipal bond funds come in many shapes and sizes just like Treasury and corporate bond funds. There are tax-free money funds, short-term municipal bond funds, long-term municipal bond funds and high-yield municipal funds.

Municipal bond interest income is free from federal income taxes. If you invest in municipal bonds issued by your state of residence, the bonds also are free of state and local taxes. So you get double or even triple tax-free income. At today's rates, it would even pay someone in the 28 percent tax bracket to invest in a double tax-free fund. That would result in a taxable equivalent yield of about 7.9 percent if the bond fund were exempt from both state and federal income taxes.

You are exposed to interest rate risk and credit risk when you invest in individual bonds or bond funds. Tax-free bonds are quoted in after-tax rates. So before you invest, you have to determine the taxable equivalent yield on the municipal bonds. Calculating your taxable equivalent yield is relatively easy. Divide the tax-free rate by 1 minus your tax bracket. For example: If the rate is 5.4 percent and your tax bracket is 36 percent, divide 5.4 by .64 (i.e., 1–.36) and you get 8.44 percent.

A word to the wise. If you are in a high tax bracket, the tax-free income from municipal bonds is nice to have. However, you will have to pay taxes for any capital gains your fund distributes at year-end. Also, you may wish to consult with your tax adviser before you invest. If you have too much tax-free income, you could be subject to the alternative minimum tax (see Chapter 11 for more details). Tax-free income also affects the taxability of Social Security payouts to retired people.

What Does It Cost You to Invest?

I'm just a no-load kind of guy. I've always encouraged people to make their money work for them, not their stockbroker.

If you invest in load funds, you'll pay through the nose. Loads or front-end sales charges range from 3 percent to 8.5 percent. That's money taken out of your pocketbook for nothing.

Let's assume the worst. You buy an 8.5 percent front-end loaded fund and invest $10,000. They takeout $850 and you have $9,150 to invest. Assuming the investment grows at an annual rate of 12 percent, your money is worth $28,419 after 10 years.

Go no-load. You have $10,000 invested from the start. Assuming the same rate of return, you have $31,058 after 10 years.

Exhibit 3–2 What Your Investment Is Worth after 10 years

The Investment Grows 12 percent per Year	
Type of Fund	**What $10,000 Grows to**
8.5 Percent Load Fund	$28,419
No Load Fund	$31,058

Many load fund groups have reduced their loads. The average front-end load is now about 5 percent. That's still a lot.

Don't worry. They've found other ways to pick your pocket. You get hit with a 12b–1 fee, also known as a sales distribution charge. The average 12b–1 fee is .50 percent or one-half-of-one-percent deducted annually from fund assets. You might pay as much as 1.25 percent or as little as .25 percent in 12b–1 fees.

Some load fund groups hit you with A and B shares. A shares charge a front-end load and no 12b–1 fee. B shares sock it to you with a back-end redemption charge and a 12b–1 fee. (see Exhibit 1–1.) Other funds just have back-end loads or contingent deferred sales charges. You might pay 6 percent if you redeem shares in the first year you own the fund. The redemption charge drops to zero after the sixth year.

Everyone pays a fund management fee. That money goes to paying the fund manager's expenses. Most stock funds have a management fee of about .5 percent. It can be higher or lower. Overseas stock funds have management fees of as much as 1 percent because of the extra cost of doing business abroad.

Fund expense ratios are important. The expense ratio is the annual charge taken out of the fund based on total assets in the fund. The average stock fund sports an expense ratio of a little over 1 percent. A bond fund's expense averages .75 percent. A good money fund charges less than .50 percent.

Read the Prospectus before You Invest

Later on in the book I'll show you how to invest in the best managed mutual funds and profit over the long-term. One of the most important things you should do before you invest is make sure you know what you are investing in.

You must read a mutual fund prospectus before you invest. By law, fund groups cannot sell you a fund unless you have obtained a prospectus.

If you don't read this important document you could run into trouble. I was speaking in the Northeast in the late 1980s, and a retired couple came up to me after the talk to have a chat "We put $10,000 in a U.S. Government Securities Fund," said the husband. "Our broker said it was 100 percent safe and backed by Uncle Sam. The fund yielded 10 percent. We thought that was great—better than the bank. But the value dropped when interest rates went up." Many people get confused by the U.S. government guarantee. You've got to read the prospectus carefully. In the mid-1980s there were hundreds of cases against securities firms that sold government funds to investors who didn't understand the U.S. government guarantee was a guarantee against default, not interest rate risk.

That's why you must read the prospectus. The document spells out the risks.

Here's what you will find in a prospectus:

- A statement about the investment objectives and investment policy of the fund.

- Fund expenses. You see a fee table. Information that shows how the fund performed, less fees, versus an index or benchmark.

- Investment restrictions.

- Portfolio turnover.

- Information that identifies the fund manager, directors, trustees, and members of the advisory board.

- The custodian bank that holds the assets in a separate account.

- Allocation of brokerage. If the funds has an organizational link with a brokerage firm, this section reveals the percentage of brokerage commissions being paid to the broker affiliate.

- Voluntary accumulation plans. The fund's policy on voluntary accumulation or automatic investment plans. That's where money is taken out of your checking account every month and put into the fund.

- Litigation. This section tells you if there are any current or pending legal actions against the fund.

- Determination of net asset value. This section explains how the fund calculates the net asset value of the fund.

- How to buy shares. The fund's initial and subsequent investments are listed. Directions on how to invest by mail or electronically. For load funds, there is information on how the sales charge is reduced if you invest large sums of money.

- How to redeem shares. Do you need an authorized signature? How to use the telephone redemption privileges.

- A special service section describes dividend and capital gain reinvestment privileges, accumulation and withdrawal plans, as well as retirement savings plans.

- Tax Information. The fund must describe its policy and tax status concerning dividends and capital gains. Keep in mind that funds must distribute at least 98 percent of their net income and realized capital gains to qualify as a regulated investment company under the Internal Revenue Code.

- Withdrawal plans. Information on how to withdraw money regularly from the fund.

- Statement of additional Information. You have to request this document from the fund group. This document may cover details that are not included in the prospectus.

A Word about Registering Your Fund

When you receive your mutual fund application, be sure to talk to your accountant, lawyer or financial adviser about how to register your fund shares. There are three ways to own property. So if you have a complex financial situation, make sure you set up the account the right way. The way you hold title to your property will affect how your loved ones will inherit your assets.

If you want to own all the shares in your name, you register you account as **fee simple.** You will designate who will receive your investments.

If you own the fund in **joint tenancy with right of survivorship,** you own all the property with someone else. You can give your interest away or sell it. But you can't leave your interest to someone else when you die. When you own property with your spouse, you both share in the ownership and control of the asset. Upon the death of one spouse, ownership of the mutual fund is automatically passed on to the surviving spouse.

With **tenancy in common,** you own part of it and can give your share away, sell or leave your part of the property to others when you die. Under this arrangement, you can own property with your spouse or others. Tenants-in-common may own unequal interests in the mutual funds. For example, you may own 50 percent of the fund assets, while your spouse and your brother own 25 percent each. When the first spouse dies, however, his or her percentage passes on to his or her designated beneficiary based on a will, trust agreement or "intestate succession."

Checking on Fund Performance

You can monitor your fund's performance daily in your local newspaper. Many tables now report a fund's total return over different time periods. *The Wall Street Journal* daily lists the year-to-date return and returns over several time periods. (See Exhibit 3–1.)

Total return is the percent gain or loss in the fund with dividends and capital gains reinvested. So say you have a fund that's up 5 percent and the distributions yield 3 percent; your total return is 8 percent.

The Wall Street Journal uses both the National Association of Securities Dealers (NASD) and Lipper Analytical Services data.

The NASD part shows you the fund's name, the investment objective, the net asset value of the fund (NAV), the offering price, and the dollars and cents change in net asset value. If there is a difference between the NAV and the offering price, that difference is the front-end load or sales charge. The Lipper data show the total return, maximum initial sales charge, and total expense ratio, as well as the fund's overall ranking compared with other funds.

There are footnotes to the table. These notes tell you if there is a back-end sales charge, a 12b–1 fee, and information on distributions.

Exhibit 3–3 Mutual Fund Quotations

What These Listings Provide . . .

		NASD Data			Lipper Analytical Data		
Monday	Inv. Obj.	NAV	Offer Price	NAV Chg.	%Ret YTD	Max Initl Chrg.	Total Exp Ratio -	
Tuesday	Inv. Obj.	NAV	Offer Price	NAV Chg.	YTD	Total Return 4 wk 1 yr		Rank
Wednesday	Inv. Obj.	NAV	Offer Price	NAV Chg.	YTD	Total Return 13 wk 3 yr*		Rank
Thursday	Inv. Obj.	NAV	Offer Price	NAV Chg.	YTD	Total Return 26 wk 4 yr*		Rank
Friday	Inv. Obj.	NAV	Offer Price	NAV Chg.	YTD	Total Return 39 wk 5 yr*		Rank

*Annualized

EXPLANTORY NOTES

Mutual fund data are supplied by two organizations. The daily Net Asset Value (NAV), Offer Price and Net Change calculations are supplied by the National Association of Securities Dealers (NASD) through Nasdaq. Its automated quotation system. Performance and cost data are supplied by Lipper Analytical Services Inc.

Daily price data are entered into Nasdaq by the fund. Its management company or agent. Performance and cost calculations are percentages provided by Lipper Analytical Services, based on prospectuses filed with the Securities and Exchange Commission, fund reports, financial reporting services and other sources believed to be authoritative, accurate and timely. Though verified, the data cannot be guaranteed by Lipper or its data sources and should be double-checked with the funds before making any investment decisions.

Performance cal culations, as percentages, assuming reinvestment of all distributions, and after all asset based charges have been deducted. Asset based charges include advisory fees, other non-advisory fees and distribution expenses (12b–1). Figures are without regard to sales, deferred sales or redemption charges.

INVESTMENT OBJECTIVE (Inv. Obj.) — Based on stated investment goals outlined in the prospectus. The Journal assembled 27 groups based on classifications used by Lipper Analytical in the daily Mutual Fund Scorecard and other calculations. A detailed breakdown of classifications appears at the bottom of this page.

NET ASSET VALUE (NAV) — Per share value prepared by the fund, based on closing quotes unless noted, and supplied to the NASD by 5:30 p.m. Eastern time.

OFFER PRICE — Net asset value plus sales commission, if any.

NAV CHG — Gain or loss, based on the previous NAV quotation.

TOTAL RETURN — Performance calculations, as percentages, assuming reinvestment of all distributions. Sales charges aren't reflected. Percentages are annualized for periods greater than one year. For funds declaring dividends daily, calculations are based on the most current data supplied by the fund within publications deadlines. A YEAR TO DATE (YTD) change is listed daily, with results ranging from 4 weeks to 5 years offered throughout the week. See chart on this page for specific schedule.

MAXIMUM INITIAL SALES COMMISSION (Max Initl Chrg) — Based on prospectus; the sales charge may be modified or suspended temporarily by the fund, but any percentage change requires format notification to the shareholders.

TOTAL EXPENSE RATIO (Total Exp Ratio) — Shown as a percentage and based on the fund's annual report, the ratio is total operating expenses for the fiscal year divided by the fund's average net assets. It includes all asset based charges such as advisory fees, other non-advisory fees and distribution expenses (12b–1).

RANKING (R) — Funds are grouped by investment objectives defined by The Wall Street Journal and ranked on longest time period listed each day. Performance measurement begins at either the closest Thursday or month-end for periods of more than one year. Gains of 100% or more are shown as a whole number, not carried out one decimal place. A = top 20%; B = next 20%; C = middle 20%; D = next 20%; E = bottom 20%.

QUOTATIONS FOOTNOTES

e–Ex-distribution, **f**–Previous day's quotation, **s**–Stock split or dividend, **x**–Ex-dividend.

p–Distribution costs apply, 12b–1 plan, **r**–Redemption charge may apply, **t**–Footnotes p and r apply.

NA–Not available due to incomplete price, performance or cost data. **NE**–Deleted by Lipper editor; data in question. **NL**–No Load (sales commission). **NN**–Fund doesn't with to be tracked. **NS**–Fund didn't exist at start of period.

k–Recalculated by Lipper, using updated data. **I**–No valid comparison with other funds because of expense structure.

Exhibit 3–4 Benham Group's Adjustable Rate Government Fund

Inv. Obj.	NAV	Offer Price	NAV Chg.		%Ret YTD	Max Initl Chrg.	Total Exp Ratio	R
Benham Group:								
AdjGov	BST	*9.94	NL	...	+3.0	0.000	0.450	..
CaTFl	IDM	11.47	NL	...	+9.2	0.000	0.520	..
CattIn	ISM	10.76	NL	+0.01	+12.4	0.000	0.550	..
CaTFS	STM	10.36	NL	...	+4.6	0.000	NA	..
CattH	MCA	9.76	NL	...	+11.7	0.000	0.560	..
CattL	MCA	12.13	NL	...	+12.7	0.000	0.520	..
EqGro	GRO	12.83	NL	−0.01	+10.9	0.000	0.750	..
EurBd	WBD	11.09	NL	+0.01	+10.8	0.000	0.510	..
GNMA	BND	10.84	NL	−0.01	+5.4	0.000	0.560	..
GoldIn	SEC	11.06	NL	+0.02	−46.5	0.000	0.750	..
IncGro	G&I	15.32	NL	...	+10.8	0.000	0.750	..
LTreas	BND	11.16	NL	−0.01	+19.6	0.000	0.000	..
NITFI	IDM	11.24	NL	...	+9.0	0.000	0.650	..
NITFL	GLM	12.40	NL	+0.01	+13.1	0.000	0.650	..
STreas	BST	10.08	NL	...	+4.8	0.000	0.000	..
Tg1995	BND	94.09	NL	+0.04	+6.4	0.000	0.620	..
Tg2000	BND	72.14	NL	+0.12	+16.4	0.000	0.660	..
Tg2005	BND	38.08	NL	−0.05	+29.0	0.000	0.700	..
Tg2015	BND	28.94	NL	+0.05	+34.6	0.000	0.620	..
Tg2020	BND	20.68	NL	+0.02	+41.9	0.000	0.660	..
TNote	BIN	10.89	NL	...	+7.6	0.000	0.530	..
UtilIn	SEC	10.92	NL	−0.05	NS	0.000	NA	..

PART II

Selecting Funds That Are Right for You

Chapter 4

How to Pick a Mutual Fund

You've got to find the right kind of fund before you start your investment game plan. No two mutual funds are quite alike. You want to invest in a fund with a good track record—one that has been around for at least one business cycle, which last about five years. That way you can tell how fund did in up and down markets.

If you invest in no-load funds, you will have to do your own legwork. You can go to the public library and look through the CDA/ Wiesenberger Investment Company Service, Value Line's Mutual Fund Survey or Morningstar Mutual Funds for a list of the best performing funds. Or you can subscribe of one of several excellent mutual fund newsletters that recommend funds.

Regardless of whether you do it yourself, rely on newsletter recommendations or pay a broker, you should use the following criteria to select the best mutual funds that meet your financial needs, goals and tolerance for risk.

How to Select a Fund

Here are the important factors you have to consider when selecting a mutual fund that's right for you.

- First, you have to compare the investment objective and risk tolerance of the fund with your objectives and investment comfort level. If you can't sleep at night because you are worrying about your hot stock fund losing money, then you should not own it. You should be investing in a conservative stock fund that gives you growth and income from dividends. Refer to Chapter 1 to review the risk characteristics of both stock and bond funds.

- Second, you want to compare fees, commissions and fund expenses. In the front of every prospectus is a section that shows you a hypothetical $1,000 investment and how it grows over one, five and ten years at 5 percent less fees, commissions and fund expenses.

  If you want to get more specific, you can compare each type of charge. You look at the front-end loads, back end-loads, 12b-1 sales distribution fees and mutual fund management fees.

  Irving Strauss, president of the 100 percent No Load Mutual Fund Council in New York, advises investors to look at the front end equivalent load of a fund that hits you with a 12b–1 charge.

  "Loads and 12b-1 fees eat into your returns," says Strauss. "Over ten years time, for example, a fund with a .5 percent 12b–1 fee would be the same as paying a 5 percent front-end load. Another way to look at is to see how you money grows."

  You should also look at the mutual fund's expense ratio. That's how much the fund spends per the net asset value of the fund. The lower the expense ratio, the more money you have in your pocket. This is particularly important when selecting fixed income or bond mutual funds. If the expense ratio is too high, it reduces the yield on your investment. It also reduces the amount of interest you can reinvest in the fund.

  Exhibit 4–1 shows you the average fees and other charges assessed by mutual funds. You want funds that give you the best returns at the lowest cost.

- Third, you have to evaluate the fund's performance or total return. A fund's total return includes price appreciation plus rein-vestment of dividends and capital gains.

Strauss says mutual fund investors should look at the following:

- A fund's annual rate of return over at least a one-, three- five-and ten-year period. The annual return is like a compound inter-est rate you get with a bank CD. It shows you the rate your money grows, assuming that you earn money on your principal plus your earnings for the year.

- The fund's yearly return over a number of time periods. You want to see from year to year how the fund performed. You want a fund that shows consistent performance compared to other funds. You can have two funds that average 10 percent. One fund may earn 9 percent in year one and 11 percent in year two. The other fund may earn 15 percent in year one and 5 percent in year two. Both average 10 percent. But you want the consistent performer. You don't want a fund that shows wild price swings every year.

You also want to look at how a fund performs in down markets. This will tell you about the quality of the professional management. You want a consistent performer that loses less per month in down markets com-pared to other funds.

Exhibit 4–2 will help you compare your fund with the peer group and market averages every year over the past 15 years, according to Morningstar Inc. data.

If a fund has been around a long time, check its 1977 track record. The S&P 500 lost 7.44 percent that year.

Check the late 1970s and see how your taxable or tax-free bond fund performed to the bond fund averages. In 1979 and 1980 the Lehman Brothers Corporate Bond Index lost 2.11 and .29 percent respectively. Tax free funds also got hit hard during those years. National municipal bond funds lost 2.31 percent in 1978, 1.29 percent in 1979 and a whop-ping 11.32 percent in 1980.

More recently, check the following years: The S&P 500 lost 5.08 per-cent in 1980. In 1987 some fund categories lost a bundle, but the average equity fund was up less than one percent. In 1991, the S&P lost 3.1 per-cent and the average equity fund lost 6.16 percent.

Bond funds have performed well over the past ten years. Interest

**Exhibit 4–1 Investment Objective Annual Ratio Averages and Total Net Assets.
Data through 12/31/94**

Objective	1980	1981	1982	1983	1984	1985
U.S. Diversified Equity Funds						
Average Expense Ratio	1.11	1.09	1.17	1.13	1.15	1.19
Average Income Ratio	3.77	4.02	4.59	3.01	3.21	2.87
Average Turnover Ratio	72.62	70.01	78.86	80.61	79.42	81.47
Total Net Assets ($Bill)	37.06	36.15	42.94	63.65	66.86	88.26
Number of Funds	232	245	262	292	331	371
International Equity Funds						
Average Expense Ratio	1.20	1.21	1.32	1.33	1.25	1.58
Average Income Ratio	2.90	2.72	3.42	1.83	1.89	1.36
Average Turnover Ratio	59.97	48.00	53.38	68.95	61.08	65.06
Total Net Assets ($Bill)	1.83	2.42	2.67	4.73	5.90	8.13
Number of Funds	16	20	23	25	33	42
Equity Funds						
Average Expense Ratio	1.13	1.11	1.20	1.17	1.18	1.24
Average Income Ratio	3.89	4.12	4.60	3.02	3.20	2.74
Average Turnover Ratio	69.86	67.82	76.91	78.17	77.83	80.56
Total Net Assets ($Bill)	41.09	40.65	48.40	73.80	78.88	103.32
Number of Funds	265	291	314	352	414	483
Hybrid Funds						
Average Expense Ratio	0.93	0094	0.99	0.96	1.02	1.05
Average Income Ratio	8.81	10.08	10.66	8.70	9.11	8.81
Average Turnover Ratio	60.41	70.81	83.79	93.91	80.01	97.24
Total Net Assets ($Bill)	8.47	7.80	9.33	12.88	14.55	22.36
Number of Funds	65	67	70	76	85	104
Taxable Fixed-Income Funds						
Average Expense Ratio	0.85	0.84	0.85	0.84	0.83	0.89
Average Income Ratio	10.57	12.45	12.90	10.96	11.38	10.70
Average Turnover Ratio	74.16	79.19	90.10	96.87	88.13	152.42
Total Net Assets ($Bill)	3.86	3.97	6.03	8.28	17.76	54.35
Number of Funds	52	54	64	74	108	413
Tax-Free Fixed-Income Funds						
Average Expense Ratio	0.81	0.82	0.83	0.78	0.77	0.82
Average Income Ratio	7.47	9.44	10.26	8.51	8.61	8.30
Average Turnover Ratio	103.03	134.80	130.04	102.14	111.50	92.44
Total Net Assets ($Bill)	3.50	3.77	7.84	15.62	21.16	38.55
Number of Funds	43	50	55	81	129	180
Total Funds						
Average Expense Ratio	1.04	13.03	1.10	1.06	1.06	1.10
Average Income Ratio	5.77	6.56	6.99	5.36	5.68	5.51
Average Turnover Ratio	72.13	76.55	84.72	85.28	83.79	94.82
Total Net Assets ($Bill)	56.91	56.18	71.60	110.57	132.36	218.58
Number of Funds	425	462	503	583	736	910

Source: Morningstar Mutual Fund Performance Report

1986	1987	1988	1989	1990	1991	1992	1993	1994
1.23	1.26	1.39	1.41	1.44	1.37	1.32	1.30	1.33
2.07	1.72	2.20	2.40	2.27	1.78	1.26	0.95	0.80
84.81	97.23	91.28	81.56	83.52	85.14	77.11	75.58	79.48
120.34	131.75	144.95	188.64	182.63	277.91	367.73	501.52	554.69
435	513	566	598	669	745	868	1274	1501
1.38	1.56	1.87	1.81	1.80	1.81	1.75	1.72	1.71
1.06	0.61	0.72	0.74	1.28	1.26	0.93	0.53	0.30
81.30	101.69	90.35	80.13	80.29	76.74	64.04	58.90	73.59
16.22	16.35	17.40	22.76	27.01	35.43	41.92	104.75	143.78
57	78	92	104	136	166	209	345	498
1.28	1.32	1.50	1.53	1.56	1.50	1.46	1.42	1.43
1.97	1.60	1.95	2.10	2.05	1.69	1.19	0.90	0.73
95.90	110.09	97.03	85.09	87.11	85.74	76.70	76.18	80.09
146.14	160.18	174.00	226.51	225.32	337.58	440.92	655.75	744.89
578	686	767	815	931	1044	1225	1817	2248
10.4	1.12	1.18	1.32	1.35	1.37	1.32	1.31	1.31
7.45	6.92	7.63	7.73	7.92	7.33	6.18	5.23	5.05
105.06	114.14	107.73	101.09	106.01	104.91	112.51	121.92	123.24
46.95	56.46	64.79	65.16	57.23	80.84	119.16	201.29	211.39
134	175	218	244	269	296	350	532	687
0.90	0.92	0.90	0.92	0.93	0.90	0.90	0.92	0.91
9.06	8.31	8.58	8.69	8.46	7.92	7.02	6.12	5.74
161.01	165.65	168.53	143.97	123.79	137.16	147.48	150.13	170.36
129.77	138.54	130.98	130.70	136.59	194.90	242.60	290.01	231.95
193	261	307	339	386	461	591	927	1094
0.74	0.77	0.77	0.75	0.75	0.75	0.75	0.76	0.78
7.34	6.75	6.90	6.76	6.61	6.42	5.98	5.37	5.08
54.32	67.01	72.84	57.75	53.38	49.54	44.99	42.04	41.91
72.24	76.25	89.31	108.00	122.90	156.57	196.51	256.43	225.52
254	350	393	416	480	523	645	1097	1514
1.09	1.11	1.19	1.21	1.23	1.20	1.17	1.15	1.13
4.74	4.46	4.93	5.11	5.04	4.69	4.07	3.58	3.41
99.50	110.83	1053.68	91.78	88.69	89.48	87.56	89.45	92.96
395.11	431.42	459.07	530.37	542.04	769.88	999.19	1403.5	1413.7
1159	1472	1685	1814	2066	2324	2811	4373	5543

Exhibit 4–2 Investment Objective Annual Total Return Averages.
Data through 08/31/95

Objective	1980	1981	1982	1983	1984	1985
Equity						
Aggressive Growth	48.50	−7.19	29.04	19.39	−14 .44	29.25
Equity Income	19.54	5.77	27.83	21.26	7.42	26.35
Growth	38.12	−1.56	27.63	21.48	−1.60	29.79
Growth and Income	26.88	−0.30	23.10	21.49	4 .17	27.20
Small Company	40.47	−1.09	25.94	26.36	−5.26	29.32
Diversified Emerging Markets Stock	31.87	−5.93	6.30	9.91	−11. 83	26.67
International–Europe Stock	NA	NA	NA	NA	NA	NA
International–Foreign Stock	27.42	−1.68	3.28	29.59	−3.29	48.24
International–Pacific Stock	35.79	17.14	−2.63	35.14	−0.55	28.93
International–World Stock	37.17	−2.37	17.55	26.74	−5.85	37.39
Specialty–Communications	NA	NA	NA	NA	22.58	20.48
Specialty–Financial	13.54	16.34	18.65	26.42	15.73	39.79
Specialty–Health	NA	NA	45.34	5.11	−3.56	39.93
Specialty–Miscellaneous	NA	NA	NA	13.46	−0.30	35.00
Specialty–Natural Resources	56.09	−17.04	−10.81	22.36	−10.77	15.10
Specialty–Precious Metals	64 .23	−24.23	48.62	1.87	−26.86	−9.35
Specialty–Real Estate	NA	NA	NA	NA	NA	NA
Specialty–Technology	41.66	−13.48	27.77	29.58	−10.17	18.13
Specialty–Utilities	6.35	20.94	23.85	14.58	19.05	26.59
Hybrid						
Asset Allocation	21.38	4.01	24.71	17.25	6.61	24.71
Balanced	19.76	4.74	28.48	17.22	8.49	27.11
Convertible Bond	33.32	3.80	36.49	22.28	2.06	24.54
Corporate Bond–High Yield	3.42	6.32	31.10	15.99	8.58	22.30
Taxable Fixed-Income						
Corporate Bond–General	1.03	4.65	32.17	9.01	12.82	21.39
Corporate Bond–High Quality	2.62	6.70	30.94	8.14	13.18	19.46
Government Bond–Adjustable-Rate Mortgage	NA	NA	NA	NA	NA	NA
Government Bond–General	6.00	7.74	26.51	7.14	12.83	18.29
Government Bond–Mortgage	−4.21	2.41	32.13	8.49	13.29	18.43
Government Bond–Treasury	NA	10.64	17.53	7.52	13.09	17.91
Short-Term World Income	NA	NA	NA	NA	NA	NA
Multi-Sector Bond	15.80	2.96	21.16	14.16	7.37	19.94
Multi-Asset Global	31.76	8.15	31.12	14.86	−5.08	18.38
World Bond	NA	NA	29.46	1.55	5.13	25.43
Tax-Free Fixed-Income						
Municipal Bond–California	−10.05	−6.32	26.39	6.23	7.00	18.78
Municipal Bond–National	−10.63	−5.95	35.67	9.74	8.94	18.16
Municipal Bond–New York	NA	NA	20.41	10.04	8.57	19.78
Municipal Bond–Single State	−19.13	−6.97	28.42	11.95	7.75	17.71
Summary						
U.S. Diversified Equity Fund Average	34.04	−1.01	26.17	21.80	−0.62	28.72
International Equity Fund Average	33.53	1.11	8.45	28.40	−4.29	41.19
Equity Fund Average	34.64	−1.48	24.91	21.82	−1.37	28.35
Hybrid Fund Average	15.15	5.24	29.35	16.95	7.65	24.45
Taxable Fixed-Income Fund Average	2.53	5.33	30.26	8.48	12.57	19.61
Tax-Free Fixed-Income Fund Average	−11.03	−6.01	34.91	9.76	8.56	18.33
Total Fund Average	23.56	−0.11	27.24	18.09	2.90	24.86
Indexes						
S&P 500 Index	32.22	−5.08	21.46	22.47	6.27	31.74
Lehman Bros Aggregate Bond Index	2.70	6.26	32.62	8.35	15.15	22.10
Lehman Bros Corporate Bond Index	−0.30	2.97	39.22	9.27	16.62	24.06
Lehman Bros Government Bond Index	5.79	9.36	27.75	7.39	14.50	20.43
Lehman Bros Municipal Bond Index	−8.92	−10.23	40.86	8.05	10.55	20.02
Morgan Stanley BAFE Index (Net Dividends)	22.58	−2.28	−1.86	23.69	7.38	56.16
U.S. Treasury Bills	11.58	14.01	10.70	8.67	9.57	7.49

Source: Morningstar Mutual Fund Performance Report

1986	1987	1988	1989	1990	1991	1992	1993	1994
12.03	−2.97	15.42	27.17	−8.29	53.59	8.49	19.49	−3.37
17.10	−2.23	16.05	21.35	−5.78	26.70	9.19	13.20	−1.73
15.36	2.82	14.82	27.55	−4.52	37.36	8.30	11.61	−1.86
15.70	2.22	15.11	23.66	−4.55	28.84	8.25	10.99	−1.15
10.79	−2.32	19.91	22.81	−10.14	49.21	14.09	16.94	−0.72
20.61	0.23	10.50	28.11	−9.74	18.10	0.26	72.16	−9.80
40.91	15.95	7.00	25.69	−5.37	7.28	−7.90	26.45	2.56
48.55	8.25	16.97	21.92	−11.57	12.57	−4.40	37.94	−2.20
72.00	32.42	22.66	27.70	−19.78	13.68	−3.98	57.82	−8.17
31.61	5.68	13.64	22.54	−9.81	21.93	−0.38	31.61	−2.27
21.70	6.59	21.89	45.01	−13.08	29.61	16.16	32.11	−1.98
15.14	−21.36	19.03	24.84	−15.86	58.98	35.08	16.75	−2.78
17.07	0.27	11.61	38.50	14.99	63.76	−4.69	3.76	4.26
17.29	−4.99	24.24	23.63	−9.19	33.54	10.60	21.48	−5.84
10.87	9.33	9.80	29.41	−8.60	6.26	2.89	21.86	−2.64
34.06	36.79	−17.72	25.65	−23.78	−3.89	−15.15	84.97	−11.66
NA	−7.68	15.60	10.57	−16.59	33.11	12.74	22.63	−4.34
4.93	2.92	2.36	22.20	−2.57	47.46	12.57	20.91	15.23
23.19	−7.00	11.61	26.95	−0.45	20.81	9.31	14.39	−8.87
13.57	2.44	9.73	15.97	1.19	21.96	8.14	11.98	−1.80
16.47	1.70	12.61	19.12	−0.43	26.22	7.41	11.17	−2.82
15.38	−3.96	11.92	14.47	−6.04	28.55	13.81	15.50	−4.58
13.37	2.02	12.82	−0.48	−9.96	36.58	17.39	18.84	−3.71
14.11	2.20	8.66	10.82	6.27	16.39	7.39	10.30	−3.50
13.36	2.41	7.14	11.65	7.63	14.25	6.35	8.33	−2.05
8.81	−1.24	5.91	12.33	8.27	10.53	4.68	3.90	−2.77
12.12	1.50	6.64	11.93	8.38	14.01	6.05	8.00	−3.58
10.95	2.16	7.68	12.92	9.39	14.64	6.43	7.20	−3.40
28.21	−0.03	9.86	14.44	6.50	15.42	6.20	10.86	−4.11
NA	−9.26	10.15	−14.29	13.43	7.99	−0.73	6.33	−2.93
8.52	1.40	13.05	6.88	1.40	24.39	8.31	14.65	−5.03
25.44	15.14	7.28	17.32	−2.06	16.60	5.16	20.36	−4.56
18.03	15.97	5.12	6.16	13.46	13.22	2.60	16.38	−6.21
17.24	−2.41	10.95	9.68	6.58	11.01	8.42	12.12	−6.77
16.85	−0.18	10.38	9.28	6.12	11.35	8.42	11.24	−5.07
16.67	−1.76	10.64	9.32	5.21	12.93	9.42	12.27	−6.56
16.27	−1.38	11.43	9.56	6.20	11.28	8.65	12.10	−6.09
14.74	1.20	15.78	25.25	−5.74	37.02	9.31	12.86	−1.54
45.48	11.23	15.76	23.22	−11.50	14.94	−3.53	38.98	−2.98
17.86	3.05	14.58	25.31	−6.94	32.17	6.72	19.43	−2.09
15.47	2.29	11.79	11.74	−3.66	27.74	10.59	14.17	−3.08
13.81	2.39	7.64	11.39	7.94	14.78	5.89	9.31	−3.57
16.75	−1.00	10.85	9.44	6.11	11.44	8.63	11.84	−5.88
16.73	1.95	12.07	17.28	−0.42	23.11	7.37	14.69	−3.51
18.58	5.26	16.61	31.68	−3.12	30.48	7.62	10.06	1.32
15.26	2.76	7.89	14.53	10.30	14.58	7.40	9.75	−2.92
16.53	2.56	9.22	13.98	7.15	18.51	8.70	12.17	−3.92
15.32	2.20	7.03	14.23	8.72	15.32	7.23	10.66	−3.37
19.32	1.50	10.16	10.79	7.30	12.14	8.82	12.28	−5.60
69.44	24.63	28.27	10.54	−23.45	12.13	−12.17	32.56	7.78
5.97	5.83	6.67	8.11	7.51	5.41	3.46	3.02	4.27

rates dropped from double digit levels to just 4 to 8 percent depending on the maturity of the bond. As a result, bond funds have grown at a staggering rate of 12.84 percent over the past ten years ending in 1991.

You won't see any negative yearly total return numbers for either taxable or tax free bond funds over the past ten years. So you have to check a couple of other factors when selecting bond funds.

- Check the average maturity of the bond fund's portfolio. The lower the average maturity the lower the price volatility.

- Check the quality of the bonds in the portfolio. Bonds rated A to triple-A (AAA) by Standard & Poor's and Moody's are issued by the most creditworthy corporations. So there is less chance a default will lower the value of your portfolio. Of course if you own a government securities bond fund, there is no risk of default. You face just interest rate risk.

- Check the bond fund's standard deviation in performance. The standard deviation (SD) is a statistical term. It's the same as the margin of error you may hear being discussed about who's favored in a presidential election. For example, a presidential candidate may have an estimated 51 percent of the vote if the election were held today, plus or minus 3 percentage points. The 3 percentage points is the margin of error or standard deviation. It means the candidate's ratings could be as low as 48 or as high as 54.

A bond fund's standard deviation is its margin of error. Robert Levy, president of CDA Technologies in Rockville, Md., says the SD highly correlates with how much the fund will gain or lose if interest rates rise or fall one percent. The SD tells you that 2/3 of the time a bond fund may swing 4 percentage points above or below its average return for the year. Say a bond fund shows a return of 6 percent for the year and has a SD of 2.5. You could expect to earn about 3.5 percent and 8.5 percent for the year in the bond fund.

Also look at a bond fund's duration. Duration tells you how much the share value of your bond fund will change when interest rates change 1 percent. The lower its duration, the lower the risk.

Assess your tolerance for risk. Longer term bonds show greater price fluctuation to changes in interest rates than short-term bonds. If you want higher yields from long-term bond funds, you have to accept that the fund's N.A.V will decline if interest rates rise a lot more than a money fund or short-term bond fund. If interest rates rise by 1 percent, a 6.5 percent long-term bond would lose almost 12 percent in value. By contrast, a one-year bond would lose 1 percent.

- Consider both the yield and total return on the bond fund. Bond funds have two yields. The Securities and Exchange Commission (SEC) mandate yield represents the rate based on interest income from the bonds. The stated yield on the bond will reflect both interest income and capital gains.

  Total return is also an important consideration when shopping for a bond fund. Total return represents both income and capital appreciation of the fund. Say a fund yields 6 percent and the fund's net asset value increases 4 percent. Your total return is 10 percent. Total return reveals the portfolio manager's ability to navigate safely in the financial markets. You could buy a fund with a whopping 10 percent yield, but a year later your total return is just 3 percent. You collected 10 percent in interest income, but you lost money on your principal.

- Consider the credit ratings of the bonds held in the portfolio. Lower credit rated bonds pay higher yields, but there is a greater risk the issuers could default or have problems paying back principal and interest.

- Consider a bond's prepayment risk. Mortgage bonds face prepayment risk. When interest rates decline, homeowners pay off their existing home loans and refinance at a lower rate. If you own a bond fund with a large stake in mortgage bonds, you face a greater chance that the investments will be prepaid.

- Consider foreign currency risk. Funds that own overseas bonds face currency risk. If the dollar gains against the value of foreign currency, the market value of bonds denominated in that currency will decline. Funds often hedge against currency risk. But the hedges are short term and are not perfect.

- Look at your tax situation. If you are in the 28 or 31 percent tax bracket, you may earn higher taxable equivalent yields from municipal bond funds.

- Check the fund's loads, fees and expense ratios. The more fees and commissions you pay, the less you have in your pocket. Bond funds with high expense ratio eat into your returns. The lower the bond fund's expense ratio the better the deal (see Exhibit 4–2).

- Whether you are investing in a bond or stock fund, check on how long the manager has been running the fund. Say a fund has a great 10-year track record. But this year the fund manager quit and a new one took over. Should you invest in the fund?

  Sheldon Jacobs, publisher of the *No Load Investor,* says you should step back from the fund. You should see how the fund performs in both up and down markets and how it performs in relation to its peers before you invest.

- Look at the fund's portfolio turnover. This will tell you whether the fund manager trades stocks or buys and holds for the long term. You will pay less taxes on funds with low portfolio turnover. High turnover funds generate capital gains during bull markets. As a result, you pay more taxes on your mutual fund distributions and the after-tax return on your fund is lower.

Chapter 5

Mutual Fund Resources

Your investments are only as good as your research.

There are several exellent source of information avaiable on mutual funds. You can subsribe to the publications or visit the public library to get your information.

Be advised, however, there is no standarized way to present mutual fund information. The reports may differ on how they rate funds.

Stick with just one or two sources to avoid confusion.

If you are shopping for a fund or want to check on how one of your funds is performing, there are several excellent source of information available.

The mutual fund reports all provide you with sufficient information to make a knowledgeable investment decision. Be advised, however, the reports are not all alike. The methods they use to evaluate fund performance may differ. Most reports give you all the important ingredients you need to pick a fund. No matter what report you look at, you get the following information:

- Current and past performance.

- Investment objective.

- How a fund ranks versus other funds.

- A risk rating that tells you whether the fund is a high, medium, or a low risk investment.

- A volatility measure that shows you how the fund's price may fluctuate over time.

- The fees, expenses, amount needed to invest, address, and toll free phone numbers.

Reports Differ

Once you go beyond the basic information, the reports differ in how they report and measure returns and risk.

One of the most notable differences occurs because the reports measure returns on different dates. It is easy to get confused. So be sure to check the dates used to figure the fund returns.

For example, *Forbes* reports a 1-year return on the Janus Fund of 15 percent for twelve months ending in June 1993.

But the Standard & Poor's/Lipper shows the Janus Fund earning 10.16 percent for one year ending in December 1993.

Meanwhile, if you are not careful, you might get confused by *Worth* magazine's data. Janus Fund registered a 15 percent annual return. Be advised that *Worth's Guide to Mutual Fund Investing* reports annually over three, five, and ten years' returns on data ending in August 1993. Janus gained 15 percent annually over three years. You also have to check on how fund performance is reported. For example, *U.S. News & World Report* reports a cumulative total return rather than a annual compound rate of return. For example, the Neuberger & Berman Partners Fund gained a total of 84.3 percent over five years ending in June 1993. But that translates into an annual rate of return of 13.01 percent.

If you want to compare *U.S News'* figures with other mutual fund surveys that use the annual rate of return, you'll have to refer to a compound interest rate table or get out the old calculator and do some fast algebra.

The method used to calculate a fund's total return may also cause a slightly different, possibly confusing picture of a fund's performance. The total return measures both the fund's price appreciation or loss with dividends and capital gains reinvested. All reporting services reviewed, with the exception of CDA/Wiesenberger and Forbes, reinvest dividends and capital gains into news shares exactly when the funds do it—either at ex-dividend, pay, or record date. Those two reports reinvest distributions at month end.

Here is what you might run up against if you compare the returns in *Forbes* or CDA with other leading services. Morningstar Mutual Funds, which also supplies data for *Business Week* and *Money* magazine, for example, reports that the Benham Long Term Treasury and Agency Fund gained 17.56 percent in 1993. By contrast, CDA reports that the fund gained 17.6 percent.

Risk or Volatility

Measures of a fund's volatility and risk adjusted performance are other areas where you find conflicting or confusing information.

Both volatility and risk adjusted returns are reported as absolute or relative numbers.

Absolute numbers are statistical calculations that show you magnitude or how much a fund's return can fluctuate. For example, *Morningstar, Value Line* and *CDA/Wiesenberger* all report volatility scores. So investors get a picture of how much the fund's returns varied during the year or over several years.

Relative numbers compare a fund's return to other funds or other investments. *Morningstar, Business Week, Money* and *Worth*, for example, report a measure of risk that looks at the downside—how much the fund has lost compared to T-bills.

Comparing a fund's volatility or risk score with a measure that looks at the risk of losing money are not the same. A fund whose returns swing widely may obtain a distorted score when measured against T-bills. The fund may register a series of small losses and just a few big losses over the years. However, one big loss could distort the information because the risk of losing measure looks at the average loss in relation to T-bills.

Volatility is measured using Modern Portfolio Theory (MPT)statistics. A fund's standard deviation (SD) and beta value are MPT measures of volatility. This data is reported by *Morningstar, Value Line,* and *CDA/ Wiesenberger.*

The SD measures how much a fund's price swings or varies from its annual return, for example, over the year. Say the XYZ Growth Stock Fund gained 12 percent annually over the past three years. The SD was 10 percent. That means that 68 percent of the time the fund earned between 2 percent and 22 percent, although it averaged 12 percent.

Beta is a measure of how volatile a fund performance is compared to the market averages, such as the S&P 500. A stock fund's beta tells you how the fund's performance varies in relation to the S&P 500. Say the PDQ Aggressive Stock Fund sports a beta value of 1.15. The S&P 500 has a beta value of 1. PDQ is 15 percent more volatile than the market. If the S&P 500 gains 10 percent, PDQ should gain about 11.5 percent. On the downside, if the market drops 8 percent, PDQ should decline about 9.2 percent because the fund is more volatile than the market average.

As a rule of thumb, the higher a fund's SD or Beta, the more volatile the fund. That means you are likely to see wider swings in your fund's returns from year to year when a fund sports a high SD or Beta value.

Up and Down Market Performance

Several of the services also report how a fund has performed in recent up and down markets. This is another measure of volatility that can be used with the funds risk rating and overall risk/return rating. You actually see how much the fund earned in up markets and declined in value in down markets.

Be advised, however, that some reports use different time periods than others when they measure bull and bear markets. Value Line, CDA and *Forbes* use the same bull and bear market time frames. The most recent up market occurred from 10/90 through 12/93, while the bear market is considered the period from 5/90 to 10/90. Standard & Poor's and Lipper consider 12/87 through 6/90 and the most recent bull market and 6/90 through 11/90 as the most recent bear market in their report.

By contrast, *Worth* magazine looks at the fund's largest quarterly loss as another way for investors to gauge a fund's volatility.

All the services covered in this chapter go one step further than reporting the absolute volatility scores. They rank the fund's volatility in relation to other funds so that you can see which funds are the riskiest compared to all funds or by investment objective.

For example, here is how the Dodge & Cox Stock Fund is rated against all other stock funds according to risk by several fund reporting services.

Value Line gives the fund a risk rating of 3 for average. The least risky funds are rated 1 and the most risky are rated 5.

To arrive at that figure, *Value Line* does some nifty calculations. They rank funds based on their 36 month SDs. Stock and bond funds are ranked separately. Funds in the top 20 percent (based on SDs) have the highest risk rankings. Funds in the bottom 20 percent (based on SDs) are consider less risky.

Standard & Poor's/Lipper give the Dodge & Cox fund a volatility rating of 4 with 5 being the highest and 1 being the lowest. But this rating differs from Value Line's for a couple of reasons. The report considers volatility to be the degree to which a fund's monthly rates of return have fluctuated over the five-year period. Every fund's volatility measure are ranked from highest to lowest. Funds in the top 20 percent are assigned a measure of 5 for highest risk and 1 for lowest risk.

By contrast the *CDA/Wiesenberger Update* has a totally different way of using rankings to rate risk. The Dodge & Cox Stock Fund carries a CDA rating of 64, which is a slightly above average rating.

What does that mean? The CDA rating is a percentile rating from 1 (best) to 99 (worst). It is based on a fund's performance two up and two down markets in the past. The best rated funds score well in both up and down markets.

Morningstar gives risks another look, even though they score the Dodge & Cox Stock Fund as having average risk. Risk is based on the "fear of losing money." To measure that *Morningstar* looks at the number of months a fund underperforms T-bills, which are considered risk free investments to come up with an average loss statistic. *Morningstar* then ranks the funds compared to other funds in the investment class. The top 10 percent of the funds are considered the highest risk funds. Above average risk funds are in the next 22.5 percent group. Average risk funds are in the next 35 percent group. The last 10 percent are low risk funds.

The magazines reporting on fund risks use variations on this data.

Kiplinger's ranks the funds SD compared to all other equity funds over the past three years. *Kiplinger's* gives the Dodge & Cox Stock fund sure and a 3-year risk adjusted performance. Growth persistency is a proprietary measure that shows which funds consistently outperform other funds. While the risk adjusted return is the return per unit of risk—

the annual return divided by the fund's standard deviation. These three measures are scored and combined into at total score. Then the funds are ranked from 1(highest) to 5(lowest) versus their peers.

So, based on its VL score, the Dodge and Cox Stock Fund earns an overall score of 3, which is average.

Kiplinger's takes a different approach to measuring risk adjusted return. But the magazine still gives the Dodge & Cox Fund an average rating of C. *Kiplinger's* measures the fund's return per unit of risk subtracting the rate of return on three-month T-bills from the fund's three-year annual rate of return. That number is divided by the fund's performance standard deviation. The best managed funds are the funds with top ranks on this risk adjusted rate of return.

Notice that the volatility ratings change if the fund is evaluated over a long time period. *Business Week's* overall risk/return rating is based on a fund's performance over five years versus the S&P 500. Using the *Morningstar* risk data, BW looks at how often a fund outperforms the S&P 500 which is also adjusted for risk. Superior funds are rates by three red up arrows. Funds with very poor ratings have three blue down arrows. The Dodge & Cox Stock Fund is rated average by this publication.

Morningstar, however, gives the fund a 4 star (out of a possible 5 star) rating. This is a composite rating based on the fund's risk and return performance of three, five and ten years. The returns are adjusted for loads, combined with the risk score to come up with an overall number. Then a fund is ranked against other stock funds.

Worth looks at risk from a different angle. They rate funds based on whether they should be owned for the short, medium or long term, considering the fund's consistency of performance over ten years. Funds with the least volatility get A ratings for a short-term holding period of up to three years. The more volatile funds score higher ratings if they are held for the longer term. Based on those markets the Dodge & Cox Stock fund earned a C rating as a short-term hold and A ratings for medium- and long-term investors willing to buy and hold the fund for over years years.

Sources of Mutual Fund Information

Standard & Poor's/Lipper *Mutual Fund Profiles* (800/221-5277), 25 Broadway, NY, NY, 10004. The directory is published quarterly and costs $145. Single issues cost $48.

Mutual Fund Profiles covers approximately 1,000 mutual funds—700 equity and 300 bond funds. You get one half-page profile on each fund that includes the following information:

- Annual compound rates of return for 1, 5, and 10 years;

- What $1,000 grows to over the past five years;

- The five top sector and stock holdings;

- Total returns for each of the past five calendar years, including the fund's performance versus the investment objective, distributions, net asset value, total assets, expense ratio, and portfolio turnover;

- Investment objective of the fund and fund size;

- Name of the fund manager and the length of time he or she has managed the fund;

- Minimum initial and subsequent investment amounts;

- Loads and other charges;

- Fund size and expenses;

- Address and toll free telephone number.

Mutual Fund Profiles also evaluates the riskiness each fund by measuring each fund's five-year volatility and phase rating performance in up and down markets. The report considers volatility the degree to which a fund's monthly rates of return have fluctuated over the five-year period. Every fund's volatility measures are ranked from highest to lowest. Funds in the top 20 percent are assigned a measure of 5 for highest risk and 1 for lowest risk. The same calculation is used to determine the average volatility for investment objective categories.

The S&P/Lipper market phase rating is an evaluation of a fund's performance relative to its peer group during the current phase of the market cycle and past up and down markets. Each fund's total reinvestment rate of return during the market phase is calculated and ranked from best to worst relative to all other funds with the same investment objective. Funds in the top quintile rating receive the highest scores.

CDA Wiesenberger *Mutual Funds Update* (800/232-2285), 1355 Picard Drive, Rockville, MD 20850. CDA Technologies and Wiesenberger Investment Company Services have merged. The monthly report covers over 3,800 funds including money market and closed-end funds. The report costs $295 annually. Along with the subscription, users receive the annual *Mutual Funds Panorama,* a directory of all funds that lists addresses, toll free phone numbers, loads, fund size and minimum investment requirements.

The *Update* is arranged into several sections. The Mutual Fund Report features articles on industry trends, interviews with portfolio managers, and summary performance statistics of 23 open end mutual fund investment categories. Over a dozen market average performance indexes are also covered.

The second section is arranged by investment objective. A performance summary of each fund class shows how the group's high, low, and average performance from 1 month to 10 years. The high, low, and average CDA rating, beta value versus the S& P 500 and versus investment objective, the funds standard deviation, alpha and R squared statistics are also listed.

The monthly and year-to-date rank of the fund compared to its peers is listed along with the latest total return for one year, three years, five years and ten years. Also listed is how the fund performed in up markets and down markets, along with how it ranks among its peers. The fund's beta value based on its objective is also listed, along with the CDA rating. Total returns on each fund are reported for one month, year to date, one year, three years, five years and ten years. In addition, each fund's performance is ranked relative to other funds in the same investment category for each time period.

The last section of the *Update* is an alphabetical listing which includes the net asset values, percentage breakdown of the portfolio holdings, modern portfolio statistics, income and capital gains distributions, the 12 month change in principal, the yield and the SEC yield.

Mutual Funds Update also rates a fund's risk using two types of measures. First, the modern portfolio statistics on each fund show a fund's return per unit of risk and volatility in relation to the market. Second, CDA gives each fund a composite rating based on its performance during four market cycles—two up markets and two down markets. Funds rated 1 have performed the best over the past market cycles. Funds rated 99 are considered to be the worst performers.

Morningstar **Mutual Funds** (800/878-5005), 225 West Wacker Dr., Chicago, IL 60606. The reports are published every other week and cover over 1,200 stock and bond funds over a 20 week cycle. An annual subscription costs $395. A three month trial offer is $55.

Morningstar Mutual Fund Values provides investors with a comprehensive report on each fund. Included in each fund report are:

- A fund description andanalysis of the fund's portfolio management strategy;

- Loads, fees, fund size, investment minimums and fund manager;

- Fund total returns are reported for year to date, three month, six month and one, three, five, ten and fifteen years; fund quarterly totalreturns;

- a 400 word analyst's evaluation of the fund;

- fund manager, fees, investment minimum;

- a tax analysis, portfolio breakdown, stock exchange allocation, top 25 portfolio holdings, historical performance and an investment style box.

Calendar year performance can go back as far as 1983. Modern portfolio theory statistics that measure a fund's return per unit of risk and volatility are covered.

Morningstar Mutual Funds takes a different approach to measuring a fund's risk and return compared to the other services. The risk measure is designed to indicate the likelihood of losing money. Risk is calculated by taking a fund's total return in each month and subtracting the total return on three-month Treasury bills. Then all the negative returns are totaled and divided by the number of months in the period. T-bills are used as a benchmark representing the risk free rate of return.

This risk statistic is computed for all funds over three, five and ten years. Next all funds are ranked into five risk categories. those in the top 10 percent are high risk; the next 22.5 percent have above average risk; the next 35 percent are rated as average; the next 22.5 percent are rated below average and the bottom 10 percent are low risk.

Value Line reports on 1,500 funds by investment objective in nine issues over an 18-week cycle. The report lists performance over the past five years. The annual subscription is $295. A three-month trial subscription is $49.

Value Line uses a dual risk rating system. There is an overall rating rank and risk rank. The risk rank is based on the SD, a measure of a fund's price volatility. A 36-month period is used to calculate risk. Stock and bond funds are ranked separately.

The SD is used because it measures the variation in a fund's return. *Value Line* considers it a conservative way to measure risk because it "overstates risk." Funds with the largest SD exhibit the greatest price volatility.

Equity, bond, and tax-free bond funds are given an overall ranking score. The three factors that determine rank include a 1- and 5-year growth persistency measure and 3-year risk adjusted performance.

Growth persistency is a proprietary measure that shows if a fund consistently outperforms other funds. The risk adjusted return is the return per unit of risk. It is the annual return over the years divided by the fund's Standard Deviation.

These three measures are scored and combined into a total score. Then the funds are ranked from 1 (highest) to 5 (lowest) versus their peers. Other "bells and whistles" include the fund's 20 largest holdings and the *Value Line's* timeliness rankings on the individual stocks. You also get the most recent up and down market performance. In the near future the report will also show the performance in both bull and bear market cycles.

You also can see what $10,000 grows to after front or back end loss. Also included is what an initial $10,000 investment, plus $100 per month, grows to over three-month to 20-year periods. In addition, you can see what the estimated taxes are on a $10,000 investment over time. The information is also included in a graph.

Shareholder information, fund description, sector weights and composition, portfolio statistics, fund manager tenure, fund management style, dividends paid over the past five years, expense structure, 15 years of historical data on the NAV, dividends, 12- month yield, capital gains, expense ratio, expense ratio relative to peers, portfolio turnover, net assets in millions, total return, return versus the S&P 500 and to peers, quintile performance relative to peers. Also: MPT statistics and rankings based on overall, risk, growth and persistency, plus a 400 word narrative on the fund.

Kiplinger's Mutual Funds 1994. The first annual mutual fund survey costs $4.95. The special edition, which is published in March, covers over 2,600 stock and bond funds. The magazine also publishes a quarterly report on over 500 funds. Individual issues of the magazine cost just $2.95.

Micropal Inc., Des Moines, Iowa, supplies the data for *Kiplinger's* mutual fund report. You get a lot of information at an attractive price. The publication lists the funds' annualized total return over 1,3, and 5 years. The total return is calculated by reinvesting fund dividend and capital gain distributions when they occur. Distributions are reinvested at either pay date, record date or ex-dividend date, depending on the fund. Total returns are less management fees and fund expenses, but not loads.

In addition to the fund's total return and investment objective, you get the following information to help you invest:

Each fund is ranked against other funds in the same category by deciles each year and over the past five years. A fund with a rank of one means that it was in the top ten percent of the performers in its class. Those rated 10 performed worse than 90 percent of all funds in their class. A fund ranked 10 means it did better than 90 percent of all funds in its investment class.

Also listed is the fund's risk adjusted rating. This is the fund's return per unit of risk. It is measured by subtracting the rate of return on 3-month T-bills from the funds 3 year annual rate of return. That number is divided by the funds performance standard deviation. The standard deviation is a complicated statistic that measures a fund's swing in price. The best managed funds are the funds with the highest risk adjusted performance numbers or the funds with the best returns per unit of risk.

Next the funds are ranked by risk adjusted performance from top to bottom in quintiles and assigned grades of A for highest and E for lowest.

The performance report also lists the decile rankings and risk adjusted grades of the fund versus all mutual funds. Stock funds in the report receive a volatility ranking with 1 being the most risky funds and 10 being the least risk. The rating is calculated by ranking the fund's standard deviation over the past three years.

The yield on bond funds is calculated by looking at the dividends of the past 12 months divided by the current share price, plus the capital gains. This yield differs from the SEC yield based on a 30-day annualized return that funds are required to report to investors. You also get information about how long the portfolio manger has been at the helm of the fund, the minimum initial investment, sales load and the expense ratio with or without the 12b-1 charge. The expense ratio is the total annual charge, excluding sales loads that is paid to run the fund.

Money **magazine.** Each monthly issue, which sells for $3.95, covers over 3000 funds by investment objective. Morningstar, Inc., provides *Money* with the data for the report. In addition to statistics, you also get "how to" investment articles on fund performance analysis, including the following:

- Annual performance. Annual compound rates of return over one, three, and five years are listed and the annual performance by year over the last five years. Also, reinvested fund distributions and the fund's specific reinvestment date, either ex-dividend date, pay date, or record date.

- Risk level weights both the likelihood that a fund will underperform a risk free T-bill in any given month and the magnitude of such under-performance based on the fund's three-year record. Money then compares each funds risk with that of all other funds and rates them on an evenly divided scale from 1 to 12. The higher the number the riskier the fund.

- Annual charges listed in the report include: Sales charges, annual charges, which are known as expense ratios, and the five-year total cost per $1,000 investment assuming a 5 percent annual return and redemption after five years. *Money* doesn't break out the 12b-1 fees which are included in the expense ratio.

Forbes **magazine's Annual Mutual Fund Survey.** Each fall *Forbes* devotes an issue of the magazine to mutual funds. Covered the over 2,000 funds by investment objective ($4). *Forbes* uses CDA/Wiesenberger's data. As a result, fund distributions are reinvested at month-end to derive the fund's total returns. Forbes lists the fund's total return for a one-year period ending in June and past ten years ending in June. Also reported are the 12-month yield, assets, weighted average p/e of the fund's holdings, median market capitalization of the fund, maximum sales charges, and annual fund expenses per $100.

Forbes evaluates a fund's risk based on up and down market performance. The report compares the funds with records over three up periods and grades them on a curve for bull market performance. Funds with only two segments of bull market performance are graded separately against one another. The same is done for bear market performance. Funds in the top 5 percent in each category are graded A+, the next 15 percent receive an A rating, the next 25 percent receive a B, the next 25 percent receive a C rating, the next 25 a D rating, and the remaining 5 percent receive an F. Also included are addresses, toll free phone numbers, and investment requirements.

Forbes' Honor Roll Funds are the top performing funds over 3 market cycles that span the most recent ten years. Funds have to earn a B rating in down market performance. A is the highest and D is the lowest.

The magazine also comes out with quarterly performance reports on over 500 funds. Each fund is rated by comparing its returns with funds of the same type and with the appropriate market indexes. Domestic funds are measured against the S&P 500. Balanced funds are rated against the S&P 500 and the Merrill Lynch corporate and government bond index. International funds are rated against Morgan Stanley's Europe Australia and Far East Index (EAFA).

Business Week's Mutual Fund Report covers 1,000 funds. But the magazine also publishes a separate mutual fund almanac that covers over 2,000 funds by investment objective. Data is supplied by Morningstar, Inc. The cost $2.75.

The report covers the average annual returns, both pre-tax and after tax over 3,5 and 10 years. In addition, you get a 10-year trend analysis on each fund. A fund's performance is evaluated relative to the performance of the stock or bond market for a 30-month period. The funds are then ranked by quartiles. The best rated stock funds, for example, outperformed 75 percent of all other stock funds relative to the S&P 500. The worst funds underperformed 75 percent of all other funds.

Business Week's risk adjusted rating is based on a 5-year measure relative to the S&P 500. BW subtracts the fund's risk of loss factor from the historical pre-tax return to get a positive number. Funds must beat the S&P 500 on a risk adjusted basis. Superior funds are designated by three "up" arrows. Poor performing funds are designated by three "down" arrows.

BW also reports the following information: Portfolio manager changes; Changes in assets over the previous year;Sales charges; Expense ratios; Last year's pre-tax and after-tax return (assuming a 31 percent tax bracket), and the pre-tax and after-tax returns over three, five and 10 years; Yield; How the fund ranks within its objective; Portfolio turnover and p/e ratio; Investment style; Untaxed gains as percent of assets; Largest holding; and risk which is based on the Morningstar methodology.

Worth magazine: reports on over 600 funds by investment objective. The magazine uses *Morningstar's* data on funds that have a 10-year track record. The cost is $3.

Worth grades funds from A on F on whether they can meet investors' needs over the short-mid and long term. Funds that exhibit the least risk, for example, carry A ratings for short-term investments.

The ratings are based on the following calculations:

- First, they look at the fund's three-, five-, and ten-year annualized returns.

- Second, they look at the fund's up-front commissions and annual fees.

- Third they look at risk which is based on the consistency of a fund's performance, as well as its largest loss.

- Fourth, they look at fund management, based on how long the fund's portfolio manager has been running the fund, the size of the fund and the portfolio turnover rate.

To find out which mutual funds do best in different time frames, *Worth* weights the grades to emphasis different factors.

- Short-term investors with a one- to three-year time horizon: *Worth* focuses on consistency, the largest one-quarter loss and the up-front commission.

- Mid-term investors with a four- to ten-year time horizon: *Worth* focuses on performance and less on commissions.

- Long term investors with greater than ten-year investment horizon: *Worth* focuses on performance and expenses.

Like other reports, *Worth* includes the following information to help you make an investment decision: Load charge; annual expense ratio; annual returns over 10, 5 and 3 years; biggest losses in single quarter; fund manger's tenure; total assets and portfolio turnover rate.

Worth's consistency rating is based on the Morningstar risk rating. It is the average percent by which a fund underperforms the risk free rate of return(T-bills) compiled during those quarters when it returns less than T-bills.

U.S. News & World Report's **Money Guide,** August, 1993, covers 150 mutual funds by investment objective. The cost, $2.

Listed are the fund's cumulative 10 year, 5-year and 12-month total returns. You can also see what $1,000 grew to in the fund over five years. The expense ratio, assets and toll free number are listed.

The funds are ranked based on an overall performance rating (OPI) by Kanon Block Carre, a Boston-based fund research firm. The OPI rating measures the relative performance of each fund over the past one, three, five and ten years and during the 1990s bear market. A fund's volatility or how much its average return fluctuates over time is factored into the equation.

The closer the OPI is to 100, the better the fund's long-term record. USNW says that funds with bear market and volatility grades lower than C+ were eliminated from the report. These funds fared worse than 50 percent of funds during the 1990s bear market and were more volatile than half the funds.

Chapter 6

Mutual Fund Risks

Before you implement an investment strategy, you must understand the investment risks, your own financial goals and your comfort level.

Here are some of the risks you run up against no matter what kind of investment tactics you use.

- Market timing. You could find yourself investing in bonds or stocks at a market peak, only to find the market is declining.

- Lost opportunity. Many investors like the safety of federally insured CDs, but buying CDs involves risk, too. You could find yourself locked into one as interest rates are rising.

- Credit risk. You could be attracted to the high yields offered by junk bonds with low credit ratings. During a recession, however, issuers with lower credit-rated companies may have a hard time paying back principal and interest to lenders.

- Interest-rate risk. Bond prices and interest rates move in opposite directions. If interest rates rise, bond prices decline. The longer the maturity on the bond, the greater the price drop. If, for example, interest rates rose one percent, your 20-year 9 percent bond would lose about ten percent of its market value. A short-term note with a maturity of ten years would lose about half that much.

- Diversification risk. If you don't plan your investments carefully, you could find yourself holding a limited number or type of stocks or bonds unhedged. You might make big profits, but you'd have nothing to balance out potential losses.

No one can eliminate risk. The best way to protect your hard-earned assets is to diversify with stocks, bonds, money funds and precious metals. Or you can use dollar cost averaging in an investment. Others may prefer to use some kind of market timing to mitigate the risk or set up a hedged investment. Before you decide how to go about the business of managing your investment portfolio, you must ask yourself how much you would be willing to lose in a given year. Are you comfortable accepting a two- or four-percent loss? Could you handle losing six or eight percent in 1990? Maybe you could even accept a ten percent loss for the chance of earning 20 percent.

How Much Are You Willing to Lose?

Try answering the questions below developed by Michael Lipper, president of Lipper Analytical Services in New York. Lipper's questionnaire is one of the best, because it clearly focuses on the risk-return relationship.

If you score 5 on the risk test, you have a low tolerance for risk. You would be better suited for dollar cost averaging into a stock fund or rebalancing a diversified portfolio of stock and bond funds.

A score of 10 means you're a moderate investor. That means you are willing to use a more aggressive tactic to move between different kinds of equity funds. You may be inclined to double up on your long-term mutual fund investments when the price drop.

Those that score 25 designates you as a risk taker. You can invest in aggressive stock and use some kinds of market timing tactics to switch between funds.

Circle your answers and just add up the numbers.

- My investment is for the long term. The end result is more important than how I went about achieving it.

(1) Totally disagree; (2) can accept variability, but not losses of capital; (3) can accept reasonable amounts of price fluctuation in total return; (4) can accept an occasional year of negative performance in the interest of building capital; (5) agree.

- Rank the importance of current income. (1) Essential and must be known; (2) essential but willing to accept uncertainty about the amount; (3) important, but there are other factors to consider; (4) modest current income is desirable; (5) irrelevant.

- Rank the amount of decline you can accept in a single quarter.

  (1) None; (2) a little, but not for the entire year; (3) consistency of results is more important than performance; (4) a few quarters of decline is a small price to pay to be invested when the stock market takes off; (5) unimportant.

- Rank the importance of beating inflation. (1) Preservation of capital and income are more important; (2,3,4) willing to invest to beat inflation, but other investment needs come first; (5) essential to ensure that you get a real return on your investment.

- Rank the importance of beating the stock market over the economic cycle. (1) Irrelevant; (2,3,4) prefer consistency over superior results; (5) critical.

What Kind of Investment Strategy Is Right for You?

Once you've zeroed in on how much risk you're willing to take, you can start investigating what investments are right for you. You don't want to sink your funds in a go-go over-the-counter growth stock if you're averse to risk. Conversely, if you need growth for the long term, you don't want to invest in bonds for interest income. You must match the riskiness of your investments with your objectives.

Chapter 7

How to Evaluate Performance

Now that you've got your mutual fund investment strategy up and running, how can you tell if it is working?

You cannot just compare a mix of stocks, bonds, metals, money funds, and real estate with the performance of the Dow Jones Industrial Average or the S&P 500—your portfolio is a different type of organism altogether.

First of all, you pay management fees and other charges when you invest in mutual funds.

Second, most mutual funds keep at least 3 percent to 6 percent of their portfolio in cash to meet redemptions.

So right off the bat you are behind the 8-ball. The S&P 500 or Lehman Brothers Corporate/Government bond index are unmanaged benchmarks or baskets of securities.

What if you are dollar cost averaging into a well managed stock fund? You are not going to outperform a buy and hold on the S&P 500 or the return on a fully invested stock fund over the longer term.

What if you're timing the market-moving in and out of stock funds and money funds to reduce downside risk or to boost returns?

You need some realistic benchmark to compare your investment tactics with. You need to see if they are working properly.

So check your returns at least every six months to see how they are doing in relation to comparable investments.

Evaluating Diversified Mutual Fund Portfolios

Asset-allocated portfolios are safer than pure stock or bond indexes, for one thing. You will not outperform the stock market during a bull market, but you will not tumble with it during a bear market, either. Even though you split up your investments among different types of individual securities or mutual funds, you still face several dangers, however. Here are a few cautionary notes:

- First, sometimes all classes of assets lose money at the same time. You could conceivably be holding onto a growth-stock mutual fund, a bond fund, and a gold fund that all decline in price at the same time.

- Second, if you split up the total too evenly among different assets, losses and gains could be equal—a result known as a washout-over the long term. You could end up squeezing out a minimal return comparable to that of a passbook savings account.

- Third, you may lose opportunity if you invest too little in stocks and the market goes into a sustained rally.

The Secret of Value-Added Gain

You really cannot compare apples to oranges. Your portfolio is safer than the stock market, so you will not rack up huge gains overnight even if the market does. One way to judge allocation performance is to apply a simple technique that pension-fund portfolio managers have been using for years. Figure the value-added gain of your portfolio—how your specific mix performs compared to several benchmark indicators. These might include T-bills or a fixed percentage of stocks and bonds based on the S&P 500 and Lehman Brothers or Salomon Brothers Corporate Bond Index.

Here's a quick and easy way to see how your investments are performing. Check a copy of *Barron's* every three months when it publishes the quarterly data on mutual funds. Look at the section that lists the mutual funds performance categories computed by Lipper Analytical Services. A certain section shows the percentage gain, with reinvestment of dividends, of stock, bond, and other types of mutual funds. We are assuming that the average performance of all stock, bond, or gold funds will be a close approximation of the market averages in those categories.

Then calculate the total return on your investments. If you do not want to perform all these calculations and you are heavily allocated with mutual funds, you can read several newsletters that list specific mutual funds and index total returns.

You also could go to the public library and check the CDA/ Wiesenberger's\ Investment Company Service, *Standard & Poor's Stock Guide, Value Line Mutual Fund Survey* or *Morningstar Mutual Funds.* You also can check *Standard & Poor's Stock and Bond Guides.*

Remember that the gain includes the price appreciation of the security and the reinvestment of dividends and/or capital gains in new shares. You will have to check the most recent statement from your mutual fund to see how many shares and at what price per share, or net asset value, distributions were reinvested.

Mutual funds are a little different because dividends and capital gains can be reinvested in new shares. You will have to calculate the total return this way: If you invested $3,000 in 100 shares of ABC Equity Income Fund at $30 a share and you reinvested dividends of $1.20 per share at $32, this equals $120 in dividend income, divided by the current price of $32. This calculation equals 3.75 new shares. Your total number of shares is now 103.75. At the end of the quarter, the market value of your investment is now $35 per share. The value of your investment is now 103.75 shares multiplied by $35 or $3,631.25. Your total return or percentage gain with reinvestment is 21.04 percent.

Next compare the return on your allocated portfolio with that of the Lipper indexes that are listed in *Barron's* every week. Calculate the percentage gain on your total investment and subtract that from the performance of the same amount in your benchmark.

Let's posit a blended portfolio with 30 percent in an aggressive-stock fund, 10 percent in a growth and income fund, 42 percent in an international fund, 12 percent in a gold fund, and 6 percent in a money fund. How might it do?

Let's say, your aggressive stock fund gained 14 percent over the past 12 months. Your growth and income fund gained 18.5 percent, the international fund which invested in Latin America and the Far East grew 19.6 percent, the gold fund lost 20 percent, and the income fund gained 8 percent. Your actual gain was: .30(14) + .10(18.5)+ .42(19.6) + .12(-20) + .06(8) = 12.30 percent. A 20 percent split against the fund averages in each category in Exhibit 7–1 resulted in a gain of .20(7.49) + .20(9.45) + .20(-3.75) + .20(-15.07) + .20(10.84) = 1.79 percent.

You had one heck of a year. The 12.30 percent increase in your portfolio, minus the 1.79 percent index gain equals a 10.51 percent value added gain, or an extra $105.10 per $1,000, on your asset allocation mix compared to the benchmark.

Of course this is just a hypothetical example. Your objective is to diversify your investments based on your risk tolerance. You may or may not outperform the average by a wide margin.

No matter what type of investment strategy you use, in addition to viewing how well you did compared to the S&P 500 or a bond market index, check to see how you did compared with balanced funds—the funds in which the portfolio manager maintains about a 60/40 stock-and-bond split.

If the average balanced fund gained 9 percent and you earned 12.3 percent, you received a value-added gain of 3.3 percent over this benchmark. You earned an extra $33 per $1,000 one your investment compared to balanced funds.

Evaluating Your Portfolio's Performance

Exhibit 7–1

Your investments			Indexes		
Fund	% mix	% return class	% mix	% return class	% differ
A.					
B.					
C.					
D.					
E.					
Total					

How to Evaluate Dollar Cost Averaging

What if you are socking away your IRA in a growth stock fund and you want to evaluate how you are doing? You won't outperform a buy and hold strategy that is fully invested from day one because you are investing a little at a time.

Fortunately, the *Value Line Mutual Fund Survey* illustrates dollar cost averaging performance on all the stock and bond funds it tracks. So you can check how your fund compares with similar funds over one year to 20 years.

Look up your fund in the *Value Line Mutual Fund Survey* and check its dollar cost averaging analysis. Then compare your fund with similar funds.

Comparing Dollar Cost Averaging Performance Using Value Line Mutual Fund Survey

Exhibit 7–2

Fund	Your Fund $ Value	Other Fund $ Value	$ Difference
A.			
B.			
C.			
D.			

How to Evaluate Your Market Timing Tactics

Of course you want to see how your fund did against the S&P 500 and the average equity fund.

If you are timing the bond markets, compare the performance with the average bond fund and Lehman or Salomon Brothers bond index.

What is your motive for using market timing? Are you trying to hit a home run? If you are, then you want to outperform the market averages over time.

Or are you switching between stock funds and money funds to protect assets? You want to avoid large losses in the event the market plunges. You want to get out before the bear market hits.

Speculative investors want to outperform the market.

Those who use market timing for asset protection must look at:

- How many times they got in and out of stock or bond funds.

- How they performed versus other funds or the market.

You goals may be to earn 85 percent of the return on the S&P 500, but with half the risk of losing money.

For example: Say your market timing tactic resulted in a 8.5 percent gain when the S&P returned 10 percent: Look at how many times your market timing strategy got you out of the market and prevented large losses. Also look at how many times you got whipsawed-exited stocks only to find the market moving higher or enter stocks only to find the market move lower.

- You can also compare how your market timing strategy performed against the pros. There are a fistful of market timing mutual funds available to investors.

The best market timing funds over the past four years ending in January 1995: Zweig Strategy A Fund (gained 12.4 percent annually), Flexfund Muirfield (grew at an 11.7 percent annual rate) and Rightime Fund (gained 11.4 percent annually).

The worst performing market timing funds over the past four years: Rightime Growth (up 5.0 percent annually), Monitrend Summation (down 1.6 percent annually) and Merriman Capital Appreciation (up 7.8 percent annually).

The Hulbert Financial Digest is another excellent source. Check to see how your strategy did with the market timing newsletters (see the directory in the appendix). This publication also rates the newsletters based on risk versus return.

Evaluating Market Timing

1. Number of switches in and out of stock or bond funds _____.

2. Number of times whipsawed_____.

3. Performance versus benchmark index over 6 months__ 1yr__ 2yr__ 3yr__ 4yr__ 5yr__

4. Performance versus market timing mutual funds 6 months__ 1yr__ 2yr__ 3yr__ 4yr__ 5yr__

5. Return/losses versus benchmark: Return on timing as a percent of S&P 500 or bond index____. Loss on index less loss on your investment_____.

Points to Remember

- Compare your portfolio to returns on the market, similar funds, and a 50 percent stock and 50 percent bond fund split.

- You want to measure apples to apples. If you have an investment that is 60 percent stock funds and 40 percent bond funds, it's not going to perform as well as a 100 percent stake in the average diversified stock fund.

- Use *Value Line Mutual Fund Survey* to compare how dollar cost averaging is working in your fund, compared to similar funds.

- Compare market timing to the performance on the S&P 500 or the average stock fund. Also look at how your market timing tactic performed in relation to market timing mutual funds.

PART III

Mutual Fund Investment Strategies

Chapter 8

Buy and Hold Investing

The buy and hold investment strategy is the simplest to use if you plan to invest for the longer term—at least five years or more, preferably twenty years if you are saving for retirement.

Buy and hold is best suited for retirement savings through an IRA, 401(k) pension plan or a variable annuity. That's because your money grows tax-deferred until you retire.

It also works well if you are saving for a young child's future college education. This is money you put away in a well managed stock fund and leave until you retire.

With buy and hold you simply invest it through thick and thin for a long period of time. Of course before you invest it's important to have a financial game plan.

- You need to have a budget and savings goals.

- You need to have disability and life insurance.

- You need to have at least six months of income in cash to meet daily needs and emergencies.

- You need to save and invest regularly.
- You need to evaluate your tolerance for risk, and determine an investment comfort level.

Loss of Volatility over the Short Term

Over the short term, stock and bond prices can move up and down. But over the long haul, when you buy and hold, you make risk work for you, not against you.

When you invest for the long term, you are investing in the economic growth of the U.S., as well as the rest of the world. We do experience booms and busts, known as "business cycles." But over time, economies worldwide grow.

Just look at the performance of stocks, bonds, Treasury bills and inflation over the past 70 years in Exhibit 8–1. You can see that a dollar invested in large company stocks in 1925 has grown to $800 by year-end 1993, according to Ibbotson Associates data.

One buck invested in small company stocks grew to $2,757 during the same period. While $1 invested in bonds and T-bills grew to $28 and $12 respectively.

Now look at inflation. One buck grew to $8 over 7 years.

Almost no one can invest for 70 years. But during our life time we can invest for periods of five years to 50 years, depending on our financial resources and investment goals. That means we are likely to earn about the historical rates of return on our investment.

Scott Lummer, vice president with Ibbotson Associates, an investment advisory firm based in Chicago, says that the longer you invest, the more likely you are to earn close to the historical rate of return on stocks.

Over a 20-year holding period, he says "common stock investors are likely to earn a 5 percent to 6 percent premium over the rate on a 20-year U.S. Treasury bond, based on historical relationships."

At the time of this writing, anyone who bought the S&P 500 could expect to see the value of that investment grow at about an 11 percent annual rate, assuming that the returns over 20 years approximate the historical rate of returns on stocks and bonds.

In the left hand corner of Exhibit 8–1 you will see the annual compound rate of returns on investments.

Exhibit 8–1 What $! Grows to 1925–1993

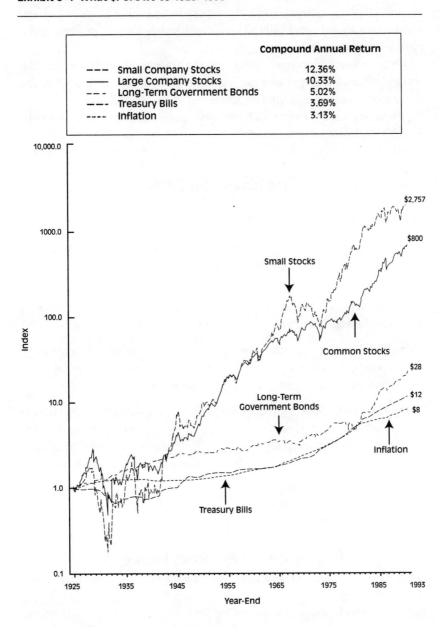

	Compound Annual Return
– – – Small Company Stocks	12.36%
—— Large Company Stocks	10.33%
– – – Long-Term Government Bonds	5.02%
– – – Treasury Bills	3.69%
- - - - Inflation	3.13%

As you can see, stocks historically have grown at an annual rate of around 10 percent. Small company stocks have grown at a 12.4 percent annual rate. Bonds and bills have earned much less—5 percent and 4 percent respectively.

Of course you don't get something for nothing. As you see from the squiggly lines that represent the returns on stocks and bonds: Over the short term, you can lose money investing in financial assets.

There are a lot of risks you have to navigate in the financial markets. That's why you can lose money in the short run.

The Risks You Face

You must contend with a number of risks when you invest.

- *Market risk.* If the overall stock or bond markets decline, your stock or bond fund investment is likely to drop in value.

- *Non-market risk.* Bad news about a company can drive the stock price down. If you own the stock or a fund with a large position in the stock, the value of your investment could drop.

- *Bond interest rate risk.* Bond price and interest rates move in opposite directions. When interest rates rise, bond prices fall. The longer the maturity, the bigger the loss in value.

- *Credit risk.* Bonds are debt obligations. So when you invest in corporate bonds, you run the risk that the issue may default on interest and principal payments. High grade corporate bonds are rated single A to triple A by Standard & Poor's and Moody's.

- *Inflation risk.* The purchasing power of your investments is eroded by inflation over the years.

The Financial Markets React to the Risks Every Day

Bond and stock prices are driven by investors' expectations of future events. The value of investments changes based on risks involved in the financial markets. That's why stock and bond returns fluctuate.

In any given year over the past 70 years, the margin of error in investment returns has been quite wide. According to Ibbotson Associates, the margin of error on the historical rate of return on large company stocks is 21 percent. Stocks average 10 percent. But 68 percent of the time over the last seven decades in any given year you could have lost 11 percent or gained 31 percent. With small company stocks the margin of error is much greater. At –32 percent, in any given year you could have earned –19 percent or gained 43 percent 68 percent of the time.

The margin of error on bonds is much smaller. But you could still lose money. In any given year over the past seven decades, your bond investment could have earned –3 percent or gained 13 percent.

Exhibit 8–2 shows you the value of long-term investing. You can see how risky it is to invest in stocks for just one or even five years. According to Ibbotson Associates data, the highest return and lowest return on stocks for one-year periods are +54 percent and –43 percent.

You can lose your shirt if you invest in a hot stock fund for one year. (See Exhibit 8–3.)

Over five-year periods, the high and low returns are +24 percent and –12 percent. You still can take a licking in a stock fund if you own it for just five years.

Now come the holding periods when it pays to invest in stock or stock funds. Over 10-year holding periods, the high and low are +20 percent and –1 percent.

For 20-year holding periods the high and the low were +17 percent and +3 percent.

You Can't Hit a Home Run

Be aware that you run the risk of losing money if you invest just for a year in the hope of making big profits. Other Ibbotson data show that investors lost money 30 percent of the time in every one-year period since 1926. But over the longer-term, the risk of losing money was greatly reduced. Eleven percent of the time there were losses in every five-year holding period since 1926. Over every 20-year investment period, however, there were no losses.

Exhibit 8–2 Value of Long-Term Investment (1926–1992)

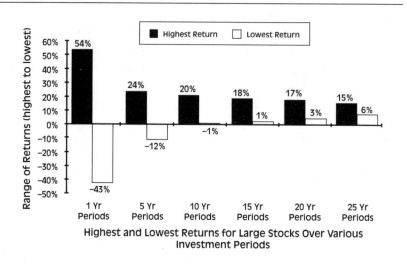

Highest and Lowest Returns for Large Stocks Over Various
Investment Periods

Exhibit 8–3 Long-Terrm Investing

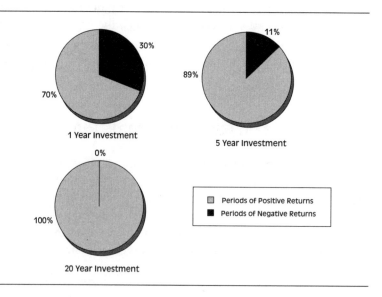

Short-Term Volatility vs. Long-Term Rewards

You also have to weigh the risks and returns of investing in stocks, bonds and cash. Stocks are riskier than bonds and bonds are riskier than cash investments such as T-bills, CDs and money funds.

There is a tradeoff, however, for the high returns from stocks. Stocks can be volatile. Although equities have averaged 10 percent a year, the returns vary from year to year. The highest and lowest returns for stocks over every one-year period since 1926 are +54 percent and –43 percent, respectively.

By contrast, the highest and lowest annual returns in long-term government bonds over the past 66 years are +40.4 percent and –9.2.

T-bills are even less risky. The highest and lowest annual returns over the past 66 years are +14.7 percent and 0 percent.

Real Returns

Don't forget inflation. During the past 15 years, T-bills registered an annual return of 8.2 percent. After inflation, however, you earned just 2.3 percent a year on your money.

The inflation-adjusted annual return over the same period is 8.2 percent on stocks and 4 percent for bonds. A 50–50 stock-bond split gave you a 6.1 percent return after inflation with half the risk of losing money if compared with a 100 percent stake in the stock market.

Equity Fund Returns

How have mutual funds performed over the longer term? According to Lipper Analytical Services, Summit, NJ, the average equity fund gained 11.6 percent annually over 30 years. Over 20, 10 and 5 years, the average equity funds grew at annual rates of 13.7 percent, 11.6 percent and 13.1 percent respectively for the periods ended in June 1993.

How long can these mutual funds' returns continue? No one knows what tomorrow might bring. Past performance is no indication of future results. All we can say is that long-term historical performance shows that it's best to have a financial game plan to invest and meet your financial goals. If you try and make a big profit and chase after hot mutual fund returns, you could lose your shirt.

The Longer You Own Stocks, the More Chances to Profit

In addition, the longer you hold onto stocks, the greater the chance you have of outperforming T-bills. You have a 61.23 percent chance of beating T-bills with a one-year holding period and a 91.7 percent chance of coming out on top, if you hold stocks for 15 years, according to Investment Information Services, Chicago.

The Longer the Holding Period, the Lower the Annual Loss

Some investment advisers scoff at buying and holding for the long haul. They claim that they can make judgments by using computer-driven buy-and-sell programs, which are based on economic and stock market price trends, to move in and out of the markets to maximize gains. These advisers may be right for a short period of time, but over the long term, market timers fail to beat the market averages. When you hold stocks for the long term, you always carefully invested to catch the turns in the market. You might take one step back as mentioned previously, but when you are in position to catch a rebound with all your money, you make two steps forward. For example, look at the worst losing periods in stock market history to give you some insight into how buy and hold investing works. According to Investment Information Services, Chicago:.

- The maximum loss you would have experienced for five years from 1928 to 1932 was an annual 12.5 percent.

- For 10 years from 1929 to 1938 you would have lost .9 percent

- For 15 years from 1929 to 1943 you would have gained .6 percent annually.

Buy and Hold versus Market Timing

Later in the book you will read about market timing. Or you can move in and out of stock or bond funds based on technical indicators for telling a rise or decline in the financial markets.

Buy and hold investors, however, scoff at market timing. The reason: There are so few periods that contribute to the rise in stock prices, that it pays to stay fully invested. If you try and time the markets and miss one of these critical periods, your returns drop like a sinking ship.

According to a study conducted by Lipper Analytical Services, from 1974 through 1993, if you bought and held the S&P 500, your 20-year investment grew at 12.8 percent annual rate. But if you missed important months of stock market performance over the past 20 years or 240 months, here is how you fared.

- Less the best month in the market. The annual return drops to 11.9 percent.

- Less the three best months in the market. The annual return drops to 10.5 percent.

- Less the five best months. The annual return drops to 9.3 percent.

- Less the 10 best months. The annual return drops to 6.5 percent.

What If You Invest a Lump Sum at the Worst Possible Time?

As long as you can buy and hold for the long term, you will be OK.

Exhibit 8–4 shows you the years of the worst possible returns in stock market history. The figure also shows you how much $1,000 grew to in each of the stock market's 20 poor performing years.

1974 ranks as one of the worst years in stock market history. The S&P 500 lost 26.5 percent. Your $1,000 initial investment was worth $735 by year end 1974. Not too great.

But if you stuck it out, you did well. By the end of 1990, your investment was worth $7,185, representing a 12.3 percent annual rate of return.

What about 1977. Your $1,000 investment lost 7.2 percent. But by year end 1990, it grew to $5,744.

Exhibit 8–4 Negative Return Years for the Standard & Poor's 500

Year	Total Return	Year	Total Return
1929	−8.4	1953	−1.0
1930	−24.9	1957	−10.8
1931	−43.3	1962	−8.7
1932	−8.2	1966	−10.1
1934	−1.4	1969	−8.5
1937	−35.0	1973	−14.3
1939	−0.4	1974	−26.5
1940	−9.8	1977	−7.2
1941	−11.6	1981	−4.9
1946	−8.1	1990	−3.2

$1,000 Invested in Each of the Stock Market's 20 Off Years

	Standard & Poor's 500		Long-Term Government Bonds	
Year	Value on 12–31–90	Average Rate of Return	Average Rate of Return	Value on 12–31–90
1929	$234,317	9.2	4.5	$15,311
1930	253,665	9.5	4.6	15,539
1931	339.544	10.2	4.6	14,856
1932	615,485	11.5	4.7	15,026
1934	424,593	11.2	4.6	12,981
1937	219,565	10.5	4.5	10,772
1939	261,667	11.3	4.5	9,864
1940	257,643	11.5	4.5	9,439
1941	289,002	12.0	4.5	9,033
1946	126,776	11.4	4.5	7,248
1953	54,593	11.1	5.3	7,117
1957	25,548	10.1	5.8	8,900
1962	14,273	9.6	6.4	6,044
1966	9,668	9.5	6.9	5,302
1969	7,821	9.8	8.2	6,127
1973	6,132	10.6	8.6	4,795
1974	7,185	12.3	9.2	4,875
1977	5,744	13.3	9.1	3,693
1981	3,675	13.9	13.7	3,611
1990	968	−3.2	6.2	1,062
Total	$3,159,864			$169,502

Source: American Society of CLU & ChFC.

Points to Remember

- Ask yourself how long you plan to invest. Over the short-term you face a strong possibility of losing money. But if you buy and hold for the long haul, you will be rewarded.

- Mutual funds are designed to be long-term investments.

- When you stay fully invested you always catch the turns in the market.

- If you buy and hold, you don't have to worry about paying capital gains taxes on investment profits. You haven't sold.

- Mutual fund distribute dividends and capital gains on stocks the fund has sold. You will have to pay taxes on the distributions unless the money is invested in a tax-deferred investment like an IRA or variable annuity.

- Stocks are riskier than bonds. Bonds are riskier than money funds and T-bills. But the higher the risk the greater return over the long haul.

Chapter 9

Dollar Cost Averaging

Not many investors can time the markets—get in at the bottom and get out at the top for a fat profit. For the average investor dollar cost averaging may be the best way to go.

Dollar cost averaging (DCA) entails making periodic payments of a fixed amount, such as $100 a month, over a time span of at least ten years to buy individual securities or mutual funds. DCA works best in retirement savings plans: It forces you to make a disciplined, long-term commitment to an investment that grows tax-deferred until you take distributions at retirement. When you buy in a disciplined manner, you buy more shares at a lower price when prices are falling. On the upside, you also accumulate shares at lower prices if the market keeps rising. Over the long term, your periodic purchases will result in an average cost that will be lower than the market price.

DCA is a safe way for the average person to invest for it eliminates market timing decisions. Most investors tend to buy at market peaks when mutual funds or stocks are receiving a great deal of media attention; unfortunately, these are the points at which the market usually plunges. Or, in a falling market, investors typically buy, hold, pray and eventually panic and sell at the worst possible times, as the market bottoms out before a rebound.

Dollar cost averaging eliminates the guesswork. You will always be fully invested to catch the turns in the market. This hypothetical example shows you how it works.

Let's say you invest $100 every three months in a stock fund that sells at $10 per share. You invest $100 and receive ten shares. The market drops and—taking an extreme, but easy example to follow—the fund goes down to $5 per share. You again invest your $100 the next quarter. At $5 per share you would receive 20 shares for your $100. Let's assume by the next quarter the market has returned to where it was when you started and your fund is now selling at $10 per share. You now receive ten shares for your $100 investment. Here is what your investment looks like.

Exhibit 9–1 Fluctuating Market

Regular Investment	Share Price	Shares Acquired
$100	$10	10
$100	$5	20
$100	$10	10
Total $300	$25	40

Average share cost: $7.50 ($300 divided by 40)

Average share price: $8.33 ($25 divided by 3)

Source: Investment Company Institute

You own 40 shares of the fund in which you invested $300. Your shares are worth more than you paid. The average price on your three investments was $8.33. The average cost was $7.50 since you invested $300 and bought a total of 40 shares.

The idea behind dollar cost averaging is to invest for the longer term. That way you will be sure to catch the down markets and be fully invested in the up markets. You have to stick with a fund in down markets, otherwise you may be forced to sell shares at a loss.

Here is what will happen on the downside assuming you invested $300 every three months:

Exhibit 9–2 Declining Market

Investment	Share Price	Shares Bought
$300	$25	12
$300	$15	20
$300	$20	15
$300	$10	30
$300	$5	60
Total $1,500	$75	137

Average share cost: $10.95 ($1,500 divided by 137)

Average share price: $15.00 ($75 divided by 5)

Source: Investment Company Institute

If you have to sell in down markets, you can take a real licking with dollar cost averaging. The share priced dropped from a high of $25 to $5. Fortunately, dollar cost averaging enables you to accumulate more shares at a lower price. The average share price of your investment over the 15-month period was $15.00. Fortunately, you were accumulating shares, so the average cost was $10.95.

The upside is where you can make money with dollar cost averaging. You rode out the tough times and bought more shares at a lower

Exhibit 9–3 Rising Market

Investment	Share Price	Shares Acquired
$300	$5	60
$300	$15	20
$300	$10	30
$300	$15	20
$300	$25	12
Total $1,500	$70	142

Average share cost: $10.57 ($1,500 divided by 142)

Average share price: $14.00 ($70 divided by 5)

Source: Investment Company Institute

cost. You continued to invest. Plus, now you can see the market value of your investment rise.

When you accumulate shares, you can profit in a rising market. The average cost of the investment was $10.57, far below the average share price of $14.00.

Dollar cost averaging is suitable for a long-term investment plan, such as saving for retirement or your child's future education.

Dollar Cost Averaging Works over the Long Term

Let's look at how a $100 monthly investment in the Massachusetts Investors Trust Fund, the first mutual fund, performed from year-end 1924 through September 30, 1994.

The 100-month investment was worth a whopping $8,504,619, while the total investments made were $2,578,880 over the past 70 years.

It's too bad we can't get into a time machine and go back to 1924 and start a saving plan. Maybe a fortunate few of us will invest in a mutual fund for 70 years. Most baby boomers will own a fund for 30 years at best or until they retire.

We can learn a lot about how dollar cost averaging worked in the Massachusetts Investors Trust Fund.

During the last half of the roaring 20s your $100 a month investment from year-end 1924 through year-end 1928 did well. Your money was worth a total of $6,016 and you invested $5,400.

The bottom fell out of the stock market in October 1929. During the Great Depression, the S&P 500 lost the following amounts in its very worst years based on total return:

- −8.4 percent in 1929,
- −24.9 percent in 1930
- −43.3 percent in 1931
- −8.2 percent in 1932
- −1.4 percent in 1934
- −3.5 percent in 1937
- −.4 percent in 1939
- −9.8 percent in 1940

Exhibit 9-4

MASSACHUSETTS INVESTORS TRUST—CLASS A (MITA)

Date	Initial Investment	Offering Price	NAV Price	Sales Charge	Dividends Reinvest	Cap Gains Reinvest	Shares Purchased	Initial Value
07/15/24	100	4.080	3.850	5.7502	Yes	Yes	24.510	84

Monthly investments of $100.00 from 08/01/24 to 08/01/94
Quantity Sales Charge Discount Included where Applicable

	COST OF SHARES					VALUE OF SHARES				
Date	Net Cumulative Investment	Period Dividend Income	Cumulative Dividend Income	Total Investment Cost	Annual Cap Gain Distribution	Direct Investment	Cap Gain Reinvestment	Dividend Reinvestment	Total Value	Shares Owned
12/31/24	600	5	5	805	0	586	0	6	802	147
12/31/25	1,600	n	78	1,878	0	1,988	0	88	2,076	427
12/31/26	3,000	144	222	3,222	0	3,281	0	247	3,538	684
12/31/27	4,200	215	438	4,638	0	5,454	0	561	6,016	837
12/31/28	5,400	302	740	6,140	80	7,967	95	1,037	9,100	1,165
12/31/29	6,600	377	1,117	7,717	0	7,982	84	1,218	9,286	1,344
12/31/30	7,600	420	1,538	9,358	0	6,443	58	1,162	7,665	1,573
12/31/31	8,000	441	1,879	10,878	0	4,132	31	803	5,067	1,649
12/31/32	10•200	338	2,318	12,518	0	4,916	28	1,175	6,121	2,660
12/31/33	11,400	388	2,707	14,107	0	7,430	35	1,52	9,358	3,174
12/31/34	12•800	481	3,188	15,788	0	9,066	38	2,503	11,807	3,700
12/31/35	13•600	578	3,768	17,568	0	12,917	48	3,832	18,788	4,184
12/31/36	15,000	786	4,562	19,562	797	16,800	857	5,438	23,087	4,796
12/31/37	18,200	821	5,484	21,684	U	11,614	551	4,246	16,412	5,295
12/31/38	17,400	681	8,148	23,546	98	15,178	750	5,781	21,711	5,955
12/31/36	18•600	885	7,031	25,631	0	15,478	708	6,358	22,95	6,447

Exhibit 9–4—Continued

| | COST OF SHARES | | | | | VALUE OF SHARES | | | | |
Date	Net Cumulative Investment	Period Dividend Income	Cumulative Dividend Income	Total Investment Cost	Annual Cap Gain Distribution	Direct Investment	Cap Gain Reinvestment	Dividend Reinvestment	Total Value	Shares Owned
12/31/40	18.600	1,068	8,101	27,801	0	14,445	610	6,98	21,605	7,161
12/31/41	21•000	1,261	8,382	30,322	0	13,441	525	6,840	20,:	9,018
12/31/42	22.200	1,266	10,658	32,858	0	15,838	589	8,772	25,181	8,845
12/31/43	23.400	1,371	12,030	35,430	0	20,119	681	11,856	32,660	8,667
12/31/44	24.600	1,612	13,842	38,242	0	24,518	786	15,424	40,732	10,448
12/31/45	25.600	1,822	15,464	41,284	810	32,048	1.205	21,322	55,277	11,304
12/31/46	27.000	2,157	17,822	44,822	1,380	28,435	3.178	20,802	53,515	12,336
12/31/47	28.200	2,613	20,235	48,435	0	28,837	3,088	22,863	5,827	13,231
12/31/48	28.400	3,185	23,422	52,822	0	28,858	2.884	25,048	57,872	14,250
12/31/49	30•600	3,485	26,818	57,518	0	35,085	3,379	32,328	70,802	15,348
12/31/50	31•800	4,711	31,828	63,428	0	43,482	4,061	43,885	61,528	18,506
12/31/51	33.000	5,235	36,864	89,864	3.158	50,807	7.870	55.333	113,812	18,081
12/31/52	34–200	5,748	42,613	76,813	1.698	55883	10.386	65.796	132,086	18,404
12/31/53	35.400	6,143	48,757	84,157	0	54,824	9.942	69.240	133,807	20,554
12/31/54	36.600	7,227	55,984	92,584	3.784	79,707	18.808	107.447	205,863	22,075
12/31/55	37.600	8,801	64,585	102,385	6.440	94,770	26.552	134,871	258,284	23.5a
12/31/56	38.000	8,657	74,242	113,242	3.433	101.866	33,791	152,880	288,648	24,818
12/31/57	40.200	10,338	84,582	124,782	4.401	86,153	32,554	137,243	255,851	26,332
12/31/58	41.400	10,432	95,015	136,415	3.279	119,744	47,863	200.366	368,084	27,572
12/31/59	42.600	11,169	106,184	148,784	6.261	128,126	58,316	220,286	402,731	26,811
12/31/60	43.600	12,317	118,502	162,302	5.983	120,436	59,161	221,015	400,613	30,416
12/31/61	45.000	11,998	130,501	175,501	18.768	143,421	68.105	273,1S	505,695	32,52n
12/31/62	46.200	13,177	143,678	188,878	10.422	124,007	86,610	247,487	458,115	34,383
12/31/63	47.400	14,620	156,288	205,698	10.988	143,201	110,147	288,185	551,543	36,166
12/31/84	48•600	16,459	174,758	223,358	6.897	161,222	128,774	348,728	640,726	37,601
12/31/65	49.600	18,838	193,388	243,198	23.232	168,459	157,660	381,475	707,816	40,034
12/31/66	51.000	20,677	214,075	265,075	28.386	144,869	184.226	345,170	654,367	43,335
12/31/67	52.200	21,929	236,004	266,204	48.785	159,865	226,576	388,882	787,424	47,636
12/31/68	53.400	21,380	257,385	310,785	55.545	182,297	265,885	422,843	870,825	52,270

Exhibit 9-4—(Continued)

	COST OF SHARES					VALUE OF SHARES				
Date	Net Cumulative Investment	Period Dividend Income	Cumulative Dividend Income	Total Investment Cost	Annual Cap Gain Distribution	Direct Investment	Cap Gain Reinvestment	Dividend Reinvestment	Total Value	Shares Owned
12/31/69	54,600	23,582	280.95	335,556	32,318	145.488	286.828	386,488	830,585	58,044
12/31/70	55,600	26,726	307.694	363,484	58.637	133.305	316.963	388,057	638,326	62,357
12/31/71	57,000	27,901	335,595	382,595	110,136	125.042	404.884	386,511	816,518	73,204
12/31/72	58,200	26,887	364,493	422,693	48,871	128.911	483.604	426,616	1,020,132	79,141
12/31/73	59,400	31,117	395,610	455,010	12,299	109,333	388,576	385,054	52,964	83,143
12/31/74	60,600	34,266	429,877	490,477	0	78,350	282,046	303,684	664,081	87,380
12/31/75	61,600	32,288	482,183	523,963	15,266	99,872	370,423	414,636	884,832	82,488
12/31/76	83,000	33,723	495,887	558,887	20,753	118,538	455,817	521,375	1,095,730	87,484
12/31/77	64,200	41,418	537,304	801,504	15,787	100,558	386,203	477,537	876,287	103,531
12/31/78	65,400	47,218	584,520	849,920	18,821	103,458	421,781	532,322	1,057,559	110,277
12/31/79	66,600	58,784	841,284	707,884	38,112	118,088	514,430	880,157	1,282,685	118,361
12/31/80	87,600	87,495	708,780	778,580	106,504	138,234	707,385	841,183	1,887,813	133,423
12/31/81	69,000	78,103	786,883	855,863	117,133	118,048	711,560	778,814	1,608,523	151,131
12/31/82	70,200	86,995	873,878	944,078	147,828	123,901	866,834	800,965	1,811,500	173,143
12/31/83	71,400	81,852	955,731	1,027,131	225,888	131,426	1,158,108	1,022,433	2,311,869	189,136
12/31/84	72,600	83,267	1,048,028	1,121,628	92,420	125,844	1,181,677	1,063,503	2,381,125	216,073
12/31/85	73,600	101,589	1,150,588	1,224,398	243,400	139,750	1,554,028	1,273,548	2,867,328	244,829
12/31/86	75,000	98,015	1,249,613	1,324,813	438,261	140,474	1,878,870	1,358,858	3,479,203	267,775
12/31/87	76,200	114,805	1,364,418	1,440,818	407,199	131,773	2,250,218	1,357,905	3,738,888	332,140
12/31/88	77,400	131,188	1,495,807	1,573,007	275,115	132,453	2,517,336	1,479,682	4,128,454	35,044
12/31/89	78,000	15,558	1,664,168	1,742,766	462,280	161,203	3–502.381	1,868,804	5,622,400	414,837
12/31/90	78,600	170,502	1,842,668	1,822,468	348,620	147,216	3–525.172	1,845,52	5,018,071	457,487
12/31/91	81,000	178,186	2,021,665	2,102,665	832,265	167,485	4,627,376	2,378,876	7,173,847	517,220
12/31/92	82•200	177,554	2,188,418	2,281,618	1,177,225	148,733	5,276,436	2,270,683	7,704,53	625,802
12/31/93	83,400	244,462	2,443,861	2,527,281	1,058,622	140,862	5,881,602	2,356,201	8,478,707	737,284
9/30/94	84•300	134,816	2,578,600	2,663,100	0	140,012	5,803,561	2,461,025	8,504,618	748,305
Totals					6.344,728					

Source: MFS

88

There were a few market rallies in the 1930s. But for the most part, everyone lost their shirts.

How did our dollar cost averaging program do during the Great Depression of the 1930s?

Fortunately, we had a cushion to help us out. We had been investing $100 a month for four years in a rising market. The total value of our investment at the end of 1929 was $9,285.

We were pretty lucky. We didn't own the market, but we did own a professionally managed mutual fund. The fund managers took action to cut losses in the 1930s. We lost money, but not as much as a 100 percent stake in the S&P 500.

Nevertheless, by the end of 1931, the total value of our investment declined to $5,067, representing a whopping 45 percent loss, and that includes the $100 a month we kicked into the fund in 1930 and 1931. We had to have a strong stomach to stay in the fund during this rough weather. But since we were dollar cost averaging, we were able to buy more shares of the fund at much lower prices.

From year-end 1929 through year-end 1931, we bought 605 more shares, including reinvestment of dividends and capital gains.

Gradually, we made a comeback. By year-end 1940, we owned a total of 7,181 shares worth $21,605. Our net cumulative investment during that time was $19,800.

Over the 16-year period, which is by far the worst in the history of the stock market, our mutual fund investment grew at an annual rate of just 1.15 percent.

Now let's look what happened in the decade of the 1940s and after World War II.

- By year-end 1939 we owned 6,447 shares of the fund, which were worth $22,545.

- By year-end 1949 we owned 15,348 shares worth a total of $70,802.

All those cheap shares of the Massachusetts Investors Trust we bought in the 1930s really shot up in value. Our investment gained a whopping 214 percent. Now you're talking! Our money grew at an annual compound rate of 12.12 percent during that decade, thanks in part to the cheap shares we bought in the 1930s.

What's Happened In the 1980s and 1990s

Let's jump in our time machine and move forward to the 1980s.

You doubled your money every 4.5 years in the stock market in the roaring decade of the 1980s. The S&P 500 grew at an annual compound rate of 16.8 percent.

This period is the exact opposite of 1930, the worst decade in stock market history.

At the beginning of the 1980s we are still socking away $100 a month into the Massachusetts Investors Trust Fund. At year-end 1979 we owned 119,381 shares of the fund. By year-end 1989 we owned a whopping 414,937 shares due to reinvestment of dividends and capital gains as well as our $100 a month or $1,200 yearly investments.

The total value of our investment increased to $5,822,400 by year-end 1989 from $1,292,813 at year end 1979, representing a 350 percent increase in the value of our investment. That means the assets in our account grew at a annual rate of 16.23 percent in the 1980s.

What Happened In the 1987 Crash

What about the stock market crash in 1987? Let's look at the Vanguard Index 500 fund, a fund that tracks the performance of the S&P 500 stock market index.

Over the past 15 years ending in October 1994, we invested $100 a month or a total of $18,000 into the fund. The market value of our investment is worth well over $63,000.

There were only three down years during that period. We lost money in 1981, 1987 and 1990. Other than that, it was all growth. The stock market crash of 1987 was not pleasant. The Dow Jones Industrial Average dropped 500 points on October 19, 1987. While in the fourth quarter of 1987, the equity fund lost 20 percent, according to Lipper Analytical Services.

If you had been in a dollar-cost-averaging program during the October 1987 stock-market plunge, you would have been able to buy more shares at a lower price in the Vanguard Index Fund and reap the ensuing gains when the market rebounded. Your $100 investment would have bought you extra shares when the fund's net asset value declined from $32.31. In October of 1987, you could have bought shares for $25.29; in

November, for $23.22. In succeeding months, you would have accumulated shares at between $5 to $7 less than the fund's high price for the year, which was $33.75. Through July of 1988, the value of your periodic payments would have grown 12 percent in ten months.

The Best Funds for Dollar Cost Averaging

When shopping for funds as dollar cost averaging candidates, invest in more volatile funds, funds with the higher risk rating.

Steve Savage, editor of the *Value Line Mutual Fund Survey,* New York, believes that dollar cost averaging can sway investment results and the risk/reward profile of a fund. Investors are prone to make the wrong investment decisions if they only compare funds on the basis of buy and hold performance.

If you have two funds with the same return, Savage says most people will pick the fund with the lower risk. This is good advice for someone who puts a lump sum into a fund. However, investors who dollar cost average should put their money in the more volatile investment, the fund that carries a higher risk rating.

The reason: Since the share prices fluctuate more, you have a greater chance of accumulating more shares at a lower cost. Then you profit when the fund rebounds. More volatile stock funds tend to show greater price appreciation when bouncing off their lows.

Take the case of the high-risk CGM Capital Development Fund (see Exhibit 9–5). While a $10,000 investment grew to $326,709 over the past 20 years, making it one of the top performing funds, the fund still trailed the low-risk Mutual Shares by $66,000. However, if a modest $100 per month in additional input for both funds is factored in over the period, CGM soared to $691,647, almost $92,000 ahead of its more conservative peer.

The reason for the difference: CGM is a more volatile investment. As a result, investors accumulated more shares at lower prices than they would have in the Mutual Shares fund in down markets. On the upside, CGM shares bought low showed a greater price appreciation.

If you are shopping for funds that you can use with a dollar cost averaging program, go to the public library and ask for the *Value Line Mutual Fund Survey.* This is the only rating service on the market that outlines the effect of dollar cost averaging on a mutual fund over time.

Exhibit 9–5 Twenty-Year Results of Three Top Performing Funds

Fund	Risk	$10,000 Grew to	$10,000+$100 a Month
Mutual Shares	Lowest	$393,574	$599,963
Lindner Fund	Lower	$410,546	$634,123
CGM Cap Dev.	Highest	$326,709	$691,647

Source: *Value Line Mutual Fund Survey*

A Few Strings

Dollar cost averaging is one of the safest ways to play the stock market, but the method does have its pitfalls. You cannot absolutely guarantee that the average cost will be lower than the market value when you redeem. You also must be careful not to invest too large a sum at once, otherwise your losses could mount up quickly.

Bull markets historically last longer than bear markets, so in many cases investors may not be able to buy enough low-cost shares during down cycles to make DCA as profitable as investing a lump sum in a bull market. For investors to accumulate enough money in a dollar-cost-averaging program for gains to become substantial profits usually takes from five to ten years. Over the short term, the performance of dollar cost averaging will lag behind other investing methods. And, although aggressive-stock funds or gold funds are the best vehicles for DCA because they are volatile and DCA capitalizes on price fluctuation, the danger always exists that the fund will not rebound sufficiently.

You must be patient to succeed at dollar cost averaging. You may experience years during which the market is flat and you are accumulating shares at about the same price. A study conducted by Sheldon Jacobs of the *No-Load Investor* newsletter found that during the flat market years of 1971 through 1976, the difference between the average share price at the beginning and at the end was only 21 cents. DCA performed poorly, he concluded, because only a small portion of money was invested at the beginning of the period. Most of the money was invested at times when prices were appreciating.

You also may experience a period when the financial markets move like a seesaw, as was the case from 1965 through 1970. A jerky market means few time periods when you can buy shares at a price low enough for regular buying to pay off.

At other times, DCA will not fare so well as a lump-sum. Let's look at the period before the stock market crash in 1987. Exhibit 9–6 shows how the strategy worked against a lump sum that was divided 50–50 between stocks and bonds. During the down market from January 1, 1973 through December 31, 1974, DCA kept its value, while a lump-sum $10,000 investment lost $1,700. During the trendless market from February 1, 1977, through January 31, 1979, both the lump-sum and the DCA programs held their initial values. In the up market from January 1, 1985, through December 31,1986, however, DCA gains lagged behind those of a buy-and-hold investment.

The pattern holds true today. DCA is a safe way to invest. You will underperform a lump sum in a bull market. But when stocks plunged in October of 1987, investors that used DCA accumulated fund shares at an attractive price. They assumed less risk because they bought at lower prices when the stock market tumbled and benefited when the market rebounded.

The S&P 500 grew at an annual rate of 14.21 percent in the five years ensuing the stock market crash of 1987. You just about double your money with a lump-sum investment.

But who had the guts to stick in a lump sum in the market after the crash? Not many. For those who wanted to play it safe and still keep a hand in the market, DCA did fine. A $100-a-month investment grew to about $8,684.

DCA is not a perfect way to invest, but in a well thought-out diversified investment plan, it is a safe way to invest for long-term horizons of ten years or more.

Points to Remember

- With dollar cost averaging you invest regularly.

- You can have as little as $50 to $100 a month automatically taken out of your checking account and invested in a mutual fund.

- You stay fully invested in your fund when you use dollar cost averaging.

Exhibit 9–6 Dollar Cost Averaging versus Buy and Hold

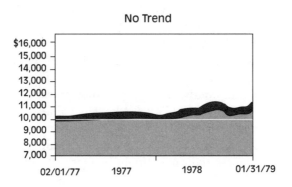

No Trend

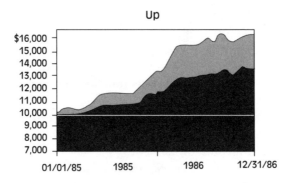

Up

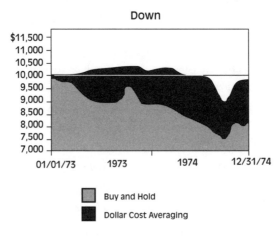

Down

Source: *Diversify Your Way to Wealth.*

- When the fund's price is down, you accumulate more shares at a lower cost. Over the longer term, the average cost of your investment will be less than the average price or market price of the shares.

- Dollar cost averaging underperforms a fully invested position in a bull market.

- You need to invest in funds that go up and down in price to make dollar cost averaging work.

Chapter 10

Constant Dollar Plan

The constant dollar investment tactic tells you when to sell high and buy low. You take your profits and sock them away in a money fund. But when your investment underperforms, you invest more money. Later, you take your profits when the investment is up.

This strategy can be used by conservative investors who want simple guidelines about when to take profits or invest.

The formula works with just a few thousand dollars to invest. It's best to have between $5,000 and $10,000 to start.

It works this way: At the end of every year, your stock fund should be worth $10,000. If you have more than $10,000, take the profits and invest them in your money fund. If you have losses, you bring the value of the investment back to $10,000.

Formula plans like constant dollar and others mentioned in the book work best for tax-deferred retirement savings investments like IRAs, 401(k)s and variable annuities. You don't pay taxes on your trades when you switch among funds in a retirement savings account.

Here's how the constant dollar strategy would work using an aggressive growth stock and a bond or money fund: You've decided to keep a constant dollar amount of $10,000 in your aggressive portfolio, but once a year you bring the portfolio back to $10,000. If the value is above $10,000, you take the profits and put them in a money fund or bond fund. If the value is below $10,000, you take money out of the money fund to bring the stock portfolio back to $10,000.

You can get more sophisticated, for example, if you are willing to accept a 15 percent gain or loss in that portfolio every six months. After six months, if the value of your stock fund has grown to $11,500, you would take out $1,500 and move it into your bond or money fund. Conversely, if the value of your stock fund has dropped to $8,500 after six months, you would switch $1,500 out of bonds or a money fund and into stocks to maintain the constant dollar value of $10,000. Use the bond fund or money fund as a parking place. The only reason to change its value is to move money in and out of stocks.

Exhibit 10–1 below shows how a simple constant dollar plan works using an aggressive stock fund and a money fund. An initial investment of $10,000 was made in an aggressive stock fund and you have $5,000 in your money fund account. Every year you rebalance the aggressive funds value back to or up to $10,000.

Over the past ten years ending in 1993, your $15,000 investment grew to almost $35,000. That represents an 8.8 percent annual rate of return. That's far below the amount earned on a buy and hold investment in the aggressive fund, which grew at a 13.81 percent annual rate. But your investment was a lot less risky. You always took your profits and dollar cost averaged into the fund when the value dropped.

As you can see from the table, you had to kick money into your aggressive stock fund in 1984 since it lost 13.21 percent. In the following year you took profits of 29.17 percent. Once again, in 1987 you had to kick a few dollars into your fund. But you took profits in the next two years.

In 1990, you had to pull $865 out of your money fund and put it into your aggressive stock fund. But as you can see from the table, you banked your profits in subsequent years.

Constant Dollar Investing

Assumes a $10,000 investment at the beginning of each year in an aggressive stock fund and a $5,000 initial investment in a money market fund.

Exhibit 10–1

Year	Ag. Growth Fund $	Money Fund $	Total $
1984	$9,669	5,479	15,148
1985	12,917	5,534	18,148
1986	11,259	8,956	20,215
1987	9,776	10,810	20,587
1988	11,562	11,292	22,854
1989	12,735	12,854	25,589
1990	9,135	14,724	24,724
1991	15,325	16,361	31,685
1992	10,855	22,436	33,291
1993	10,842	23,994	34,836

Source: Alan Lavine

Points to Remember

- You set a rule governing when to buy and sell with constant dollar investing.

- Every three, six, nine or twelve months you take profits and bring the value of your stock fund back to the initial investment.

- You take money out of the money fund and invest it in the stock fund when the price has declined.

- More aggressive investors check the constant dollar amount every three to six months. Conservative investors wait an entire year before they make the changes.

- Invest with a mutual fund family when you use constant dollar investment. It is easier to make the trades.

- You can use more than one stock fund. You can set constant dollar amounts for international funds, small company stock funds and value stock funds.

Chapter 11

Constant-Ratio Investing

The constant-ratio investment plan is another way to buy more shares when prices decline. By maintaining a constant ratio of stocks to bonds or cash over a period of time, you are rebalancing your portfolio by taking profits on the upside and dollar cost averaging on the down-side when the investment declines.

If you keep one-third of your investment in a growth stock fund and two-thirds in a money or bond fund, that combination would translate into a ratio of 50 percent-one-third divided by two-thirds equals .50. Every six months you would check the ratio of stocks to bonds or cash and bring it back to 50 percent, if necessary. You would rebalance the portfolio to keep the right mix.

With the constant-ratio strategy you have a predetermined sell point and you dollar cost average as prices fall. You won't make as much as you would if you bought and held a fund in a bull market. Most likely is you split the investment between stocks and bonds, you will earn half way between the buy and hold on a stock fund and a bond fund.

You will not hit a home run with a constant ratio investment plan. It's not designed for that. It's a trade rule that forces you to take profits and dollar cost average when your investments are down.

The following hypothetical example computed by Ray Linder, money manager and publisher of the *Linder Letter,* Herdon, VA, shows the value of investing according to the constant ratio plan. This example assumes a $10,000 investing in January 1977 which is split equally between the Vanguard Index 500 equity fund and T-bills. At the begining of each year, the portfolio was rebalanced so that half of the portfolio's value was in the stock fund and half was in T-bills. See Exhibit 11–1. .

By year-end December 1993 the $10,000 investment grew to $55,700, representing a annual compound rate of return of 10.63 percent.

While this return is less than the $82,200 an investor could have earned if he or she bought and held the stock fund, it is greater than the return on T-bills. The $10,000 invested in T-bills grew to $35,300.

"The real attraction of the Constant Ratio Plan," says

Linder, "is the ablilty to earn higher rates of return with less risk."

Linder says that the month to month volatility of the mixed portfolio was half that of the equity fund portfolio.

In addition, this investment tactic worked well in difficult markets. Most of the difference between the constant ratio portfolio and the equity only portfolio was achieved during the 1980s market that was consistently going up.

During an extended bear market such as that which accompanied the recession in the early 1980s, the Constant Ratio Plan offers investors protection of capital. An investor with a 100 percent postion in the stock fund saw the value of his or her investment decline 16.7 percent from November 1980 to July 1982.

But the Constant Ratio investor's capital would have grown 1 percent over the same time.

The market crash of 1987 is another example of how constant ratio investing saves the day. The stock fund investor would have lost 30 percent between September and November 1987. Many investors left the stock market after that. Those that stayed had to wait until May 1989 to recoup their losses.

By contrast the constant ratio investor would have lost 17 percent and regained his or her losses by January 1989.

Exhibit 11–1 Constant Ratio Investing

Date	Index 500	T-Bill	Stock $	T-Bill $	Total $	% Gain	Excess Rtn	Stock Only	Excess	Bills Only
Jan-77	-5	0.36	$4,750	$5,018	$9,768	-2.3°/a	-2.7%	$9,500	-5.4%	$10,036
Feb-77	-1.4	0.35	$4,684	$5,036	$9,719	-0.5%	-0.9%	$9,367	-1.8°7a	$10,071
Mar-77	-1.3	0.38	$4,623	$5,055	$9,677	-0.4%	-0.8%	$9,245	-1.7%	$10,109
Apr-77	0	0.38	$4,623	$5,074	$9,697	0.2%	-0.2%	$9,245	-0.4%	$10,148
May-77	-1.5	0.37	$4,553	$5,093	$9,646	-0.5°7a	-0.9%	$9,107	-1.9%	$10,185
Jun-77	4.5	0.4	$4,758	$5,113	$9,871	2.3%	1.9%	$9,516	4.1%	$10,226
Jul-77	-1.5	0.42	$4,687	$5,135	$9,821	-0.5%	-0.9%	$9,374	-1.9%	$10,269
Aug-77	-1.4	0.44	$4,621	$5,157	$9,778	-0.4%	-0.9%	$9,242	-1.8%	$10,314
Sep-77	0	0.43	$4,621	$5,179	$9,800	0.2%	-0.2%	$9,242	-0.4%	$10,359
Oct-77	-4.2	0.49	$4,427	$5,205	$9,632	-1.7%	-2.2%	$8,854	-4.7%	$10,409
Nov-77	3.5	0.5	$4,582	$5,231	$9,813	1.9%	1.4%	$9,164	3.0%	$10,461
Dec-77	0.5	0.49	$4,605	$5,256	$9,861	0.5%	0.0%	$9,210	0.0%	$10,513
Jan-78	-6	0.49	$4,635	$4,955	$9,590	-2.8%	-3.2%	$8,657	-6.5%	$10,564
Feb-78	-1.7	0.46	$4,556	$4,978	$9,534	-0.6%	-1.0%	$8,510	-2.2%	$10,613
Mar-78	2.6	0.53	$4,674	$5,004	$9,678	1.5%	1.0%	$8,731	2.1%	$10,669
Apr-78	8.5	0.54	$5,072	$5,031	$10,103	4.4%	3.8%	$9,474	8.0%	$10,727
May-78	1.3	0.51	$5,138	$5,057	$10,194	0.9%	0.4%	$9,597	0.8%	$10,781
Jun-78	-1.6	0.54	$5,056	$5,084	$10,139	-0.5%	-1.1%	$9,443	-2.1%	$10,840
Jul-78	5.7	0.56	$5,344	$5,112	$10,456	3.1%	2.6%	$9,981	5.1%	$10,900
Aug-78	3.4	0.55	$5,525	$5,141	$10,666	2.0%	1.5%	$10,321	2.9%	$10,960
Sep-78	-0.6	0.62	$5,492	$5,172	$10,665	-0.0%	-0.6%	$10,259	-1.2%	$11,028
Oct-78	-8.9	0.68	$5,003	$5,208	$10,211	-4.3%	-4.9%	$9,346	-9.6%	$11,103
Nov-78	2.6	0.7	$5,134	$5,244	$10,378	1.6%	0.9%	$9,589	1.9%	$11,181
Dec-78	1.7	0.78	$5,221	$5,285	$10,506	1.2%	0.5%	$9,752	0.9%	$11,268
Jan-79	4.1	0.77	$5,468	$5,293	$10,762	2.4%	1.7%	$10,152	3.3%	$11,355

Exhibit 11-1 (Continued)

Date	Index 500	T-Bill	Stock $	T-Bill $	Total $	% Gain	Excess Rtn	Stock Only	Excess	Bills Only
Feb-79	-2.9	0.73	$5,310	$5,332	$10,642	-1.1%	-1.8%	$9,857	-3.6%	$11,438
Mar-79	5.7	0.81	$5,612	$5,375	$10,987	3.2%	2.4%	$10,419	4.9%	$11,530
Apr-79	0.4	0.8	$5,635	$5,418	$11,053	0.6%	-0.2%	$10,461	-0.4%	$11,623
May-79	-1.6	0.82	$5,545	$5,463	$11,007	-0.4%	-1.2%	$10,293	-2.4%	$11,718
Jun-79	4	0.81	$5,766	$5,507	$11,273	2.4%	1.6%	$10,705	3.2%	$11,813
Jul-79	1.1	0.77	$5,830	$5,549	$11,379	0.9%	0.2%	$10,823	0.3%	$11,904
Aug-79	6.1	0.77	$6,185	$5,592	$11,777	3.5%	2.7%	$11,483	5.3%	$11,995
Sep-79	0.2	0.83	$6,198	$5,638	$11,836	0.5%	-0.3%	$11,506	-0.6%	$12,095
Oct-79	-6.5	0.87	$5,795	$5,687	$11,482	-3.0%	-3.9%	$10,758	-7.4%	$12,200
Nov-79	5.1	0.99	$6,090	$5,744	$11,834	3.1%	2.1%	$11,307	4.1%	$12,321
Dec-79	1.8	0.95	$6,200	$5,798	$11,998	1.4%	0.4%	$11,510	0.9%	$12,438
Jan-80	5.9	0.8	$6,353	$6,047	$12,400	3.3%	2.5%	$12,190	5.1%	$12,538
Feb-80	0.4	0.89	$6,379	$6,101	$12,480	0.6%	-0.3%	$12,238	-0.5%	$12,649
Mar-80	-9.8	1.21	$5,753	$6,175	$11,928	-4.4%	-5.6%	$11,039	-11.0%	$12,802
Apr-80	4.3	1.26	$6,001	$6,253	$12,253	2.7%	1.5%	$11,514	3.0%	$12,964
May-80	5.5	0.81	$6,331	$6,303	$12,634	3.1%	2.3%	$12,147	4.7%	$13,069
Jun-80	2.8	0.61	$6,508	$6,342	$12,850	1.7%	1.1%	$12,487	2.2%	$13,148
Jul-80	6.6	0.53	$6,938	$6,375	$13,313	3.6%	3.1%	$13,311	6.1%	$13,218
Aug-80	1.3	0.64	$7,028	$6,416	$13,444	1.0%	0.3%	$13,484	0.7%	$13,303
Sep-80	2.7	0.75	$7,218	$6,464	$13,682	1.8%	1.0%	$13,848	2.0%	$13,402
Oct-80	2	0.95	$7,362	$6,526	$13,888	1.5%	0.6%	$14,125	1.0%	$13,530
Nov-80	11	0.96	$8,172	$6,588	$14,760	6.3%	5.3%	$15,679	10.0%	$13,660
Dec-80	-3.1	1.31	$7,919	$6,675	$14,593	-1.1%	-2.4%	$15,193	-4.4%	$13,838
Jan-81	-4.4	1.04	$6,976	$7,372	$14,348	-1.7%	-2.7%	$14,524	-5.4%	$13,982
Feb-81	2.1	1.07	$7,122	$7,451	$14,573	1.6%	0.5%	$14,829	1.0%	$14,132
Mar-81	3.7	1.21	$7,386	$7,541	$14,927	2.4%	1.2%	$15,378	2.5%	$14,303

Exhibit 11–1 (Continued)

Date	Index 500	T-Bill	Stock $	T-Bill $	Total $	% Gain	Excess Rtn	Stock Only	Excess	Bills Only
Apr-81	-2.2	1.08	$7,223	$7,623	$14,846	-0.5%	-1.6%	$15,040	-3.3%	$14,457
May-81	0.6	1.15	$7,266	$7,711	$14,977	0.9%	-0.3%	$15,130	-0.5%	$14,624
Jun-81	-0.9	1.35	$7,201	$7,815	$15,016	0.3%	-1.1%	$14,994	-2.3%	$14,821
Jul-81	0	1.24	$7,201	$7,912	$15,113	0.6%	-0.6%	$14,994	-1.2%	$15,005
Aug-81	-5.4	1.28	$6,812	$8,013	$14,825	-1.9%	-3.2%	$14,184	-6.7%	$15,197
Sep-81	-5	1.24	$6,472	$8,112	$14,584	-1.6%	-2.9%	$13,475	-6.2%	$15,385
Oct-81	5.2	1.21	$6,808	$8,210	$15,018	3.0%	1.8%	$14,176	4.0%	$15,572
Nov-81	4.4	1.07	$7,108	$8,298	$15,406	2.6%	1.5%	$14,799	3.3%	$15,738
Dec-81	-2.8	0.87	$6,909	$8,370	$15,279	-0.8%	-1.7%	$14,385	-3.7%	$15,875
Jan-82	-1.5	0.8	$7,525	$7,701	$15,226	-0.4%	-1.2%	$14,169	-2.3%	$16,002
Feb-82	-5.1	0.92	$7,141	$7,771	$14,913	-2.1%	-3.0%	$13,447	-6.0%	$16,149
Mar-82	-0.7	0.98	$7,091	$7,848	$14,939	0.2%	-0.8%	$13,352	-1.7%	$16,308
Apr-82	4.2	1.13	$7,389	$7,936	$15,325	2.6%	1.5%	$13,913	3.1%	$16,492
May-82	-2.8	1.06	$7,182	$8,020	$15,203	-0.8%	-1.9%	$13,524	-3.9%	$16,667
Jun-82	-1.6	0.96	$7,067	$8,097	$15,165	-0.2%	-1.2%	$13,307	-2.6%	$16,827
Jul-82	-2.2	1.05	$6,912	$8,182	$15,094	-0.5%	-1.5%	$13,015	-3.3%	$17,003
Aug-82	12.4	0.76	$7,769	$8,245	$16,013	6.1%	5.3%	$14,628	11.6%	$17,133
Sep-82	1	0.51	$7,846	$8,287	$16,133	0.7%	0.2%	$14,775	0.5%	$17,220
Oct-82	11.1	0.59	$8,717	$8,336	$17,053	5.7%	5.1%	$16,415	10.5%	$17,322
Nov-82	4.2	0.63	$9,084	$8,388	$17,472	2.5%	1.8%	$17,104	3.6%	$17,431
Dec-82	1.7	0.67	$9,238	$8,444	$17,682	1.2%	0.5%	$17,395	1.0%	$17,547
Jan-83	3.4	0.69	$9,142	$8,902	$18,044	2.0%	1.4%	$17,986	2.7%	$17,669
Feb-83	2.5	0.62	$9,370	$8,957	$18,328	1.6%	1.0%	$18,436	1.9%	$17,778
Mar-83	3.5	0.63	$9,698	$9,014	$18,712	2.1%	1.5%	$19,081	2.9%	$17,890
Apr-83	7.6	0.71	$10,435	$9,078	$19,513	4.3%	3.6%	$20,531	6.9%	$18,017

Exhibit 11-1 (Continued)

Date	Index 500	T-Bill	Stock $	T-Bill $	Total $	% Gain	Excess Rtn	Stock Only	Excess	Bills Only
May-83	-0.9	0.69	$10,341	$9,140	$19,482	-0.2%	-0.9%	$20,347	-1.6%	$18,141
Jun-83	3.8	0.67	$10,734	$9,202	$19,936	2.3%	1.7%	$21,120	3.1%	$18,263
Jul-83	-3.2	0.74	$10,391	$9,270	$19,661	-1.4%	-2.1%	$20,444	-3.9%	$18,398
Aug-83	1.8	0.76	$10,578	$9,340	$19,918	1.3%	0.5%	$20,812	1.0%	$18,538
Sep-83	1.2	0.76	$10,705	$9,411	$20,116	1.0%	0.2%	$21,062	0.4%	$18,679
Oct-83	-1.4	0.76	$10,555	$9,483	$20,038	-0.4%	-1.1%	$20,767	-2.2%	$18,821
Nov-83	2.2	0.7	$10,787	$9,549	$20,336	1.5%	0.8%	$21,224	1.5°/a	$18,953
Dec-83	-0.6	0.73	$10,722	$9,619	$20,341	0.0%	-0.7%	$21,096	-1.3%	$19,091
Jan-84	-0.5	0.76	$10,120	$10,248	$20,368	0.1°/a	-0.6%	$20,991	-1.3%	$19,236
Feb-84	-3.3	0.71	$9,786	$10,321	$20,106	-1.3%	-2.0%	$20,298	-4.0%	$19,373
Mar-84	1.6	0.73	$9,942	$10,396	$20,338	1.2%	0.4%	$20,623	0.9%	$19,514
Apr-84	0.7	0.81	$10,012	$10,480	$20,492	0.8%	-0.1%	$20,767	-0.1%	$19,672
May-84	-5.4	0.78	$9,471	$10,562	$20,033	-2.2%	-3.0%	$19,646	-6.2%	$19,825
Jun-84	2.2	0.75	$9,680	$10,641	$20,321	1.4%	0.7%	$20,078	1.5%	$19,974
Jul-84	-1.5	0.82	$9,534	$10,728	$20,263	-0.3%	-1.1%	$19,777	-2.3%	$20,138
Aug-84	11.2	0.83	$10,602	$10,817	$21,420	5.7%	4.9%	$21,992	10.4%	$20,305
Sep-84	0	0.86	$10,602	$10,910	$21,513	0.4%	-0.4%	$21,992	-0.9%	$20,480
Oct-84	0.2	1	$10,624	$11,020	$21,643	0.6%	-0.4%	$22,036	-0.8%	$20,685
Nov-84	-1	0.73	$10,517	$11,100	$21,617	-0.1%	-0.8%	$21,816	-1.7%	$20,836
Dec-84	2.6	0.64	$10,791	$11,171	$21,962	1.6%	1.0%	$22,383	2.0%	$20,969
Jan-85	7.6	0.65	$11,815	$11,052	$22,868	4.1%	3.5%	$24,084	7.0%	$21,105
Feb-85	1.4	0.58	$11,981	$11,116	$23,097	1.0%	0.4%	$24,421	0.8%	$21,228
Mar-85	0	0.62	$11,981	$11,185	$23,166	0.3%	-0.3%	$24,421	-0.6%	$21,359
Apr-85	-0.3	0.72	$11,945	$11,266	$23,211	0.2%	-0.5%	$24,348	-1.0%	$21,513
May-85	6	0.66	$12,662	$11,340	$24,002	3.4%	2.7%	$25,809	5.3%	$21,655

Exhibit 11-1 (Continued)

Date	Index 500	T-Bill	Stock $	T-Bill $	Total $	% Gain	Excess Rtn	Stock Only	Excess	Bills Only
Jun–85	1.4	0.55	$12,839	$11,403	$24,241	1.0%	0.4%	$26,170	0.9%	$21,774
Jul–85	-0.2	0.62	$12,813	$11,473	$24,287	0.2%	-0.4%	$26,118	-0.8%	$21,909
Aug–85	-0.7	0.55	$12,724	$11,536	$24,260	-0.1%	-0.7%	$25,935	-1.3%	$22,030
Sep–85	-3.1	0.6	$12,329	$11,606	$23,935	-1.3%	-1.9%	$25,131	-3.7%	$22,162
Oct–85	4.4	0.65	$12,872	$11,681	$24,553	2.6%	1.9%	$26,236	3.8%	$22,306
Nov–85	6.9	0.61	$13,760	$11,752	$25,512	3.9%	3.3%	$28,047	6.3%	$22,442
Dec–85	4.7	0.65	$14,406	$11,829	$26,235	2.8%	2.2%	$29,365	4.0%	$22,588
Jan–86	0.4	0.56	$13,170	$13,191	$26,361	0.5%	-0.1%	$29,482	-0.2%	$22,714
Feb–86	7.6	0.53	$14,171	$13,261	$27,432	4.1%	3.5%	$31,723	7.1%	$22,835
Mar–86	5.5	0.6	$14,950	$13,340	$28,291	3.1%	2.5%	$33,468	4.9%	$22,972
Apr–86	-1.4	0.52	$14,741	$13,410	$28,151	-0.5%	-1.0%	$32,999	-1.9%	$23,091
May–86	5.4	0.49	$15,537	$13,476	$29,013	3.1%	2.6%	$34,781	4.9%	$23,204
Jun–86	1.7	0.52	$15,801	$13,546	$29,347	1.2%	0.6%	$35,373	1.2%	$23,325
Jul–86	-5.7	0.52	$14,901	$13,616	$28,517	-2.8%	-3.3%	$33,356	-6.2%	$23,446
Aug–86	7.4	0.46	$16,003	$13,679	$29,682	4.1%	3.6%	$35,825	6.9%	$23,554
Sep–86	-8.3	0.45	$14,675	$13,740	$28,415	-4.3%	-4.7%	$32,851	-8.8%	$23,660
Oct–86	5.6	0.46	$15,497	$13,803	$29,300	3.1%	2.7%	$34,691	5.1%	$23,769
Nov–86	2.5	0.39	$15,884	$13,857	$29,741	1.5%	1.1%	$35,558	2.1%	$23,862
Dec–86	-2.6	0.49	$15,471	$13,925	$29,396	-1.2%	-1.7%	$34,634	-3.1%	$23,978
Jan–87	13.3	0.42	$16,653	$14,760	$31,413	6.9%	6.4%	$39,240	12.9%	$24,079
Feb–87	4	0.43	$17,319	$14,823	$32,143	2.3%	1.9%	$40,810	3.6%	$24,183
Mar–87	2.9	0.47	$17,821	$14,893	$32,714	1.8%	1.3%	$41,993	2.4%	$24,296
Apr–87	-1	0.44	$17,643	$14,959	$32,602	-0.3%	-0.8%	$41,573	-1.4%	$24,403
May–87	1	0.38	$17,820	$15,015	$32,835	0.7%	0.3%	$41,989	0.6%	$24,496
Jun–87	5	0.48	$18,711	$15,087	$33,798	2.9%	2.5%	$44,088	4.5%	$24,614

Exhibit 11–1 (Continued)

Date	Index 500	T-Bill	Stock $	T-Bill $	Total $	% Gain	Excess Rtn	Stock Only	Excess	Bills Only
Jul–87	4.9	0.46	$19,627	$15,157	$34,784	2.9%	2.5%	$46,249	4.4%	$24,727
Aug–87	3.8	0.47	$20,373	$15,228	$35,601	2.3%	1.9%	$48,006	3.3%	$24,843
Sep–87	-2.3	0.45	$19,905	$15,297	$35,201	-1.1%	-1.6%	$46,902	-2.8%	$24,955
Oct–87	-21.7	0.6	$15,585	$15,388	$30,974	-12.0%	-12.6%	$36,724	-22.3%	$25,105
Nov–87	-8.2	0.3	$14,307	$15,435	$29,742	-4.0%	-4.3%	$33,713	-8.5%	$25,180
Dec–87	7.6	0.39	$15,395	$15,495	$30,890	3.9%	3.5%	$36,275	7.2%	$25,278
Jan–88	4.2	0.29	$16,093	$15,490	$31,583	2.2%	2.0%	$37,799	3.9%	$25,351
Feb–88	4.6	0.46	$16,834	$15,561	$32,395	2.6%	2.1%	$39,537	4.1%	$25,468
Mar–88	-3	0.44	$16,329	$15,629	$31,958	-1.3%	-1.8%	$38,351	-3.4%	$25,580
Apr–88	1	0.46	$16,492	$15,701	$32,193	0.7%	0.3%	$38,735	0.5%	$25,698
May–88	0.8	0.51	$16,624	$15,781	$32,405	0.7%	0.1%	$39,045	0.3%	$25,829
Jun–88	4.6	0.49	$17,389	$15,859	$33,247	2.6%	2.1%	$40,841	4.1%	$25,955
Jul–88	-0.4	0.51	$17,319	$15,939	$33,259	0.0%	-0.5%	$40,677	-0.9%	$26,088
Aug–88	-3.4	0.59	$16,730	$16,033	$32,764	-1.5%	-2.1%	$39,294	-4.0%	$26,242
Sep–88	4.3	0.62	$17,450	$16,133	$33,583	2.5%	1.9%	$40,984	3.7%	$26,404
Oct–88	2.7	0.61	$17,921	$16,231	$34,152	1.7%	1.1%	$42,090	2.1%	$26,565
Nov–88	-1.5	0.57	$17,652	$16,324	$33,976	-0.5%	-1.1%	$41,459	-2.1%	$26,717
Dec–88	1.7	0.63	$17,952	$16,427	$34,379	1.2%	0.6%	$42,164	1.1%	$26,885
Jan–89	7.3	0.55	$18,444	$17,284	$35,728	3.9%	3.4%	$45,242	6.8%	$27,033
Feb–89	-2.5	0.61	$17,983	$17,389	$35,372	-1.0%	-1.6%	$44,111	-3.1%	$27,198
Mar–89	2.3	0.67	$18,397	$17,506	$35,903	1.5%	0.8%	$45,125	1.6%	$27,380
Apr–89	5.2	0.67	$19,353	$17,623	$36,976	3.0%	2.3%	$47,472	4.5%	$27,564
May–89	4	0.79	$20,127	$17,762	$37,890	2.5%	1.7%	$49,371	3.2%	$27,781
Jun–89	-0.6	0.71	$20,007	$17,888	$37,895	0.0%	-0.7%	$49,075	-1.3%	$27,979
Jul–89	9	0.7	$21,807	$18,014	$39,821	5.1%	4.4%	$53,491	8.3%	$28,174

Exhibit 11–1 (Continued)

Date	Index 500	T-Bill	Stock $	T-Bill $	Total $	% Gain	Excess Rtn	Stock Only	Excess	Bills Only
Aug-89	1.9	0.74	$22,222	$18,147	$40,369	1.4%	0.6%	$54,508	1.2%	$28,383
Sep-89	-0.4	0.65	$22,133	$18,265	$40,398	0.1%	-0.6%	$54,290	-1.0%	$28,567
Oct-89	-2.3	0.68	$21,624	$18,389	$40,013	-1.0%	-1.6%	$53,041	-3.0%	$28,762
Nov-89	2	0.69	$22,056	$18,516	$40,572	1.4%	0.7%	$54,102	1.3%	$28,960
Dec-89	2.4	0.61	$22,586	$18,629	$41,214	1.6%	1.0%	$55,400	1.8%	$29,137
Jan-90	-6.7	0.57	$19,227	$20,725	$39,951	-3.1%	-3.6%	$51,688	-7.3%	$29,303
Feb-90	1.3	0.57	$19,477	$20,843	$40,319	0.9%	0.4%	$52,360	0.7%	$29,470
Mar-90	2.6	0.64	$19,983	$20,976	$40,959	1.6%	0.9%	$53,722	2.0%	$29,659
Apr-90	-2.5	0.69	$19,483	$21,121	$40,604	-0.9%	-1.6%	$52,379	-3.2%	$29,863
May-90	9.7	0.68	$21,373	$21,265	$42,638	5.0%	4.3%	$57,459	9.0%	$30,066
Jun-90	-0.7	0.63	$21,224	$21,399	$42,622	-0.0%	-0.7%	$57,057	-1.3%	$30,256
Jul-90	-0.3	0.68	$21,160	$21,544	$42,704	0.2%	-0.5%	$56,886	-1.0%	$30,461
Aug-90	-9	0.66	$19,256	$21,686	$40,942	-4.1%	-4.8%	$51,766	-9.7%	$30,662
Sep-90	-4.9	0.6	$18,312	$21,816	$40,128	-2.0%	-2.6%	$49,250	-5.5%	$30,846
Oct-90	-0.4	0.68	$18,239	$21,965	$40,203	0.2%	-0.5%	$49,033	-1.1%	$31,056
Nov-90	6.4	0.57	$19,406	$22,090	$41,496	3.2%	2.6%	$52,171	5.8%	$31,233
Dec-90	2.7	0.6	$19,930	$22,222	$42,152	1.6%	1.0%	$53,579	2.1%	$31,421
Jan-91	4.3	0.52	$21,983	$22,186	$43,168	2.4%	1.9%	$55,883	3.8%	$31,584
Feb-91	7.1	0.48	$23,543	$21,288	$44,831	3.9%	3.4%	$59,851	6.6%	$31,736
Mar-91	2.4	0.44	$24,108	$21,381	$45,489	1.5%	1.0%	$61,288	2.0%	$31,875
Apr-91	0.2	0.53	$24,157	$21,495	$45,651	0.4%	-0.2%	$61,410	-0.3%	$32,044
May-91	4.3	0.47	$25,195	$21,596	$46,791	2.5%	2.0%	$64,051	3.8%	$32,195
Jun-91	-4.6	0.42	$24,036	$21,686	$45,723	-2.3%	-2.7%	$61,104	-5.0%	$32,330
Jul-91	4.6	0.49	$25,142	$21,792	$46,934	2.7%	2.2%	$63,915	4.1%	$32,488
Aug-91	2.3	0.46	$25,720	$21,893	$47,613	1.4%	1.0%	$65,385	1.8%	$32,638
Sep-91	-1.7	0.46	$25,283	$21,993	$47,276	-0.7%	-1.2%	$64,274	-2.2%	$32,788
Oct-91	1.3	0.42	$25,612	$22,086	$47,697	0.9%	0.5%	$65,109	0.9%	$32,926

Exhibit 11–1 (Concluded)

Date	Index 500	T-Bill	Stock $	T-Bill $	Total $	% Gain	Excess Rtn	Stock Only	Excess	Bills Only
Nov-91	-4	0.39	$24,587	$22,172	$46,759	-2.0%	-2.4%	$62,505	-4.4%	$33,054
Dec-91	11.4	0.38	$27,390	$22,256	$49,646	6.2%	5.8%	$69,630	11.0%	$33,180
Jan-92	-1.9	0.34	$24,352	$24,908	$49,259	-0.8%	-1.1%	$68,307	-2.2%	$33,292
Feb-92	1.2	0.28	$24,644	$24,977	$49,621	0.7%	0.5%	$69,127	0.9%	$33,386
Mar-92	-1.9	0.34	$24,176	$25,062	$49,238	-0.8%	-1.1%	$67,814	-2.2%	$33,499
Apr-92	2.9	0.32	$24,877	$25,142	$50,019	1.6%	1.3%	$69,780	2.6%	$33,606
May-92	0.5	0.28	$25,001	$25,213	$50,214	0.4%	0.1%	$70,129	0.2%	$33,701
Jun-92	-1.5	0.32	$24,626	$25,294	$49,919	-0.6%	-0.9%	$69,077	-1.8%	$33,808
Jul-92	4	0.31	$25,611	$25,372	$50,983	2.1%	1.8%	$71,840	3.7%	$33,913
Aug-92	-2.1	0.26	$25,073	$25,438	$50,511	-0.9%	-1.2%	$70,332	-2.4%	$34,001
Sep-92	1.2	0.26	$25,374	$25,504	$50,878	0.7%	0.5%	$71,176	0.9%	$34,090
Oct-92	0.3	0.23	$25,450	$25,563	$51,013	0.3%	0.0%	$71,389	0.1%	$34,168
Nov-92	3.4	0.23	$26,315	$25,621	$51,937	1.8%	1.6%	$73,817	3.2%	$34,247
Dec-92	1.2	0.28	$26,631	$25,693	$52,324	0.7%	0.5%	$74,702	0.9%	$34,343
Jan-93	0.8	0.23	$26,372	$26,222	$52,594	0.5%	0.3%	$75,300	0.6%	$34,422
Feb-93	1.4	0.22	$26,741	$26,280	$53,021	0.8%	0.6%	$76,354	1.2%	$34,497
Mar-93	2.1	0.25	$27,302	$26,346	$53,648	1.2%	0.9%	$77,958	1.8%	$34,584
Apr-93	-2.4	0.24	$26,647	$26,409	$53,056	-1.1%	-1.3%	$76,087	-2.6%	$34,667
May-93	2.7	0.22	$27,367	$26,467	$53,834	1.5%	1.2%	$78,141	2.5%	$34,743
Jun-93	0.3	0.25	$27,449	$26,533	$53,982	0.3%	0.0%	$78,375	0.1%	$34,830
Jul-93	-0.4	0.24	$27,339	$26,597	$53,936	-0.1%	-0.3%	$78,062	-0.6%	$34,913
Aug-93	3.8	0.25	$28,378	$26,663	$55,041	2.0%	1.8%	$81,028	3.6%	$35,001
Sep-93	-0.8	0.26	$28,151	$26,733	$54,883	-0.3%	-0.5%	$80,380	-1.1%	$35,092
Oct-93	2.1	0.22	$28,742	$26,792	$55,533	1.2%	1.0%	$82,068	1.9%	$35,169
Nov-93	-1	0.25	$28,454	$26,859	$55,313	-0.4%	-0.6%	$81,247	-1.3%	$35,257
Dec-93	1.2	0.23	$28,796	$26,920	$55,716	0.7%	0.5%	$82,222	1.0%	$35,338

Source: *Linder Letter*

108

Points to Remember

- Constant ratio investing goes one step beyond dollar cost averaging.

- You redistribute profits to maintain a constant investment ratio.

- More aggressive investors will reset the ratio every three to six months.

- Conservative investors can reset the ratio every 12 months.

- The constant ratio is used when you have an investment goal. You need to accumulate a certain amount of money over a certain period of time, but you don't want to assume too much investment risk.

- You will pay taxes on your trades unless the money is invested in a tax-deferred investment such as an IRA or variable annuity.

Chapter 12

Asset Allocation

Whether you are a conservative or aggressive investor, it's important to spread your risk by diversifying investments. When you split up the investment pie among different kinds of mutual funds, you can earn solid returns for years to come. You can do that because you cushion the impact of a stock or bond market correction when you split your investments among different assets.

Diversification works to reduce losses because gains in one asset often offset losses in others. It is important because you face a number of risks when you invest in stock or bond funds, such as:

- Systematic risk. This is also known as market risk. This means that if the entire stock market moves higher or lower, there's a good chance your stock fund will follow the market. Although your Value Line Fund may not own the same stocks as the S&P 500, for example, the stocks in the fund's portfolio still are correlated with the performance of the overall stock market.

  Bondholders also face market risk. Bond prices move in opposite directions to interest rates. So if interest rates rise bond prices fall. Conversely, if interest rates fall, bond prices rise. The longer the maturity of the bond or bond portfolio, the greater the price fluctuation due to the change in interest rates.

- Unsystematic risk. This is the risk that affects a particular firm. Bad news about a company could drive down the price of its security. Say, for example, the Value Line Leveraged Growth Fund owns stock in a company and the chief executive officer of the firm dies unexpectedly. The stock's price could tumble due to the bad news.

  By contrast, another firm owned by the fund reports fourth quarter earnings that are better than expected. Wall Street gets wind of this, buys the stock and drives up the price.

- If you own bonds or bond funds, you also face credit risk, or the risk that a company will fall on hard times and default on its debt interest and principal payments.

Don't Put All Your Eggs in One Basket

How do you protect yourself against market and non-market risk?

The answer: Invest in mutual funds and diversify your fund holdings.

Mutual funds, by definition, own a diversified portfolio of stocks. As a result, bad news about a specific company (unsystematic risk) will not hurt the overall performance of a fund. For simplicity's sake, say you own 100 shares in four stocks all priced at $10 a share for a total investment of $4,000. Bad news about a failed business venture drives the price of one stock down to $8 per share. If you owned just that stock, you sit on a 20 percent loss. However, because the other stocks in your portfolio rose an average of $1.50 a share, the market value of your portfolio rose to $4,250.

Owning a diversified portfolio of securities reduces unsystematic risk. While you still face market or systematic risk, you reduce that risk when you split up your mutual fund investments among different types of assets. Over the past six decades, for example, a 60-40 percent stock-bond split grew at an annual rate of 8.5 percent. You earned 85 percent of the return on stocks. But your investment was half as risky as it would have been had you been fully invested in stocks.

How to Split Up the Investment Pie

According to CDA Weisenberger's asset optimizer, a computer software program that helps allocate assets, there are a number of ways you can diversify your investments:

- A low-risk investor could put 6.5 percent in an aggressive growth fund, 18 percent in a growth and income fund, 13.5 percent in an international stock fund, 6.5 percent in a precious metals fund and 55.5 percent in a money fund. The expected rate of return on this portfolio is 8.6 percent with a "standard deviation," or margin of error, of 6.4 percent.

- A moderate risk investor could put 14 percent in an aggressive stock fund, 33.5 percent in a growth and income fund, 26.5 percent in an international fund, 12 percent in precious metals fund and 14 percent in a money fund. The expected rate of return on the portfolio is 11 percent with a standard deviation of 12.5 percent.

- An aggressive investor could put 45 percent in an aggressive stock fund, 3.5 percent in a growth and income fund, 35 percent in an international fund and 16.5 percent in a precious metals fund. The expected rate of return on the portfolio is 12.7 percent with a standard deviation of 17 percent.

Consider Your Age and How Long
You Have to Invest

The younger you are the more risks you can take. Refer back to Chapter 8 on long-term investment. You can lose 10 percent or more in a stock fund in a year's time. But if you can hang on to a well-managed fund for 10 years or more, the gains will far outweigh the losses.

Preservation of principal becomes more of a concern as you get older. Nevertheless, those who have just retired still need some growth so that their capital maintains its purchasing power.

There may be times when the value of your principal declines, perhaps by 15 percent or more in a year. But, historically, keeping part of an investment in stock funds would have provided a return that beat both inflation and taxes.

Exhibit 12–1 A Profile of Vanguard LIFEStrategy Funds

Target Allocation*	Vanguard Fund Components	Suitable For Investors...
Growth Portfolio 	45% Total Stock Market 15% European and Pacific 10% Fixed Income Securities 30% Asset Allocation	Seeking capital growth and will to accept substantial short-term declines. *Example:* Those seeking to accumulate savings for retirement (ages 20–49).
Moderate Growth Portfolio 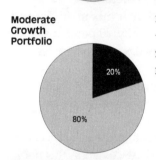	35% Total Stock Market 10% European and Pacific 25% Fixed Income Securities 30% Asset Allocation	Seeking reasonable exposure to stocks and willing to accept potentially large short-term declines. *Example:* Those approaching their retirement years (ages 50–59).
Conservative Growth Portfolio 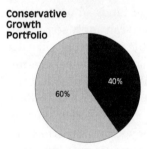	17% Total Stock Market 5% European and Pacific 28% Fixed Income Securities 20% Short-Term Corporate 30% Asset Allocation	Seeking current income and low-to-moderate growth and willing to accept periodic short-term declines. *Example:* Those in their early retirement years (ages 60–75).
Income Portfolio 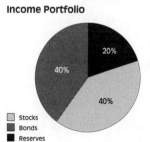	5% Total Stock Market 45% European and Pacific 20% Short-Term Corporate 30% Asset Allocation	Seeking current income and will to accept moderate short-term declines. *Example:* Those in their later retirement years (age 75 and over).

■ Stocks
■ Bonds
■ Reserves

Source: Vanguard Group of Funds

Exhibit 12–1 suggests several asset-allocation mixes based on your age and the historical rate of return on that mix from 1926 through 1993. The mixes are broken down into just stock and bond funds. But consider dividing stocks even further among growth and income funds, small company stock funds and international stock funds. On the bond side, stick with money funds and short-term bond funds.

For example, someone age 29 through 49 should invest 80 percent in stocks and 20 percent in bonds. The historical average annual return on this investment mix is 9.6 percent.

Those age 50 though 59 should consider a mix of 60 percent stocks and 40 percent bonds. This historical return is 8.6 percent.

Retirees and senior citizens should reduce their mix of stocks and bonds, and keep more in money funds. Historically, 40 percent stocks, 40 percent bonds and 20 percent money funds has grown at a 7.4 percent historical rate of return.

If you are age 74 and above, keep just 20 percent in stocks, 20 percent money funds and 60 percent in bond funds. Historically, this mix has grown at a 6.2 percent annual rate.

Once you have diversified based on your age and risk tolerance, you can apply other mutual fund investment tactics discussed in this book.

You can dollar cost average into your mix of funds. You can rebalance your portfolio once or twice a year. You also can apply some market timing to the portfolio—to cut losses when the market looks like it is in for a big decline or to invest in the funds that show the best performance trends. Perhaps it's the beginning of a bull market and small company stock fund prices show strong relative strength and have broken their 39-week moving average. The trend may continue for a year or more. So you may want to switch money out of your underperforming stock funds or money fund and reallocate your investments into small company stock funds.

Points to Remember

- Diversification reduces risk.

- More aggressive investors should put a greater percentage of their investments in stock funds.

- Conservative investors should have less in stocks and more in bonds and money funds.

- Investing in small company stock funds, international funds, precious metals funds and money funds gives you an extra layer of diversification.

- You want to get the best possible return by taking the least amount of risk.

Chapter 13

Invest Early and Often

So far, we have covered long-term investment plans like dollar cost averaging and portfolio rebalancing. These are easy-to-use tactics you can employ annually.

But there is a missing piece to this puzzle. To maximize your returns, you need to invest early and often. It particularly pays to do so an IRA, 401(k) or 403(b) pension plan.

Keep in mind that what happened over the last several decades may not occur in the future. But at least the past can give us an idea of how a diversified portfolio of mutual funds might react to both bull and bear markets.

Asset allocation was discussed in Chapter 12. But to refresh your memory, here is how a mix of stock, bond and cash investments that's well-suited for retirement savers performed from year-end 1949 through year-end 1993, according to T. Rowe Price Associates, Baltimore.

- 40 percent stocks, 40 percent bonds and 20 percent cash grew at an annual rate of 8.5 percent. The best year was 26.8 percent, the worst year was –7.2 percent. The average loss in the seven down years was –3 percent.

- 60 percent stocks, 30 percent bonds and 10 percent cash grew at an annual rate of 9.9 percent. The best year was 33.8 percent. the worst year was –13.8 percent. The average loss in the eight down years was –5.6 percent.

- 80 percent stocks and 20 percent bonds grew at an average rate of 11.2 percent. The best year was 43.5 percent and the worst year –20.3 percent. In the ten down years, the average loss was –7.1 percent.

The Early Bird Gets the Worm

Once you have a fix on your risk level, it is important to have a retirement savings plan. Experts say you should set up a budget and start saving now, rather than later. Review your monthly spending habits and cut wasteful spending. Use the savings to make tax-deductible contributions to your IRA.

"You will need somewhere between 60 percent and 80 percent of your pre-retirement income in your post-retirement years," warns Andrew Herkus, director of retirement services for Neuberger & Berman Management, New York. "Needless to say, it is better to start saving now rather than later."

Look what happens if you invest sooner, rather than later.

Assume a $2,000 annual investment earns 10 percent annually: Exhibit 13–1 shows how an early starter who opened an IRA at age 30 and stopped investing at age 40 will have more at retirement than a late starter who invests between ages 40 and 65.

The early starter would accumulate $401,560 by age 65, while the late starter would accumulate $218,364.

Another way to look at it: Here is what you will need to save by age 65, assuming an 8 percent annual return to provide you with the following annual income.

- For a $22,500 annual income, you will need to save $224,000.

- For a $30,000 annual income, you will need to save $299,000.

- For a $37,500 annual income, you will need to save $374,000.

- For a $45,000 annual income, you will need to save $448,000.

- For a $52,500 annual income, you will need to save $523,000.

Do It for the Long Haul

What if the stock market is at record levels and everyone is forecasting a steep correction—maybe a 10 percent to 20 percent decline from its highs?

Invest and don't worry. Following are results of Neuberger & Berman Management's analysis of how investors have been able to improve their returns by investing early rather than trying to time the market.

The results show that a hypothetical investor who bought each year at the stock market's high could have beat an investor who waited until later in life and bought on the day of a stock market low.

The early bird who was a poor market timer amassed $264,207 in the Neuberger & Berman Guardian Fund. By contrast, the perfect market timer who invested later in life only had $256,037.

Even more surprising is that the poor timer still could have beat the perfect timer by simply starting earlier, even if the perfect timer invested twice as much money.

To illustrate, three sets of hypothetical investment results were compared—those of two broadly used stock indexes (S&P 500, Dow Jones Industrial Average) and one actively managed mutual fund (Neuberger & Berman Guardian Fund). In all cases, share purchases were assumed to occur on the day of the yearly high/low of the Dow Jones Industrial Average (DJIA).

The results show that, based on historical performance, starting early may be the single most important factor affecting the bottom line. The extra time to compound made it possible for Early Bird to beat Late Bird, even with lower average annual returns.

Analysis Summary:
Comparison of Two Hypothetical Portfolios

1. Early Bird

   - Started early: Invested $2,000 each year from 1963–1972 ($20,000), held portfolio until June 30, 1994.

   - Poor market timer: Invested each year on day of stock market high.

2. Late Bird

- Started late: Invested $2,000 each year from 1973–1992 ($40,000); held portfolio until June 30, 1994.

- Perfect market timer: Invested each year on day of stock market low (stock market high/low as measured by the Dow Jones Industrial Average).

Points to Remember

- Start a savings plan by budgeting money to invest in a mutual fund for the long term.

- Invest early and often. Your money goes to work for you right away. You benefit because your investment earnings compound over time. Your earnings earn money.

- Take advantage of IRAs and company pensions plans. You make tax-deductible contributions and your money grows tax-deferred.

- If you invest for the long-term, don't worry about short-term losses.

Exhibit 13–1 Performance Results

	Timing Skill	Portfolio Value as of 6/30/94	Total $ Invested	Years Adding $	$ per Year
Standard & Poors 500					
Early Bird:	Poor	$264,207	$20,000	1963–72	$2,000
Late Bird:	Perfect	$256,037	$40,000	1973–92	$2,000

Avg. annualized total return as of June 30, 1994

Early Bird	10.1%
Late Bird	14.5%

	Timing Skill	Portfolio Value	Total $	Years	$ per Year
Neuberger & Berman Guardian Fund					
Early Bird:	Poor	$477,624	$20,000	1963–72	$2,000
Late Bird:	Perfect	$331,614	$40,000	1973–92	$2,000

Avg. annualized total return as of 6/30/94

Early Bird	12.6%
Late Bird	16.5%

	Timing Skill	Portfolio Value	Total $	Years	$ per Year
Dow Jones Industrial Average					
Early Bird:	Poor	$246,957	$20,000	1963–72	$2,000
Late Bird:	Perfect	$262,816	$40,000	1973–92	$2,000

Avg. annualized total return as of 6/30/94

Early Bird	9.9%
Late Bird	14.8%

Note: 6.73%, 12.92%, and 15.62% were the average annual total returns for the 1-, 5- and 10-year periods ended June 30, 1994. Results are shown on a "total return" basis and include reinvestment of all dividends and capital gains distributions. The Neuberger & Berman Equity Funds were reorganized in August, 1993. Performance and information for periods prior to August, 1993 refer to the predecessor of the Funds. Past performance is not a guarantee of future results. Investment returns and principal fluctuate. Redemption proceeds may be higher or lower than original cost.

Source: Neuberger & Berman Management

Chapter 14

Growth versus Value and Small versus Large

Here is a more sophisticated play on the old buy and hold strategy that looks at mutual fund investment styles. Investment style is nothing more than the way a fund manager invests—how he or she goes about it.

An equity mutual fund investment style can be broken down as follows:

- Large company growth stocks

- Midsize company growth stocks

- Small company growth stocks

- Large company value stocks

- Midsize company value stocks

- Small company value stocks

You also can throw an international stock component into the pot. These funds also have different investment styles.

Now the idea is to buy and hold funds by stock picking style or make a few switches to take advantage of the stock picking style that will be in favor.

Growth versus Value

No one style of stock fund remains the "king of the hill" forever. The reason: Growth stocks and value stocks go in and out of favor on Wall Street. This chapter looks at performance cycles in the financial markets. Later in this book, you'll read about the best-performing funds based on investment style.

Stock rotation plays a major role in determining what types of funds pop up on our buy list. According to *Money Magazine's Money Guide*, 75 percentage of an equity mutual fund's performance is attributable to whether a fund's investment discipline is growth or value. Funds that invest in growth stocks buy companies with rapidly increasing earnings. By contrast, value stocks sell at bargain basement prices. Other data published by the Luthold Group, Minneapolis, MN, show that value stocks dominated the market in the mid-1970s and early 1980s. Then growth stocks exhibited superior performance from the mid-1980s through 1991.

Exhibit 14–1 Growth versus Value Stocks

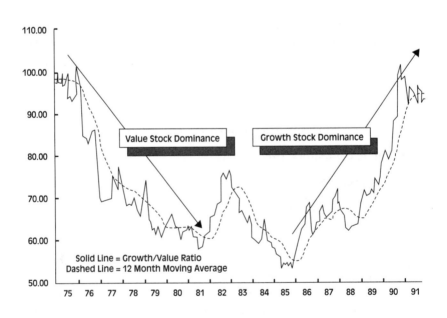

Source: The Leuthold Group

The relationship between growth and value doesn't go in a straight line. Over the last 20 years, as Exhibit 14–1 shows, there have been four alternating growth-value cycles, each lasting from three to seven years. During two of these cycles, growth stocks outperformed value stocks, while value stocks performed better during the other two cycles. There may also be mini-cycles that last from six months to 18 months, in which growth or value stock performance either leads or lags each other.

Over the longer-term there is not much difference in how they perform, according to Morningstar's statistics. For example over the past 10 years ending in May of 1994, the average growth fund, irrespective of company size, grew at an annual rate of 13.21 percent. By contrast, the average value fund, irrespective of company size, grew at an annual rate of 13 percent.

Growth funds, however, were more volatile investments than value funds. Their prices swing more from year to year compared with funds that buy beaten-down stocks.

Price volatility is often measured by what is known as a fund's standard deviation (SD) in performance. SD is the margin of error that is used to evaluate, for example, how much performance can fluctuate from its average.

Growth funds have a margin of error of 18.97 percent. Value funds have a margin of error of 13.5 percent.

This means that two-thirds of the time over the past 10 years, growth fund returns varied from –5.65 percent to +32.28 percent.

By contrast, value fund returns varied by –.47 percent to +26.47 percent.

Exhibit 14–2 Growth versus Value by Size

	1 yr %	3 yr %	5 yr %	10 yr %	SD %
All Growth	6.76	10.84	10.88	13.32	18.97
All Value	7.66	11.27	9.84	13.00	13.47
Small Cap Value	8.46	13.38	10.22	12.26	14.50
Small Cap Growth	7.33	12.38	11.23	11.77	19.49
Medium Cap Value	6.84	11.13	9.70	12.65	13.06
Medium Cap Growth	7.05	11.02	11.00	13.87	19.47
Large Cap Value	8.11	10.10	9.74	14.09	13.16
Large Cap Growth	5.20	7.66	10.01	13.95	15.87

Source: *Mutual Fund Performance Reports*, Morningstar Inc.

What Are Value Stocks?

Mutual funds that buy on value invest in stocks that have been beaten down in price, although the companies are or may be profitable in the future. Here are some of the ways value fund managers select stocks:

- Value fund managers buy companies with strong balance sheets that sell cheap to the market and their peer groups. These are low P/E stocks.

- Pure value funds often own companies whose private market value per share, or value if the company were sold, is more than the current price per share.

- Value fund managers also look at a firm's cash flow and debt coverage ratios. They want to invest in low P/E stocks that are likely to rebound when the economy improves because the companies have cut costs, reduced debt and improved their products' market share.

- Other value managers want to own stocks that are not widely followed. When the companies become profitable, the fund managers profit when Wall Street jumps on the bandwagon.

- Some value managers bottom-fish in a problem stock market. Shrewd value investors often can uncover stocks that either are misunderstood or too severely penalized for some sort of short-term misfortune. The managers buy when the stock's price does not fairly represent either the company's underlying business value or future earnings potential.

Call them turnaround specialists, bargain hunters or just plain cheap, but value investing is a specialized discipline that is the flip side of the coin to growth investing. Value investors must have the patience of a saint. It can take years for a company to recover from whatever ailments put them on the cheap list in the first place and even then, the market may take a few more years to acknowledge their profitable transformation. Chrysler is a classic example of a value stock. When Chrysler was teetering on the brink of extinction, the vast majority of investors dropped Chrysler stock like a bad habit. Chrysler eventually reached a low of $7 per share in the early 1980s. However, some value investors who really understood the underlying business value of the Chrysler franchise, Lee Iacocca's business ability, and the government's reluctance to see tens of thousands of jobs disappear, loaded up on Chrysler stock. With Chrysler now trading at $48 1/2, value investors have been handsomely rewarded.

What Are Growth Stocks?

By contrast, growth funds and earnings momentum funds frequently look at a firm's recent two to three quarters of earnings performance in relation to the company's historical rate of growth.

Growth stocks tend to trade at high price-to-earnings multiples. Stock prices get bid up fast due to expectations about future earnings.

Growth stock funds buy companies with earnings that are growing much faster than the economy and inflation. Since growth companies pay out little or no dividends, portfolio managers want to see a firm's profits successfully reinvested in the company's plant, products and equipment. As a result, fund managers evaluate firms based on earnings growth rates. In today's market, a growth fund must buy companies that are growing faster than S&P 500 companies, which are growing at an annual average of 22 percent.

Growth companies, for the most part, don't pay dividends. They are growing companies, as opposed to mature companies like AT&T, GE or Dow Chemical. Growth companies reinvest their profits into the business.

In a nutshell, growth stock pickers look at a firm's return on equity in relation to its retention ratio to derive an internal growth rate. Next, the managers look at the stock's price to future earnings ratio. If the P/E ratio is low compared with the company's growth rate, the stock is a good buy, provided that stockholders' equity is substantial in relation to the firm's profits.

Profitable Growth versus Value Trading Strategy

Dan Wiener, editor of the Independent Advisor for Vanguard Investors, NY, developed a simple trading tactic that has outperformed the S&P 500 in every rolling 10-year period since 1975.

Here is how it works:

1. Use the Vanguard Growth Index Fund and Vanguard Value Index Fund as your investment vehicles. The Growth Index Fund is made up of S&P 500 stocks with the higher price to book values. Price to book value is the price of a stock divided by the book value per share. The Value Index Fund owns the S&P 500 stocks with the lowest price to book values.

2. Review the performance of each fund every three months.

3. Invest in the fund that is underperforming. For example, say the Growth Index Fund gained 2 percent over the first quarter of the year and the Value Fund gained 2.5 percent. Put all your money in the Growth Index Fund.

4. Always switch to the underperforming index fund every three months. If you are invested in the fund that is underperforming, stay put.

Wiener found that over 39 rolling 10-year periods from 1975 to the present, shifting back and forth from growth to value resulted in an annual compound rate of return of 16.5 percent. By contrast, the S&P 500 gained 15.6 percent.

A $10,000 investment using style switching grew to $212,089. By contrast, an investment in the S&P 500 gained $181,617.

For each 10-year period shows that style switching outperformed the buy and hold on the S&P 500 by over 1 percentage point in annual return. For example:

*   In 10-year periods ending in 1985 and 1986 the buy and hold and style shifting were dead even.

*   Shifting outperformed the buy and hold in 1987 by a wide margin of 2 percentage points.

*   For 10-year periods ending in 1988 and beyond, style shifting consistently outpaced the buy and hold on the S&P 500.

Exhibit 14–3

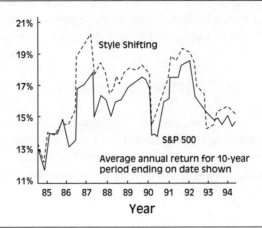

Source: Independent Investmenmt Advisor

Small versus Large

There are some other cycles to consider. Within the growth versus value universe, you could see stocks rotate between small companies and large companies.

The size of a company depends upon its market capitalization, which is the value of the outstanding shares times the current market price of the stock.

Small company stocks have market capitalizations of under $1 billion.

Midsize company stocks have market capitalizations between $1 billion and $5 billion.

Large company stocks have market capitalizations greater than $5 billion.

You Can Profit from Small Company Stocks

Small company stock funds could perform well with the economic recovery, coupled with the Clinton Administration's proposed small business tax incentives.

Listed on the NASDAQ (the stock exchange for small company stocks), small company stocks have represented some of the fastest-growing companies and industries. Often small company earnings grow at a faster rate than the economy and large companies combined.

Volatile Performers

Despite the profit potential, small company stocks are volatile performers. The stocks are thinly traded, and their earnings can fluctuate more than blue chip issues. Currently, the NASDAQ index is at a record high level. Small company stocks shot up 51 percent in 1991. The following year they gained just 12.94 percent.

Small Company Stock Cycle

Small company stocks tend to outperform large company stocks in roughly four-to-five-year cycles. Within the small company sector, you can expect small company growth stocks and small company value stocks to take turns outperforming each other.

Statistics published by Ibbotson Associates, Chicago, indicate that investing in small company stock funds is a good bet for the long term. For example:

- Small company stocks have registered 12 percent annual returns compared to 10 percent annual returns on the S&P 500 over the last six decades.

- In every period just following a recession since 1954, small company stocks have outperformed large company stocks in the ensuing 12 months.

- Small company stocks exhibit a pattern of leading and lagging the S&P 500 for several years at a time. For example, they outpaced the S&P 500 from 1961 through 1968, then fell behind for eight years. Small company stocks then beat the broad market from 1974 through 1983. Large company stocks outpaced their smaller cousins for the next seven years. But now small company stocks are performing well.

Strategy for Investing in Small Company Stock Funds

Look at the P/E ratios of the stocks held by the T. Rowe Price New Horizons Fund, a small company stock fund that is considered a benchmark indicator for the performance of small company stocks.

Consider other important factors that might indicate small company stock funds should rebound.

Here are important points to review before you invest in small company stocks, according to John Laporte, manager of the fund:

1. Review the P/E of the fund's securities in relation to the S&P 500 (see Exhibits 14–4 and 14–5). The lowest levels since 1961 are around 1 and the highest are relative P/E ratios twice the S&P 500's P/E.

2. Look at what's happened in the past. Have small stocks underperformed large company stocks over the past several years or have they outperformed their larger cousins?

3. Have small company stocks experienced some stiff corrections? Over the past four years ending in 1994, small company stocks have gone through three big corrections of 15 percent.

Exhibit 14–4 T. Rowe Price New Horizons Fund, Inc.
P/E Ratio of Fund's Portfolio Securities Relative to the S&P 500 P/E Ratio (12 Months Forward) September 30, 1994

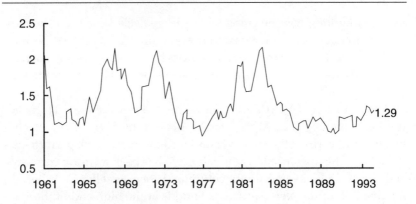

Source: T. Rowe Price Associates, Inc.

Exhibit 14–5 Business and Investment Cycle

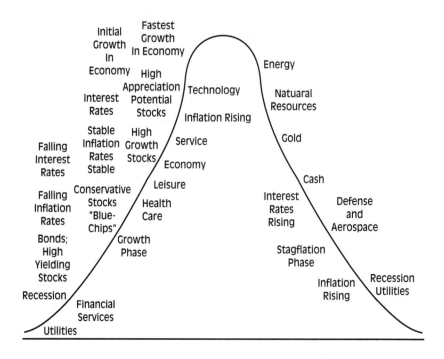

4. How long has the small versus large cycle lasted? In the most recent cycle over the past four years, small company stocks have outperformed large company stocks. The cycles usually last five to seven years based on historical performance, Laporte stresses.

When to buy: (A). If the relative P/E ratio of the New Horizon's fund is at the low end. At the time of this writing it was 1.29, which is below normal. (B). If the small versus large company stock performance cycle has some distance to go. (C). If there has been a strong correction and the cycle looks like it will continue. When to sell: (A). When the relative P/E of the New Horizon's Fund is at the high end of the spectrum. (B). If the small stocks have outperformed large stocks for more than five to seven years.

Strategy: Using the Business Cycle to Invest

The granddaddy of all cycles is the business cycle. On average, a business cycle lasts four years. In most cases, we get about two years of economic growth, followed by about two years of recession.

The business cycle moves through different stages in its growth to recession cycle. Exhibit 14–6 shows how different stocks perform during the business cycle. (This is an oversimplified example. In reality, you may see different stocks perform better than expected because of expectations about the future.)

Conversely, some stock sectors that should do well will perform poorly due to other investors' expectations about earnings and future profitability.

Exhibit 14–6 T. Rowe Price New Horizons Fund, Inc.
P/E Ratio of S&P/BARRA Indexes (Based on Trailing 12-Month Earnings)

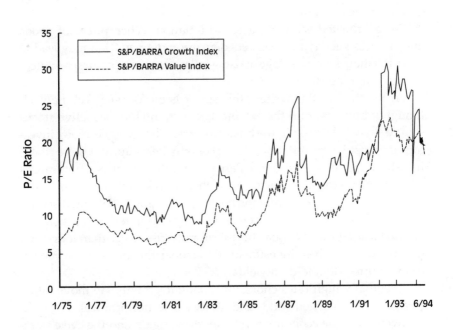

Source: T. Rowe Price Associates, Inc.

Whether a fund buys large company, small company, growth, or value stocks, its profitability depends upon anticipating which stocks will do well. To determine this requires knowing how different industries perform during the business cycle.

During the initial stages of an economic rebound, interest rates and inflation are low (see the left side of the exhibit). That's what's happening today. Utility stocks still are doing well because interest rates are low. Financial services stocks also are top performers. Many investors are rolling over their bank CDs into high-yielding blue chip stocks.

Economic indicators show that the economy is improving, albeit very slowly. In the second quarter of 1993 the Gross Domestic Product (GDP) grew at a rate of 1.8 percent.

If we get some healthy improvement, you may see the blue chip stocks perform well. In the recent past, it's been the small company stocks and mid-cap stocks that have registered the biggest gains.

Once the economy really starts growing, you see high P/E growth stocks get hot. Investors reward earnings growth with a vengeance. You will begin to see hot growth stocks in the leisure, service and technology sectors of the economy.

An overheated economy leads to inflation. When prices of goods and services keep rising, workers demand more pay. That may lead to more inflation. During a stage of rising inflation, energy, natural resources and gold mining stocks do well.

At the time of this writing this sector is performing well now, although it appears from the exhibit that such inflation-sensitive stocks should do well later on in the business cycle. The reason is many investors anticipate more inflation as the economy heats up, and these stocks have been the cheapest around. Perhaps investors in energy, natural gas and mining sectors are a bit ahead of themselves. Only time will tell.

What happens when inflation heats up? You guessed it. Interest rates rise. Fixed-income investors demand high yields in return for their loss of purchasing power. When short-term rates rise faster than long-term rates, cash is the best investment. Remember the 1980s when money funds sported double-digit yields?

Eventually high rates choke off economic growth. We move into a recession. That's when bonds and utility stocks perform well.

Eventually the economy turns the corner again and the cycle starts over.

Strategy: More Ways to Profit from Investment

Styles Make the Adjustments or Buy and Hold

There are couple of ways to invest using fund investment styles.

1. First, you can invest across the board and own all investment styles and size companies. This is just a variation on the buy and hold strategy. You cover your bases and earn a blended rate of return on your equity fund investments. Of course, you can also use dollar cost averaging, as well as portfolio rebalancing to keep things in line with your tolerance for risk.

2. Second, you can use a moving average or trend following indicator to invest in the style of fund that shows the strongest relative performance—funds that are outperforming other funds and the market. If the fund shows a positive performance trend, the trend is likely to continue.

There are several newsletters that track fund trends using momentum indicators like moving averages, relative strength and other momentum indicators. They include:

- *NoLoad Fund X,* 235 Montgomery St., Suite 662, San Francisco, CA 94104. Editor Burton Berry rates funds based on current trend performance. He tracks five different risk categories. His report will show which funds are rising to the top of the performance list. So you can see whether growth or value by small, medium or large company stocks are performing well. Berry uses a formula which looks at the average of the funds' twelve, six, three and one-month results.

- *Fundline,* P.O. Box 663, Woodland Hills, CA. David Menashe, editor, uses technical indicators to track fund performance. He uses a variation on moving averages and relative strength to spot trends.

- *Mutual Fund Strategies,* P.O. Box 446, Burlington, VT. Charles Hopper, editor, also uses moving averages and other trend indicators to spot the best investments.

- *Fabians Investment Resource,* P.O. Box 2538, Huntington Beach, CA 92647. Richard Fabian Jr., editor, also uses moving averages to recommend funds that show the best chances of outperforming the stock market on the up side.

- *Mutual Fund Trends*, Growth Fund Research Bld, Box 6600, Rapid City, SD. Walther Rouleau, editor, lists the moving averages and rankings of no-load funds. This chart book will show you which types of funds have broken through their short- and longer-term moving averages. By using this report on fund trends, you also can spot when a new investment style cycle will begin.

3. Use dollar cost averaging along with the business cycle trends. This isn't a precise formula that tells you when to exactly readjust your portfolio based on investment style. But then again, growth and value, small and large company stock funds, don't precisely turn on a dime and start moving higher. You can use the business cycle as a guide to tell you when different stock groups will come in and out of favor. Then you look at your funds' investment style, and make a decision.

For example: Keep an eye on the business and economic news. Say that interest rates start to decline and bonds and utility stocks have been outperforming other kinds of investments: The business cycle shows that before we move into a economic recovery bonds and utilities perform well. But when we start a recovery, small company stocks lead the pack.

Now check the performance of small company stocks during this phase in the business cycle. Small stock funds are underperforming and may be losing money. Is it time to invest and catch the turnaround?

Of course, no one knows when a recovery will start or when small company stocks will take off. If you dollar cost average into some well-managed small company stock funds, you will be in good position to catch the rebound and the beginning of the next bull market.

What about large company stocks? Later in the recovery large company stocks perform well. So you have an opportunity to take a position in large company stocks after small company stocks have run their course.

What is in store for today?

It looks like growth stocks are moving back into the limelight. According to a report published by T. Rowe Price, the Baltimore-based mutual fund company, the main reasons zero in on an anticipated slowdown in the economy and the attractive valuations quality growth stocks offer today.

When the path of the economic growth slows, investors will look for companies with more assured growth. The focus usually shifts from economically sensitive cyclical companies that enjoyed earnings momentum to reliable growth companies that have demonstrated a history of maintaining steady earnings growth year in and year out.

You can't always tell when growth or value stocks will turn around. But looking at the price to earnings ratios (P/E) of the stock groups can give you some insight.

The P/E ratio is the price of the stock divided by the last 12 months' earnings per share. If a company's earnings are good but the stock price is low, the company may be considered undervalued because of the low P/E ratio. By contrast, if a company's earnings are real strong, growing at a 20 percent annual rate, the price of the stock could be very high because everyone is buying it. As a result, the P/E ratio is very high.

Growth stocks tend to have high P/E ratio because investors anticipate that a company's future earnings will be great. Thus, investors buy today and drive up the stock's price.

Value stocks tend to have low P/E ratios. Few buy the stock and many have sold it. But the company may have a new product in the pipeline or is under new management. Some think the stock is undervalued because the stock could turn around.

At the time of this writing growth stocks began looking attractive due to their relatively low P/E ratios (see Exhibit 14-6, indicating the P/E ratios of growth stocks and value stocks.) Growth stocks, as mentioned above, usually sell at a premium to the market, but after the performance trends of the past few years, they are selling at P/E ratios similar to that of value stocks.

As you can see from the exhibit, the P/E ratios on growth and value stocks are both hovering around 20. Growth stock P/Es have been lower than value P/Es for more than two years.

Could this be a harbinger of things to come?

Another reason growth stocks look attractive: The price to earnings ratio of growth stocks is on the same level as value stocks. Usually growth stocks have much higher price to earnings ratios than value stocks.

When you combine the understanding of market capitalization with portfolio management style (growth or value), you get a mighty arsenal of investment power. The trick is to identify the trends, go with the flow and invest in funds that are on target with their stock selection. But John Laporte, a fund manager with T. Rowe Price says that you have to make some judgments because "there is no formula that tells you when the market focus will shift growth to value or vice versa."

The trick is to look at which group has lagged behind and is selling at a cheaper value based on price to earnings multiples: then invest and wait for the turnaround.

Points to Remember

- Stock performance goes in cycles. They are not precise but there is a trend.

- Growth stocks and value stocks take turns outperforming one another about every two years.

- Small company stocks tend to outperform large company stocks in runs of about five years.

- When the P/E ratios of either large company stocks or small company stocks lag behind, it is an indication that this group will eventually turn around. If it's been about two years that one group has underperformed the other, there could be a turnaround.

- The business cycle lasts about four years. The economy moves from growth to recession and back again.

- During a recession or economic slowdown, bond and interest rate-sensitive stocks, such as utilities, perform well.

- During the initial stages of an economic recovery, small company stocks perform well.

- As the economy picks up steam, growth stocks perform well.

- When inflation is expected to increase, precious metals mutual funds do well. So do money funds because short-term interest rates rise. But long-term bond funds lose money.

- As the economy slows, interest rates come down and bonds perform well.

Chapter 15

Rebalancing an Allocated Portfolio

The rebalancing strategy goes one step further than the constant ratio tactic. When you rebalance, you maintain the same constant percentage mix in your diversified portfolio. The size and allocation of the percentage portions can be tailored to your specific situation. To cut your risk in the stock and bond markets, you could divide your portfolio into fifths. You put 20 percent, for example, in U.S. government bond funds, 20 percent in international stock funds, 20 percent in growth and income funds, 20 percent in an aggressive stock funds and 20 percent in a precious metals fund as an inflation hedge or a money fund as a safety valve.

To keep it simple, every year you total up the value of your portfolio and divide by five. You have rebalanced the portfolio because you now have 20 percent of the portfolio in each asset.

Say you put $1,000 into five different kinds of mutual funds—a growth and income fund, a small company stock fund, an international fund, a money fund and a precious metals fund:

- In year one the investment is worth $5,000.

- The next year some of the funds gain in value while others drop. However at the end of the year you now have a total investment worth $6,000.

Now you rebalance the portfolio by dividing $6,000 by five. You have a $1,200 investment in each fund for the following year.

How Much Do You Put Into Each Fund?

You can set up a mix that fits your tolerance for risk. Chapter 12 shows that you have to zero in on your risk level. More aggressive investors can keep an 80 percent stock fund and 20 percent money fund mix. Conservative investors can go with a 60 percent stock fund and 40 percent money fund or bond fund mix. Safety-minded investors can keep 30 percent in a blue chip stock fund and the rest in money funds and bond funds.

With these kinds of mixes, you are diversified, so that gains in one type of mutual fund will offset some of the losses in other types of funds. Want an inflation hedge? You can put a small percentage of your portfolio in a precious metals fund.

A Lower Risk Investment than a
100 Percent Stake in Stocks

If you had rebalanced a portfolio that was one-third invested in a diversified U.S. stock fund, an international stock fund, and a U.S. taxable bond fund, the investment grew at an annual rate of 6.9 percent over five years ending in 1994.

The S&P 500 grew at a 8.7 percent annual rate. So you underperformed the market averages. But you were diversifying your investment to reduce risk.

Your rebalanced portfolio gave you 80 percent of the return on the market with one-third the risk. That's not bad. That is what a rebalanced investment is supposed to do.

Rebalancing Your Diversified Portfolio

The rebalancing strategy goes one step further than the other formula plans. When you rebalance, you maintain the same constant percentage mix in your diversified portfolio. The size and allocation of the percentage portions can be tailored to your specific situation. This rebalancing usually dictates some switching around and some tax consequences if the money is not invested in a retirement savings plan. By rebalancing, though, you actualize your profits and dollar-cost-average with the investments that have faltered temporarily.

How It Works

Let's look at how rebalancing a diversified portfolio works using some of the Scudder Mutual Fund Group's funds for 10 years ending in 1994.

Assume that you invested in each of the following funds on Dec. 31, 1984 through Oct. 31, 1994:

- $1,000 in Scudder International Fund, an international stock fund.

- $1,000 in Scudder Capital Growth Fund, a growth stock fund.

- $1,000 in Scudder Development Fund, a small company stock fund.

- $1,000 in Scudder Cash Investment Trust, a money fund.

Also assume that every year you totaled up your investment and divided by four. Then you resplit the money equally among the four funds.

The results show (see Exhibit 15–1) that the $4,000 initial investment grew to $14,697. Over 9.75 years, your investment grew at an annual compound rate of 14.23 percent.

Your investment performed well for a couple of reasons: You took your profits and reinvested the money in your underperforming funds. Later the poorer performers registered big gains.

For example, in 1987, investors took a licking in the Scudder Development and the Scudder Capital Growth funds. The exhibit shows that they lost money in both funds. Not much, but they lost.

But at the end of 1987, the portfolio was rebalanced. More money was placed in both funds to equalize the investment mix.

Look what happened in the following year. The Capital Growth Fund gained 33.8 percent and the Development Fund gained 23.21 percent.

Exhbit 15–1 Portfolio Rebalancing

Scudder International Fund	Scudder Capital Growth Fund	Scudder Development Fund	Scudder Cash Investment Trust		Portfolio Total
$1,000.00	$1,000.00	$1,000.00	$1,000.00	12/31/84	$4,000.00
49.01%	36.70%	19.65%	7.79%	12/31/85 Annual Return	28.29%
$1,490.10	$1,367.00	$1,196.50	$1,077.90	12/31/85	$5,131.50
$1,282.88	$1,282.88	$1,282.88	$1,282.88	12/31/85 Rebalance	$5,131.52
50.47%	16.58%	7.79%	6.40%	12/31/86 Annual Return	20.31%
$1,930.34	$1,495.58	$1,382.82	$1,364.98	12/31/86	%6,173.72
$1,543.43	$1,543.43	$1,543.43	$1,543.43	12/31/86 Rebalance	$6,173.72
1.91%	-0.73%	-1.42%	6.10%	12/31/87 Annual Return	1.24%
$1,559.02	$1,532.16	$1,521.51	$1,637.58	12/31/87	$6,250.28
$1,562.57	$1,562.57	$1,562.57	$1,562.57	12/31/87 Rebalance	$6,250.28
18.84%	29.71%	11.06%	7.18%	12/31/88 Annual Return	16.70%
$1,856.96	$2,026.81	$1,735.39	$1,674.76	13/31/88	$7,294.92
$1,823.48	$1,823.48	$1,823.48	$1,823.48	12/31/88 Rebalarce	$7,293.92
27.04%	33.80%	23.21%	8.86%	12/31/88 Annual Return	23.23%
$2,316.55	$2,439.82	$2,246.71	$1,985.01	12/31/89	$8,988.11
$2,247.03	$2,247.03	$2,247.03	$2,247.03	12/31/89 Rebalance	$8,988.12
-8.92%	16.98%	1.48%	7.84%	12/31/90 Annual Return	4.35%
$2,046.59	$2,628.58	$2,280.29	$2,423.20	12/31/90	$9,378.65
$2,344.66	$2,344.66	$2,344.66	$2,344.66	12/31/90 Rebalance	$9,378.64
11.78%	42.96%	71.83%	5.96%	12/31/91 Annual Return	33.13%
$2,5620.86	$3,351.92	$4,028.83	$2,484.40	12/31/91	$12,486.02
$3,121.51	$3,121.51	$3,121.51	$3,121.51	12/31/91 Rebalance	$12,486.04
-2.64%	7.09%	-1.82%	3.51%	12/31/92 Annual Return	1.54%
$3,039.10	$3,342.83	$3,064.70	$3,231.08	12/31/92	$12,677.70
$3,169.42	$3,169.42	$3,169.42	$3,169.42	12/31/92 Rebalance	$12,677.68
36.50%	20.07%	8.84%	2.58%	12/31/93 Annual Return	17.00%
$4,326.26	$3,805.52	$3,449.60	$3,251.19	12/31/93	$14,832.57
$3,708.14	$3,708.14	$3,708.14	$3,708.14	12/31/93 Rebalance	$14,832.56
4.08%	-6.87%	-3.73%	2.87%	10/31/94 YTD REturn	-0.91%
$3,859.44	$3,453.39	$3,569.83	$3,814.56	10/31/94	$14,697.22

Source: Scudder Stevens & Clark

The Scudder International Fund lost almost 9 percent in 1990. Then you rebalanced your portfolios. Money went into this fund. In the following year the fund gained almost 12 percent.

In 1992 the same thing happened with the International Fund and the Development Fund. They both lost money. But you rebalanced and the investments bounced back in 1993.

Rebalancing works well for several reasons. Investments such as those listed previously tend to move in contrary directions. If one does poorly, another may produce offsetting gains. Because you are dollar-cost-averaging, you buy low and sell high when you rebalance. Rebalancing eliminates market timing decisions.

The worksheet below will help you set up a mutual fund portfolio rebalancing plan.

Safety Is the Key

The important point about rebalancing is the process: spreading your risks and realizing your profits without trying to guess the best time to buy or sell.

Rebalance Based on Your Risk Level

The 25 percent rebalancing tactic works well to reduce risk. This percentage breakdown may not be ideal for everyone, however. A couple approaching retirement should take less risk than a young professional couple with a combined income of more than $125,000 a year.

Younger people can afford to seek growth and take more risk because they can buy and hold for a longer time as well as anticipate a longer period of generating (probably rising) income. The pre-retirement couple may want some growth, but they also need safety. They would be aghast to see the value of their portfolio drop 20 percent a few years before they retire.

This is why it is important to match investment risk with financial needs and risk tolerance. When you look at your risk level and income and growth requirements, you can set a better investment mix. Examine the following factors:

- How closely do investments move in tandem with each other? You want a mix where the investments will move in opposite directions part of the time. In the halls of finance, that is known as how well investments "correlate" with one another.

- You want to combine investments to obtain the best return with the least amount of price volatility. Ideally, you will lower your margin of error every month and still receive the kind of return you need to build your wealth. If you could choose between an investment offering an annual return of 16 percent with a price fluctuation, or margin of error, of 24 percent, or an investment mix providing a 12 percent return with a 12 percent margin of error, which would you choose? The answer depends on how much you want to risk. Hint: Before choosing the former offering, think honestly about how you would feel if you lost nearly $2,500 on each $10,000 you invested in a single year.

Constructing an investment mix to obtain the best return with the lowest margin of error—taking into account an individual's risk parameters—is known in finance as "optimizing your portfolio." (I wonder what academic coined a word as forbidding as "optimization" to explain a concept as simple as finding the best investment mix with the least amount of risk?)

Rebalancing a Higher Risk Mix for Profits

When you mix your portfolio properly, you can boost your return and lower the monthly price hit, or risk of losses, in the event you have to sell. If you were a low risk investor who wanted some growth from stocks, but also safety, you simply could adopt one of our model portfolios. Using that, you would put 40 percent in a growth and income fund, 43 percent in an international stock fund, 5 percent in precious metals fund, and 12 percent in a money fund.

Rebalancing based on these percentages over the ten years ending in March 1993 would have given you an annual rate of return of 13.3 percent. During that same period, the S&P 500 gained 14.40 percent a year. You earned 92 percent of the return on the market, but with about one-third less risk.

This mix of funds gives you the best return with just a tad more risk based on the annual margin of error, which also is known as the "standard deviation." You earned over 13 percent a year with a margin of error of about 13.

Because you put more assets into stock funds than a portfolio that was equally weighted, you boosted the return on your investment. You took on more risk than an equally weighted portfolio. But your investment still was less volatile than a 100 percent stake in the stock market.

Flexibility

It is best to rebalance your portfolio in a tax-deferred investment like an IRA, 401(k) company pension, variable annuity or variable life insurance policy. That way you don't have to pay taxes on your trades.

Every year use the worksheet below to total up the value of your investment pie. Then call your fund representative, toll-free, and indicate how much you want in each fund. Some variable annuities make it easy. You can get automatic rebalancing.

You also can combine rebalancing with dollar cost averaging. Say that you have money automatically taken out of your checking account and deposited in your IRA's money fund: At the end of the year, you total what your investment is worth and rebalance. The extra money you have accumulated in the money fund will get redistributed at the end of the year.

And don't forget you get a tax deduction for making your IRA or 401(k) contributions.

Points to Remember

- Diversify your investment mix to match your risk tolerance.

- Rebalance the portfolio at least once a year.

- More aggressive investors can rebalance their portfolios every three or six months.

- Rebalancing enables you to take profits in winning investments and dollar cost average into underperforming investments.

- It works best in retirement savings plans because you don't pay taxes on the trades.

- If you invest 100 percent of your money in a stock fund, you will earn more than if you split up your investment pie and rebalanced the portfolio.

- Rebalancing is a lower-risk way to invest in stocks and bonds.

Fund Rebalancing Work Sheet

Year	Fund A$	Fund B$	Fund C$	Total$	Rebalance: Divide by 4
1995					
Beginning					
Ending					
1996					
Beginning					
Ending					
1997					
Beginning					
Ending					
1998					
Beginning					
Ending					
1999					
Beginning					
Ending					
2000					
Beginning					
Ending					

Chapter 16

Value Averaging

Value Averaging is an aggressive form of dollar cost averaging. This tactic is for investors who can tolerate greater price volatility in their investments.

Instead of investing a fixed amount regularly over the long term, your goal is to have the investment's value increase by a specific amount over a specific timeframe. That means you could be investing more in some months when the investment has declined, or less when the investment increased beyond expectations.

For that reason, this system requires you to invest more when the market declines and the value of your mutual fund investments plunge.

The book, *Value Averaging,* by Harvard business professor Michael Edleson, published by International Publishing Corp. (Chicago), discusses an aggressive adaptation of dollar cost averaging.

Edleson says value averaging is similar to dollar cost averaging, in which you invest a fixed dollar amount every month. But with value averaging, you make the value of the portfolio increase by a fixed amount every month.

If you want, for example, the value of your investments to increase $100 a month, your actual purchase may range from zero to $100 depending on how much your existing stock or equity mutual fund has increased. You would sell shares when prices rise and the value of the portfolio increases more than $100. That way you take excess profits out of your investment. If share prices drop, however, you have to kick in extra money.

It works this way: Say you want the value of your investment to increase by $100 a month, so you invest $100 in the first month. You have to make your holdings rise by $100 so your investment is worth $200 in month two. Say the market value of your initial investment went up to $115 by the end of the second month. All you need to kick in is $185.

In month three, for example, the market value of your holdings increases to a whopping $350. You just kick in another $50. But say in the next month your investment is worth $425. You take out the excess profits of $25 and sock it away in a money fund.

But what happens if the market value of your investment drops?

Edleson says you should make up the difference. At the end of month five, your investment will then be worth $500. But say we had a stock market correction and the value of your investment dropped to $375. You then have to kick in another $125 to bring the value back up to $500.

The reason value averaging works well over the long term is due to the volatility of the stock market. Edleson says that the stock market overreacts over the shorter-term to bad news such as rising interest rates or declining corporate earnings. However, as time goes by, the market will bounce back and correct itself from the overreaction.

For example, if you refer back to the exhibit in Chapter 1, you will see that the longer you own stocks, the greater your chance of making money. The number of periods stocks have provided positive returns over every rolling 10-year period in stock market history is 57 out of 59 times, or 97 percent of the time. Drop down to rolling five year periods and the pluses outweigh the negatives 58 to 64 or 90 percent of the time.

Over one year it's a different ballgame. The number of positive years is 48 of 68 years.

You want to use value averaging over at least a five-year period. But investing regularly, you take advantage of the down periods in the stock market to buy low. The idea is to accumulate more shares at a lower prices. Then take profits on the upside.

How often do you up the ante or take profits when you use value averaging? Edleson says it's best to adjust your portfolio from once to four times a year for the best results. Over time, that can lead to solid investment returns. For example, his studies show that value averaging outperformed dollar cost averaging over the last six decades from 1926 through 1989. If you adjusted your portfolio quarterly using value averaging, your investment grew at an annual rate of 12.76 percent compared with 11.42 percent using dollar cost averaging. If you adjusted your portfolio once a year, you would have earned 12.54 percent annually with value averaging compared with 11.41 percent with dollar cost averaging.

Let's look at how value averaging performed before and after the great stock market plunge of 1987, when the Dow dropped 500 points in one day and the average growth stock fund lost a whopping 20 percent in the fourth quarter of that year. The data are based on a study conducted by the American Association of Individual Investors in the October 1992 issue of *Computerized Investing.*

The study assumes that a $1,000 initial investment was made in the Twentieth Century Ultra Fund, a small stock growth fund. The dollar amount of increase every quarter should be $1,000.

The study also shows that you have to have deep pockets to invest using value averaging.

As you can see, $1,000 was initially invested in the 20th Century Ultra fund at the year-end, 1986. You purchased 112.108 shares at a NAV (net asset value) of $8.92.

Look at column B. Your target was a desired value of $2,000 by the end of March 1987; $3,000 by the end of June; and, $4,000 by the end of September.

Look at column C. The NAV of the fund steadily rose over the following nine months. It hit a high of $12.97 by the end of September of 1987.

Now look at column F, which shows you what the value of the account was before you make the adjustments so that your account increases to the desired value. Comparing column B to column F shows that you did not reach the desired value at the end of the period. That means you had to kick in more money.

Look at column G. It shows how much you have to invest or sell to reach your desired level. Column H shows you how many shares of the fund you had to buy or sell to reach that level, while column I shows you the total number of shares you own after you add or subtract from the account to reach the desired value.

Exhbit 16–1 Value Averaging Worksheet

September/October 1992 Computerized Investing, A.A.I.I.
By John Baikowski
Twentieth Century Ultra
TWCUX
$1,000 Dollar Amount of Initial Investment
$1,000 Dollar Amount of Increase (Decrease) Desired Each Period
1 Do You Wish to Sell Shares to Force Portfolio to Maintain Desired Level?
      (Enter 1 if Yes, 0 if No)
Shares WILL be sold to keep portfolio change at desired level

A	B	C	D	E
			No. of Shares Acquired since Last	Shares Owned before
Date	Desired Value	NAV	Rebalancing	Rebalancing
Dec 86	$1000.00	8.92		0.000
Mar 87	1000.00	12.55	0.071	112.179
Jun 87	3000.00	12.07		159.363
Sep 87	4000.00	12.97		248.550
Dec 87	5000.00	6.23	161.271	469.685
Mar 88	6000.00	6.89		802.568
Jun 88	7000.00	7.59		870.827
Sep 88	8000.00	7.00		922.266
Dec 88	9000.00	7.06		1142.857
Mar 89	10000.00	8.34		1274.788
Jun 89	11000.00	9.21		1199.041
Sep 89	12000.00	10.26		1194.354
Dec 89	13000.00	8.53	156.722	1326.313
Mar 90	14000.00	8.16		1524.033
Jun 90	15000.00	9.47		1715.686
Sep 90	16000.00	7.94		1583.949
Dec 90	17000.00	9.30	6.067	2021.180
Mar 91	18000.00	13.09		1827.957
Jun 91	19000.00	12.28		1375.095
Sep 91	20000.00	14.48		1547.231
Dec 91	21000.00	17.34		1373.626
Mar 92	22000.00	16.14		1211.073
Jun 92	23000.00	14.36		1363.073
Sep 92	24000.00		1601.671	
Dec 92	25000.00		#DIV/OI	

Source: *Computerized Investing*, American Association of Individual Investors

F	G	H	I
Total Value before Rebalancing	Amount to Invest (Redeem)	No. of Shares to Buy (Sell)	No. of Shares Owned after Rebalancing
$0.00	$1000.00	112.108	112.108
1407.85	592.15	47.184	159.363
1923.51	1076.49	89.187	248.550
3223.69	776.31	59.854	3083.404
2926.14	2073.86	332.883	802.568
5529.69	470.31	68.259	870.827
6609.58	390.42	51.439	922.266
6455.86	1544.14	220.591	1142.857
8068.57	931.43	131.931	1274.788
10631.73	(631.73)	(75.747)	1199.354
11043.17	(43.17)	(4.687)	1194.354
12254.07	(254.07)	(24.763)	1169.591
11313.45	1686.55	197.720	1524.033
12436.11	1563.89	191.653	1715.686
16247.55	(1247.55)	(131.737)	1583.949
12576.56	3423.44	431.164	2015.113
18796.97	(1796.97)	(193.223)	1827.957
23927.96	(5927.96)	(452.862)	1375.095
16886.17	2113.83	172.136	1547.231
22527.68	(2527.68)	(173.605)	1373.626
23818.67	(2818.67)	(162.553)	1211.073
19546.72	2453.28	152.000	1363.073
19573.73	3426.27	238.598	1601.671
0.00	24000.00	DIV/OI	#DIV/OI
#DIV/OI	#DIV/OI	#DIV/OI	#DIV/OI

As you can see from column G, you had to add money into the account in each of the three-month periods in 1987. You kicked in $592 in March, $1,0876 in June and $776 in September.

The Stock Market Plunge

You really took a licking in the last quarter of 1987. The 20th Century Ultra Fund dropped a whopping 52 percent from its high of $12.97 in September 1987.

Get Out Your Pocketbook

You had to kick in an extra $2,074 (column G) to bring your account up to the desired value of $5,000.

Of course, you bought more shares because the fund NAV was sliced in half. You bought 333 shares of Ultra at that time. As you can see, you are aggressively dollar cost averaging using this method.

You Keep Buying

You had to keep kicking in extra money into the fund until September 1988. For the first 21 months of your investment, you had invested a total of $8,853 so that your investment hit its desired value of $9,000 by year-end 1988.

Now Comes the Gravy Train

In 1989, the NAV of the fund shot up to $10.26 by the end of September 1989 from $7.06 at year-end 1988. Now you had to take profits from the fund to keep the investment at the desired level.It wasn't much. You withdrew a total of $928 and your investment stood at $12,000.

The stock market took a severe hit in late 1989 and 1990 due to the recession and a war in the Middle East. By September of 1990 (see columns B and C) you had to have an account value of $16,000 and the fund NAV plunged to $7.94 for a high of $10.26. You had to add a total of $5,427 into the fund to hit your target. From September 1990 though June 1992, the fund's NAV rallied to a high of $16.14 before pulling back to $14.36. Your desired account value stood at $23,000. And you took profits totaling $5,079 out of the investment.

You Put a Lot In, Took a Lot Out and Ended Up Fine

At the end of June 1992, the desired value of your account stood at $23,000. During the entire period from December 1986 though the end of June 1992, you invested a total of $18,155 into the 20th Century Ultra Fund to maintain your desired account level during down periods of the fund. During that same period you also withdrew a total of $15,248 to maintain the desired account level during periods in which the fund registered gains.

Volatility over the Short Term

Over short periods, you can get some whopping returns with value averaging if you happen to start your investment program after a severe stock market correction. Look how much you invested after the stock market crash in 1987 at cheap prices as the fund's net asset value shot up to a high of $17.34 at year-end 1991 from a low of $6.23 at year-end 1987 (see Exhibit 16–1). The account value grew to a whopping $21,000 from $5,000.

Be advised, however, that over the longer term, Dr. Edleson warns that the law of averages catches up with you. About the best you can do if you invest over a lifetime: Your investment will approximate the historic return on a value-averaged investment of 12 percent since 1926.

Value averaging is an aggressive systematic way to invest in mutual funds. Be advised. You are not going to get rich quick using this system. Plus, with value averaging, you need to be aware of the following:

- You will need a computer program to carry out this tactic. So you must be willing to spend the extra time monitoring your investment.

- If you use load funds, you will increase your transaction costs due to numerous trades.

- If you invest in load funds, avoid Class A front-end loaded shares and Class C back-end load shares. It's best to stick with Class B shares that charge a flat 1 percent annual fee. Otherwise you pay too much to move in and out of the funds.

- If you invest in load funds, check the break points on the fund commissions. Load funds lower their commissions if you invest large sums with them.

- Unless the investment is in a tax-sheltered account, such as an IRA, 401(k), or variable annuity, you could be forced to pay a lot of taxes on those capital gains due to profitable trades.

- You must be willing to invest large sums of money in down markets and hold on for unknown periods of time waiting for your stock fund to rebound.

- You have to invest in a stock fund that stays fully invested in stocks. You don't want to invest in a fund that can move a large percentage of the fund to cash during bad periods. That defeats the purpose of your investment.

- You must invest with fund families that will permit numerous trades. Some funds will limit the number of times you can switch from stock funds to money funds to just two round-trips annually.

Points to Remember

- Value averaging is an aggressive form of dollar cost averaging.

- Since you want the value of your mutual fund investment to increase by a specific amount, you must be prepared to kick in extra money when the fund underperforms.

- Over the long term, your value averaging will outperform dollar cost averaging.

- Over the short-term, value averaging could underperform dollar cost averaging.

- To make value averaging work, you need to invest in growth, aggressive growth or small company stock fund that always stay fully invested.

Chapter 17

Value Ratio Investing

Conservative investors looking to become just aggressive enough to catch major long-term trends might consider the value ratio method of mutual fund investing.

Walter Rouleau, publisher of *Growth Fund Guide* in Rapid City, SD, designed this system to determine when the markets are over- or undervalued.

He simply says that as the stock market goes higher, investors should salt more into conservative equity mutual funds or cash, then wait out the declines and reinvest in stocks when the market again looks overvalued.

There is no surefire way to time the markets. However, Rouleau's strategy is a disciplined way to make investment decisions by examining how much it will cost to buy a dollar's worth of stock dividends, and investing accordingly.

Here is how it works. You invest based on the price to dividend ratio (P/D) on the S&P 500 stock market index. P/D is calculated by dividing the dividend yield on the index into the number one. For example, if the stock market yields 4 percent, the P/D is 25 or 1 divided by 4. This tells you that it costs $25 to buy $1 worth of dividends.

Historically, the market is overvalued when it costs $30 to $34 for $1 of dividends. At $20 for a $1 dividend, however, the stock market is undervalued. Great buying opportunities exist when the P/D is below 20, or when stocks yield 5 percent or more.

Rouleau says that over the past 100 years, whenever the P/D ratio has climbed into the 30s or higher range, a major stock market decline eventually has followed. The 13 highest P/D ratio readings have averaged almost 34 to 1 and declines thereafter have averaged 40 percent.

At the time of this writing, the P/D ratio stood at 35.46. That means investors should take a risk averse stance in the market. They need to stay in cash or invest in hedge funds like precious metals and contrarian funds—funds that perform well in down markets because they hedge their losses.

Rouleau says that when the stock market plunges, the P/D ratio usually declines to an average or below-average reading of about 23. At the low extreme in late 1974 and late 1982, P/D ratios fell to the mid-teens. Readings in the middle-teens or below are very rare and usually last only for a short time. As P/D ratios fall, your portfolio becomes more invested in stock funds that should lead the way up when the market goes higher.

Which funds will be big winners when the market moves higher? Which funds should you invest in when the market is overvalued? Your cue is the fund's beta value.

Beta is a measure of how a fund moves in relation to the market as measured by the S&P 500. The S&P 500 has a beta value of 1. A fund with a beta of 1.2 will move 20 percent higher than the market when it goes up. By contrast, it will lose 20 percent more than the market on the downside. A fund with a beta value of .8 gives up 80 percent of the upside on the S&P 500. On the downside, you will lose 20 percent less than the market.

For example, let's say the S&P 500 goes up 10 percent: You own a well-managed stock fund with a beta value of 1.2. Your fund will be up 12 percent. Now the market loses 10 percent. Your fund will probably drop 12 percent in value.

By taking advantage of a fund's beta value, the Value Ratio form of investing puts you in the high beta stock funds when the market is undervalued and has the potential to rise. By contrast, when stock prices are too high, you invest in low beta funds that will lose less when prices decline.

Rouleau's strategy is an easy one. You always stay fully invested and split the portfolio into three, depending on your risk tolerance:

- **Strategy 1.** Stay 100 percent invested and use conservative and aggressive equity funds.

- **Strategy 2.** You also can use a money fund as a conservative investment. When the price-to-dividend ratio is rising, you put more money in conservative growth and income funds until you are 100 percent invested in safer mutual funds when the P/D hits 34. As the P/D declines you put more into aggressive growth funds. When the P/D goes below 20, you maintain a 100 percent position in aggressive stock funds.

- **Strategy 3.** This is an aggressive tactic. You move between money funds and stock funds. You also use leverage. You invest in money funds when the market is overvalued and the P/D ratio is high. When the P/D ratio is low, you invest in high beta stock funds or borrow on margin to invest in the stock funds.

Strategies 1 and 3

For the stock and cash portfolio, the breakdown is as follows:

- If the P/D is 34, you put 50 percent in money funds and 50 percent in conservative stock funds.

- When the P/D equals 32 to 33.99, you invest 15 percent in money funds, 75 percent in conservative stock funds and 10 percent in aggressive stock funds.

- When the P/D equals 30 to 31.99, you invest 10 percent in money funds, 55 percent in conservative stock funds and 35 in aggressive stock funds.

- A P/D of 23 to 29.99 calls for 50 percent in conservative stock funds and 50 percent in aggressive stock funds.

- When the P/D ranges from 20 to 22.99, you put 37.5 percent in conservative stock funds and 62.5 in aggressive stock funds.

- You are 100 percent invested in aggressive funds when the P/D is below 19.99.

Strategy 2

The exact breakdown using this strategy is as follows for a fully invested portfolio:

- If the P/D is 34, you are 100 percent in conservative stock funds.

- When it drops to between 30 to 33.99, you are 87.5 percent in conservative stock funds and 12.5 percent in aggressive stock funds.

- At a P/D ranging between 23 and 29.99, you are 67.5 percent in conservative and 32.5 percent in aggressive funds.

- At a P/D of 20 to 23.99 you are 37.5 percent conservative and 62.5 percent aggressive. When the P/D is below 20, you are 100 percent aggressive.

What Specific Funds Should You Use?

Rouleau makes specific fund recommendations in Growth Fund Guide. He based his fund picks on trend indicators—which funds show the best performance today based on current market conditions. These are the funds that are outperforming other funds. For example, in October 1994, when the P/D ratio registered 35, he recommended the following funds in the fully invested portfolio: Benham Gold, Dreyfus Strategic Growth, Lexington Gold, Robertson Contrarian, Linder Bulwark—all low beta value funds that hedge against stock market declines.

You can keep it simple and stick to just three funds. Rouleau's model portfolio includes the following recommended no-load funds:

- Mutual Shares. This is a conservative growth and income fund that invests in larger company stocks. This fund buys undervalued, out-of-favor and beaten-down stocks. The fund manager looks for turnaround situations—a new manager, a new product or new market tactics. Since the fund invests in beaten-down stocks, there is less downside risk. Many of the stocks in the portfolio have already experienced major declines. The fund can invest in both U.S. and foreign stocks and has a beta value of just .40. It is the investment of choice for those who remain fully invested when the stock market is in overvalued territory.

- Twentieth Century Growth, a growth fund that buys large company stocks. The fund invests in companies that show strong trends earnings growth rates. The fund manager wants to own companies that are growing faster than the economy, the rate of inflation and other companies. The fund, which can invest in both U.S. and foreign stocks, has a beta value of 1.4. It is the investment of choice when the stock market is undervalued.

- Vanguard Prime Portfolio, a money market fund. This is one of the lowest-cost money funds on the market. The fund keeps expenses to the bone and invests in only the highest quality and safest money market instruments.

A Lower-Risk Way to Move into and out of the Market

Rouleau notes that his Value Ratio tactic is a low-risk way to earn mutual fund profits. According to *Growth Fund Guide's* data: The model portfolio for a fully invested portfolio, which only uses the funds mentioned above, grew 9.8 percent over the 12 months ending in September 1994.

The cash portfolio and leveraged portfolio, which has been 100 percent in the money fund, is up 3.5 percent over the same 12-month period.

From Dec. 30, 1966 to Sept. 30, 1994, Rouleau says the fully invested portfolio has grown at a 19.6 percent annual compound rate of return. The equity and cash portfolio gained at a 23.4 percent annual rate and the equity, cash and leveraged portfolio gained 25.7 percent annually.

The *Hulbert Financial Digest,* an Alexandria, VA-based newsletter that tracks and measures newsletter performance advice, reports that over the past five years ending in July 1994, the Value Ratio fully invested portfolio gained 31.1 percent, which translates into a 5.5 percent annual return.

The cash portfolio gained 32.3 percent, which is a 5.8 percent annual return.

The equities, cash and leveraged portfolio gained 36.4 percent, which is a 6.4 percent annual return.

During the same period, the Wilshire 5000 gained 61.6 percent, which translates into a 10.1 percent annual return.

T-bills gained 27.9 percent, which translates into a 5.2 percent annual return.

Rouleau's portfolios barely outperformed T-bills over the past five years. The reason: The stock market has been overvalued and traded at historically high price-to-dividend ratios during that period. Only for a brief time in 1990 did the P/D ratio drop to 25, when the stock market yielded 4 percent. For most of the past five years, the dividend yield on the market has been hovering around 3 percent or less. As a result, the value ratio system keeps its investors in a low-risk position.

Points to Remember

- Value ratio investing is a low-risk way to diversify and manage your mutual funds.

- When the stock market is overvalued, you invest in conservative stock funds or money funds.

- When the stock market is undervalued or has gone through a correction, you invest in growth stock funds.

- You must be patient when you apply the value ratio investment strategy. Over the past three years, investors have had the majority of their money in either conservative stock funds or money funds.

- You can combine value ratio investing with dollar cost averaging.

Chapter 18

Variable Ratio Investing

If you want to buy low and sell high, then consider the variable ratio formula investment plan. It's a variation of the constant ratio plan discussed in Chapter 11. This strategy can be used by more aggressive investors who are willing to invest more when their fund loses money.

You start with a fixed mix of funds, as with the constant ratio plan. Then you periodically rebalance the portfolio to maintain that mix.

The variable ratio investment plan goes one step further. You increase your percentage invested in a common stock fund when it declines in value. On the upside, you decrease the proportion you invest in a stock fund when the market price rises.

Let's look at a period of high stock market volatility to gain insight into how the variable ratio plan can work.

A study conducted by Gerald Perritt, Ph.D., publisher of the *Mutual Fund Letter,* shows how the variable ratio plan works during a volatile period of stock market behavior over an eight-year period from January 1977 through year-end 1984. During this time there were big changes in the Dow Jones Industrial Average. Twice, the market declined 200 points then surged during a bull market that saw the Dow increase from 945 to 1211 by year-end 1984.

Perritt began with a $10,000 initial investment split evenly between the Vanguard Index Trust and one-month Treasury bills. This plan calls for an increase in the proportion committed to common stocks when market prices fall by 20 percent, and a decrease in the common stocks proportion when the stock market prices increase by 25 percent.

This variable ratio calls for buying more shares when the fund value declines, and taking profits when prices rise.

In this study, Perritt decreased the stock fund proportion of the overall portfolio from 50 percent to 25 percent on the first 25 percent rise in stock prices. If the stock market continued to rise by another 25 percent, he put 100 percent of the portfolio in T-bills.

By contrast, if the stock fund price fell by 20 percent, the 50-50 ratio would be changed to 75-25 in favor of common stocks. That split would become 100 percent common stocks if the market continued to fall by another 20 percent.

The results show that the variable ratio method was a profitable tactic used during a period of several market increases and declines. After starting out with a 50 percent stock fund and 50 percent T-bill mix in January 1977, the portfolio was readjusted five times in the ensuing eight years. For example:

- In February, 1978, the portfolio shifted to a 75 percent stock fund and 25 percent T-bill mix. Note that after making a stock purchase in July 1982, which resulted in a 75-25 stock–Treasury bill ratio, two successive stock sales and portfolio realignments were made in October 1982 and April 1983 which resulted in a 25-75 stock–Treasury bill ratio.

- In August, 1980, profits were taken in the stock fund and the mix was reduced to 50-50.

- In July, 1982, following a market decline, the mix was readjusted to 75-25.

- In October, 1982, profits were taken and the mix was readjusted to 50-50.

- In April, 1983 following a surge in stock prices as a result of the bull market, the mix was readjusted to 25-75 until the end of the study in December 1984.

Exhibit 18–1 Variable Ratio Plan

Event	Date	DJIA	Equity Portion	T-Bill Portion	Action	Split between Stock and T-bill
A	1/77	945	$5000	$5000	Initial Investment	50/50
B	2/78	756	4260	5306	Sell $2915 T-bills and reinvest in equities	75/25
C	8/80	945	11365	2983	Sell $4191 equities and reinvest in T-bills	50/50
D	7/82	756	6916	9169	Sell %5148 T-bills and reinvest in equities	75/25
E	10/82	945	15222	4108	Sell $5557 equities and reinvest in T-bills	50/50
F	4/83	1181	12103	10063	Sell $6561 equities and reinvest in T-bills	25/75
G	12/84	1211	6049	19349	End of period— Total Portfolio Value	$25,398

Source: Dr. Gerald Perritt

An initial $10,000 investment using the variable ratio plan grew to $25,398 over the eight years, representing a 12.36 percent annual rate of return on the investment.

By contrast, a $10,000 investment in the Vanguard Index 500 grew to $22,440, representing a 10.63 percent annual rate of return on the investment.

Perritt believes formal investment plans, such as the constant ratio and variable ratio investment tactics, are useful.

"Formal investment plans improve investment results," Perritt says. "While they come nowhere near the results that could be achieved if an investor were able to take full advantage of each rise and fall in the market, they avoid the disasters which result from the implementation of poorly thought-out market timing schemes."

But variable ratio investing isn't fool-proof. First, you have to ask yourself if the improved returns over a buy-and-hold investment are worth the time and effort it takes to use the variable ratio strategy.

Second, the after-tax returns on the variable ratio tactic will be reduced by taxes. At the time of this writing, short-term profits for investments held under one year were taxed as ordinary income at rates as high as 39.6 percent. Long-term capital gains were taxed at 28 percent. However, if capital gains tax rates are lowered, the variable ratio investment tactic is an attractive way to invest in mutual funds because you always buy shares at lower prices and take profits on price increases.

Third, Perritt says conservative or risk adverse investors should avoid using this strategy. The reason: An investor using such a plan must be able to make accurate forecasts about future stock prices. An assumption must be made about the outlook for stock prices over the coming year. Then the trading rules must be established. As a result, there is an element of risk that stock prices may not rise or fall in the same periodic manner.

Perritt emphasizes that to make variable ratio investing work, you have to diversify your investment between a stock fund and money fund or other cash investment. If you want to get more complicated, you can set up a strategy that tells you when to buy and sell a portfolio of U.S. and international stock funds. Or a portfolio that may contain a small companies stock fund.

"When implementing any investment strategy, I cannot over-emphasize the need for proper diversification," Perritt says. "Formula plans are built on the assumption that the assets being managed will fall in value periodically, then track back upward and, at the very least, return to values reached at previous points in time. That is, formula plans will not produce a positive investment return if a portfolio only falls in value. Thus, it appears that formula plans are best suited for investment in mutual funds."

Points to Remember

- This is used by sophisticated investors who have strong ideas about the direction of the financial markets and the economy.

- Variable ratio plan is an aggressive cousin of the constant ratio investment strategy.

- When your stock fund increases in value, you reduce your ratio of stock to bond funds.

- When your stock fund loses money, you increase the ratio of stock fund investments to bond fund investments.

- To make this tactic work you need a game plan.

Chapter 19

Double Percentage Adjustment

If you want to protect yourself against big losses, yet perform as well as or better than the average stock fund over the longer term, consider using the Double Percentage Adjustment (DPA) formula. It's another type of trend-following indicator that tells you went to buy and sell stock funds.

This tactic works well for investors who want to invest in a well managed fund for the long term, but also want to protect themselves from major losses.

It's a "scaredy cat's" way to be more aggressive with your mutual fund investments. All you need is a common stock fund that tracks the performance of the S&P 500 and you are all set to go.

DPA can be used in tax-advantage investments or in taxable accounts. And speculators may want to use this method if they think a fund will show strong performance in up markets. They'll have a formula telling them when to sell. Here is how it works:

- First, keep track of how your fund performs every week.

- Second, record the net asset values (NAV) of the fund for each month.

- Third, calculate the average of the weekly NAV's for the month.

- Fourth, calculate the percentage change in the NAV from month to month.

Buy Signal

When the monthly percent change in the fund's NAV is up one percent or more: Invest twice the percentage change in the NAV in new shares of the fund.

For example, if the NAV is up 1 percent from the previous month, then you buy 2 percent of the value of your fund in more shares.

Sell Signal

When the percent change in the NAV is negative, sell twice the percentage change and invest the proceeds in a money market fund.

For example, say the current month's average fund price declines by 2 percent: You sell 4 percent of the value of your fund and invest in a money fund.

You have the flexibility to adjust how much you want to buy or sell. The greater the percentage change in the NAV of the fund from the previous month, the fewer switches you make each year. The smaller the percentage change in NAV from month to month, the greater the number of times you trade.

Daniel Todzia, president of Southeast Financial Planning, Stuart, FL, believes that the DPA adds value to your portfolio in declining markets.

"It can stop panic selling," says Todzia. " Investors buy on greed and sell on fear. They usually buy at the top of the market and sell at the bottom. This method gets you in and out of the market consistently."

If we are in a prolonged bear market and your fund is declining, for example, at about 1.5 percent a month, you would be reducing your ownership by 3 percent a month. That way you cut your losses.

On the upside it works the same way. In a sustained bull market you invest twice as much.

How It Worked

Over the two years ending in 1994 the trading tactic performed well. But the real value in the Double Percentage Adjustment Formula rests in its ability to reduce losses. Exhibit 19-1 shows how you increased your investments in up periods, for example, from January 29, 1993 through March 26, 1993. But during the period of sustained losses from November 26, 1993 through March 31, 1994, a greater percentage of the investment was withdrawn, thus avoiding large losses.

A hypothetical study using the Janus Fund gives you an inkling of how this tactic performed. Taxes on trades were not taken into consideration. A $25,000 investment was made in the Janus fund for the period of 12/31/92 to 12/29/94. The trading strategy called for trades with the NAV of the fund increased or decreased .50 percent or more every month. It was assumed that a money fund earned $\frac{1}{4}\%$ a month or 3 percent per year. All fund distributions were reinvested at ex-dividend date.

The Results

Buying and holding the Janus Fund over two years resulted in the $25,000 investment growing to $27,444.17, representing a $2,444.17 gain. The investment grew at a 9.8 percent annual rate.

Using the Double Percentage Adjustment tactic resulted in $25,000 growing to $28,494.05, representing a profit of $3,494.05. The investment grew at a 14 percent annual rate.

Of course you would have had to pay taxes on the trade. The profitable trades would have been taxed as ordinary income since you did not hold the investment for a year. But the 14 percent gain gave you plenty of cushion. At one point the DPA tactic was up $5,950.84.

The important point, however, is that you cut your losses and let your profits run. You didn't know how long the market would decline. So you protected yourself by reducing your stake in the Janus Fund.

How many times has an investor found a fund with a good track record only to see it decline just after buying it? A common reaction, says Todzia, might be to panic, cut your losses and get out. But he says that the DPA timing strategy can help the investor get out of a tough spot by reducing the funds at risk while maintaining a long term position.

Exhibit 19–1 Janus Fund

B/H	1338.3 shs
Inv	$25,000
% Cash	0%

Week		Price	Mo Ave	% Chg	Fund Adj	# Shs	Fund Value	MM Fund	Amt Invested	Value
1	12/31/92	$18.68	$18.68			1338.33	$25000.00	$0.00	$25000.00	$25000.00
2	1/8/93	18.65								
3	15-Jan	19.01								
4	22-Jan	18.92								
5	29-Jan	18.68	18.82	0.77%	1.54%	1358.96	25630.05	(389.15)	25000.00	25240.90
6	5-Feb	19.42								
7	12Feb	19.18								
8	19-Feb	18.94								
9	26-Feb	19.17	19.11	1.54	3.087	1400.84	26854.02	(1192.81)	25000.00	25661.21
10	5-Mar	19.28								
11	12-Mar	19.56								
12	19-Mar	19.49								
13	26-Mar	19.52	19.40	1.52	3.03	1443.34	28174.05	(2025.54)	25000.00	26148.52
14	2-Apr	19.42								
15	8-Apr	19.39								
16	16-Apr	19.56								
17	23-Apr	18.96								
18	30-Apr	19.06	19.28	−0.65	−1.30	1424.60	27152.84	(1673.33)	25000.00	25479.51
19	7-May	19.06								
20	17-May	18.87								
21	21-May	19.12								
22	28-May	19.37	19.10	−0.94	−1.88	1397.70	27073.44	(1156.48)	25000.00	25916.96
23	4-Jun	19.36								
24	11-Jun	19.12								
25	18-Jun	19.12								
26	25-Jun	19.42	19.28	0.95	1.91	1424.34	27660.72	(1676.77)	25000.00	25983.95
27	2-Jul	19.47								
28	9-Jul	19.54								
29	16-Jul	19.48								
30	23-Jul	19.44								
31	30-Jul	19.65	19.52	1.23	2.47	1459.51	28679.39	(2372.03)	25000.00	26307.36
32	6-Aug	19.81								
33	13-Aug	19.83								
34	20-Aug	20.00								
35	27-Aug	20.12	19.88	1.88	3.75	1514.25	30466.78	(3479.39)	25000.00	26987.40
36	3-Sep	20.11								

Exhibit 19–1 (Continued)

Week		Mo Ave	% Chg	Fund Adj	# Shs	Fund Value	MM Fund	Amt Invested	Value
37	10-Sep	20.16							
38	17-Sep	20.09							
39	24-Sep	20.18	20.13	1.26	2.51	1552.33	31326.11	(4256.56)	25000.00	27069.55
40	1-Oct	20.38							
41	8-Oct	20.56							
42	15-Oct	20.82							
43	22-Oct	20.69							
44	29.-Oct	20.81	20.65	2.58	5.17	1632.53	33972.88	(5936.00)	25000.00	28036.88
45	5-Mov	20.40							
46	12-Nov	20.71							
47	19-Nov	20.52							
48	26-Nov	20.52	20.59	-0.29	0.00	1632.53	33499.45	(5950.84)	25000.00	27548.61
49	3-Dec	20.69							
50	10-Dec	20.62							
51	17-Dec	20.67							
52	23-Dec	20.78							
53	31-Dec	19.39	1.33	Dist		1744.51			
54	31-Dec	19.39	20.43	-0.49	-1.57	1717.06	33293.73	(5433.49)	25000.00	27860.24
55	1/7/94	19.42							
56	14-Jan	19.57							
57	21-Jan	19.68							
58	28-Jan	19.82	19.55	-4.33	-8.66	1568.30	31083.62	(2498.63)	25000.00	28584.99
59	4-Feb	19.73							
60	11-Feb	19.53							
61	18-Feb	19.70							
62	25-Feb	19.52	19.66	0.59	1.18	1586.75	30973.37	(2865.12)	25000.00	28108.25
63	4-Mar	19.51							
64	11-Mar	19.55							
65	18-Mar	19.59							
66	25-Mar	19.28							
67	31-Mar	18.88	19.36	-1.52	-3.03	1538.65	29049.67	(1964.10)	25000.00	27085.57
68	8-Apr	19.00							
69	15-Apr	19.00							
70	22-Apr	18.92							
71	29-Apr	19.10	19.01	-1.84	-3.69	1481.91	28304.44	(885.28)	25000.00	27419.16
72	6-May	18.93							
73	13-May	18.79							
74	20-May	19.19							
75	27-May	19.24	19.04	0.17	0.00	1481.91	28511.91	(887.49)	25000.00	27624.42

Exhibit 19–1 (Concluded)

Week		Mo Ave	% Chg	Fund Adj	# Shs	Fund Value	MM Fund	Amt Invested	Value
76	6/3/94	19.24							
77	10-Jun	19.27							
78	17-Jun	19.21							
79	24-Jun	18.61	19.08	0.24	0.00	1481.91	27578.31	(889.71)	25000.00	26688.60
80	1-Jul	18.71							
81	8-Jul	18.79							
82	15-Jul	19.11							
83	22-Jul	19.03							
84	29-Jul	19.18	18.96	-0.62	-1.24	1463.50	28069.99	(538.93)	25000.00	27531.06
85	5-Aug	19.17							
86	12-Aug	19.30							
87	19-Aug	19.40							
88	26-Aug	19.69	19.39	2.25	4.49	1529.25	30111.02	(1834.92)	25000.00	28276.10
89	2-Sep	19.67							
90	9-Sep	19.52							
91	16-Sep	19.57							
92	23-Sep	19.06							
93	30-Sep	19.15	19.39	0.02	0.00	1529.25	29285.22	(1839.51)	25000.00	27445.71
94	7-Oct	18.84							
95	14-Oct	19.38							
96	21-Oct	19.22							
97	28-Oct	19.61	19.26	-0.68	-1.36	1508.52	29582.00	(1437.43)	25000.00	28144.57
98	4-Nov	19.33							
99	11-Nov	19.27							
100	18-Nov	19.25							
101	25-Nov	18.99	19.21	-0.28	0.00	1508.52	28646.72	(1441.02)	25000.00	27205.70
102	2-Dec	19.03							
103	9-Dec	18.82							
104	16-Dec	19.07							
105	23-Dec	19.18							
106	29-Dec	19.19	19.06	-0.78	-1.57	1484.84	28494.05	(990.25)	25000.00	27503.80

Source: Southeast Financial Planning and Consulting Inc.

A second study looks at how DPA performed in 1994, a miserable period when the average stock fund lost 3 percent.

An initial investment of $25,000 was made into the Janus Fund on 12/31/93 through 12/29/94. It was assumed that the money fund earned 1/4 percent a month.

Exhibit 19–2 Double Percentage Adjustment Formula Results from 12/31/92 through 12/29/94

Strategy	What $25,000 Grew to	Total Percent Gain
Buy & Hold	$27,444.17	9.78%
Double Percent Adjustment	28,494.05	13.98

Source: Southeast Financial Planning

The results showed how DPA helped reduce your losses. Buying and holding the Janus Fund in 1994 resulted in a 1.03 percent loss. You lost just .54 percent using the DPA strategy (see Exhibit 19–3).

Exhibit 19–3 Double Percentage Adjustment Formula Results from 12/31/93 through 12/29/94

Strategy	What $25,000 Grew to	Total Gain
Buy & Hold	$24,742.14	–1.03%
DPA	24,863.00	–.54

Source: Southeast Financial Planning

As you can see from Exhibit 19–3, DPA helped get you out at an increasing rate during the sustained losses that occurred from January 28, 1994 through July 29, 1994. There were only two periods where you kicked in extra money when the fund's NAV headed north—August 26 up to October 28. You got whipsawed a bit. But then again, what if prices went higher? Starting in October, you began to systematically withdraw money from the fund.

Don't forget, you pay taxes on the trades. In this case, however, you've got some short-term losses that you can write off against your short- or long-term gains for the year.

DPA is far from being a foolproof method of investing. The trick is finding the right percentage gain or loss to use as an investment signal. In choppy markets, you can get whipsawed if you use .50 percent or 1 percent gain.

But during a long-term uptrend, you will always be adding more money into your fund. By contrast, during a bear market, you will always be taking more out of your fund to protect against increasing losses.

The method seems to work best during periods when there is sudden and sustained surge in the stock market.

Of course there are drawbacks to this strategy. Every time you sell funds it is considered a taxable event. So your profits will be reduced by the capital gains taxes paid. Because this is a rapid fire strategy that may generate short-term capital gains, your profits will be taxed as ordinary income. For some investors, that means they will pay 39.6 percent of their gains to the tax man. So if your gains are minimal, your after-tax return on the investment will be miserable. Then you would be better off buying and holding an investment. Or using this tactic in your retirement plan or variable annuity.

In addition, many fund families place limits on switching. So if you are moving in and out more than a half dozen times a year, you may be asked to stop trading or leave the fund family.

If you trade in a no transaction fee discount brokerage account, there are limits on trades. Charles Schawb account-holders are required to own a fund for 90 days before they can trade transaction-free. Otherwise you must pay a transaction fee. You have leeway after three months. You can make 15 trades free of charge per year.

Points to Remember

- You should adhere to strict buy and sell rules when you use the Double Percentage Adjustment Formula (DPA).

- DPA is a trend-following strategy that has you investing more when the fund is rising and selling more when the fund is declining.

- DPA at its best helps reduce losses. But don't expect to hit a home run with this over the long term.

- DPA works best when the net asset value of the fund changes .5 percent (one half of one percent) or more.

- DPA doesn't work well in choppy markets.

- You will pay taxes on your trades unless the money is invested in an IRA, 401(k), variable life or variable annuity policy.

Chapter 20

Investment Cycle Methods

Some investment strategies are more art than science. There are some long-term cycles that analysts have noticed repeat themselves. You shouldn't bet the ranch on any patterns of stock or bond market performance. However, if you are aware of the trends, they may aid you in making investment decisions. Every little piece of information helps.

Here is a rundown on some prominent investment cycles.

Fifth Year of Every Decade

One strategy may be akin to flipping a coin ten times and winning every time because it comes up heads.

There has never been a down year in the stock market in the fifth year of any decade since 1890. This phenomenon was first discovered by Edgar Lawrence Smith in a book he wrote fifty years ago titled *Common Stocks and Business Cycles*, published by William-Fredrick Press, New York.

Exhibit 20–1 The Ten–Year Stock Market Cycle

	Annual % change in Standard & Poor's Composite Index Year of Decade									
Decades	1st	2nd	3rd	4th	5th	6th	7th	8th	9th	10th
1885–1890					20	9	–7	–2	3	–14
1891–1900	18	1	–20	–3	1	–2	13	19	7	14
1901–1910	16	1	–19	25	16	3	–33	37	14	–12
1911–1920	1	3	–14	–9	32	3	–31	16	13	–24
1921–1930	7	20	–3	19	23	5	26	36	–15	–29
1931–1940	–47	–18	48	–2	39	28	–34	13	0	–12
1941–1950	–15	6	21	14	33	–10	–2	–2	11	20
1951–1960	15	7	–3	39	23	4	–13	33	11	–4
1961–1970	27	–13	18	13	9	–11	17	12	–14	–1
1971–1980	10	12	–19	–32	32	18	–10	2	11	26
1981–1990	–7	13	18	0	26	20	–3	15	26	–6
1991–2000	18	12	7							
Up Years	8	9	5	6	11	8	3	9	9	3
Down Years	3	2	6	4	0	3	8	2	2	8
Total% Change	43%	44%	34%	64%	254%	67%	–77%	179%	67%	–42%

Based on average December prices.

Source: *Stock Traders Almanac* The Hirsch Organization, Inc.

Over the past 110 years, during 11 periods, the S&P 500 gained a total of 254 percent in the fifth year of the decade for an average return of 23 percent, according to Yale Hirsch, Old Tappan, NJ. In recent history, we have had some big gains: 32 percent in 1975 and 26 percent in 1985. So far in 1995, the market is up. Overall since 1890, there have been no negative years in the fifth year of a decade and 11 positive years.

Years ending each decade (i.e., with a zero) are the worst performance years. Stocks lost a total of –42 percent for an average of –3.82 percent during each zero year of the decade. In zero years of decades there were eight down years and only three up years for stocks. The worst years were 1920, down 24 percent and 1930, down 29 percent. The year 1990 was no exception to this trend as the S&P 500 lost 6 percent.

Although the zero year of the decade may be the lousiest year to invest, those that like to buy low and sell high may find it profitable. In the first year of every decade since 1890 there have been eight plus years and three negative years. You will have to keep your eyes open, however: stocks gained a big fat 43 percent in total during this year of each decade. So unless you are a good mutual fund bottom fisher, you might skip this tactic.

The eighth year of the decade is second most profitable. Stocks gained a total 179 percent for an average 16.3 percent. There were nine plus years and two negative ones. Most recently, we had a 12 percent gain in 1998.

How has this system worked with mutual funds? Let's look at the performance of the State Street Investment Trust, one of the oldest mutual funds in existence today. The fund opened its doors for business in 1924 and has been buying and selling growth stocks ever since.

As you can see from Exhibit 20–2, the fund gained 32 percent in 1985. Thus far in 1995, the fund is up 21 percent. In 1975 the fund gained 36 percent and in 1965 is was up 17.5 percent. In a total of seven periods since 1925, the fund gained a whopping 228 percent or an average of 32.5 percent. There were seven up years and no down years.

Again the zero years were the worst. In seven periods since 1930, the fund gained just 11.2 percent. There were four down years and only three up years.

The eighth year of the decade was the next best time to invest in the fund. It gained a total of 185 percent during these periods for an average gain of 26.4 percent.

Exhibit 20–2 State Street Investment Trust

					Year % Return					
Decade	0	1	2	3	4	5	6	7	8	9
20	–	–	–	–	66.0	85.5	13.2	53.2	85.5	–7.2
30	–23.7	–27.7	2.4	57.1	2.7	39.3	45.8	–32.2	17.5	1.8
40	–10.5	–6.0	21.6	28.6	23.5	34.9	–2.7	1.8	4.4	22.6
50	22.2	24.6	13.6	–6.0	35.4	18.0	8.3	–11.7	41.0	7.1
60	4.6	27.6	–9.9	16.8	13.5	17.5	2.0	26.0	14.0	–6.9
70	–5.3	19.2	18.3	–19.9	–25.4	36.1	24.5	–0.8	12.2	29.2
80	24.9	–1.4	12.7	19.6	1.3	32.0	11.7	6.9	10.2	32.1
90	–1.0	28.1	6.3	10.2	–3.47					
Total	11.2	64.4	65.9	111.8	113.5	228.4	102.8	43.2	185.1	79.4

As of December 31, 1994

Source: Alan Lavine

Many seasoned money managers may scoff at the "fifth year of decades" strategy write the performance off as just random chance.

Peter Eliades, publisher of *Stockmarket Cycles,* Los Angeles, CA, is one who doesn't. He says that if you look at the 10-year performance charts of each 10-year period, you will notice that each decade is characterized by three bull markets and three bear markets.

Eliades, whose publication was rated as the top-performing mutual fund newsletter over the past eight years ending in 1993 by the *Hulbert Financial Digest,* is bearish. His technical analysis and cycle trends indicate the stock market is headed lower.

By switching between sector funds and money funds, the adviser gained a whopping 389 percent over the past eight years ending in 1993. By contrast, the Wilshire 5000 grew 176 percent during the same time frame.

Eliades made just a few switches out of money funds and into the hedge funds in 1994. This year, however, he is more optimistic. The two and four year stock market cycles indicated that the stock market hit bottom at year end 1994. As a result, stock prices should rebound in the coming two year cycle.

Meanwhile, he is also optimistic because 1995 because it is the fifth year of the decade. No one can predict the future. But based on the past trends, he thinks this is a favorable sign for profitable year.

The Presidential Election Cycle

The four-year presidential election cycle is another helpful barometer of where the market may be going.

Yale Hirsch, publisher of the *Stock Traders Almanac,* also says that the 162-year saga of the Presidential Election/stock market cycle continues. It is no mere coincidence that the last two years of the 41 administrations since 1932 produced a total net gain of 557 percent, dwarfing the 74 percent gain of the first two years of these administrations.

The presidential election every four years has a profound effect on the economy and the stock market. Wars, recessions, and bear markets tend to start or occur in the first half of the term—more prosperous times and bull markets, in the latter half.

But there is no free lunch with this cycle. Hirsch notes that the cycle did not ring true in 1985 and 1986. It came back on track in 1990 with a war, recession and a bear market.

Seasonal Trends to Help You Invest

Seasonal trends can add a few percentage points to your returns. Other trends can save you money. Here are a few trends to look for when you invest in mutual funds or individual securities. The information is based on research published by the Hirsch Organization of Old Tappan, NJ., publishers of the *Stock Traders Almanac*.

- Small stocks gain in January. January is an important month to invest. Small stocks historically outperform the market this time of year.

But look out for a big correction. Yale Hirsch adds that the greatest concentration of downturns in the market since 1949 occurred in the month's first six trading days.

In addition, the performance of stocks during the first five trading days of the new year serve as a signal as to how stocks will perform in the remainder of the year. The batting average, says Hirsch, is about 8 for 10.

- January barometer. Since 1950, the performance of the stock market in January predicts the performance for the entire year. Based on whether the S&P 500 is up or down in January, most years have followed suit 38 out of 43 times or 88 percent of the time, adds Hirsch.

Hirsch stresses that with the exception of 1987, the top 23 Januaries had gains of 1 percent and started bull markets. Twenty Januaries had poor years. All were followed by bear markets. Only one good year followed a January loss. Errors occurred in 1966, 1968 and 1982. Vietnam affected the returns in the 1960s.

- November through April are the best months to invest. Hirsch says a number of profitable seasonal patterns in the stock market come together during the months of November, December and January. If you invested every November through April over the past 42 years in the S&P 500, the money grew at an annually compounded rate of 6.8 percent. Over the past 15 years, the six-month investment period registered a 7.9 percent annual return.

Exhibit 20–3 Stock Market Action Since 1832

Net change from year to year based on average December prices

Presdient Elected	4–year Cycle Beginning	Election Year	Post Election Year	Mid-term	Pre– Election Year
Jackson (D)	1832	15%	–3%	10%	2%
Van Buren (D)	1836	–8	–8	1	–13
W.H. Harrrison (W)**	1840*	5	–14	–13	36
Polk (D)	1844*	8	6	–15	1
Taylor (W)**	1848*	–4	0	19	–3
Pierce (D)	1852*	20	–13	–30	1
Buchanan (D)	1856	4	–30	–7	–7
Lincoln (R)	1860*	–4	–4	43	30
Lincoln (R)**	1864	0	–14	–3	–6
Grant (R)	1868	2	–7	–4	7
Grant (R)	1872	7	–13	3	–4
Hayes (R)	1876	–18	–10	6	43
Garfield (R)**	1880	19	3	–3	–9
Cleveland (D)	1884*	–19	20	9	–7
B. Harrison (R)	1888*	–2	3	–14	18
Cleveland (D)	1892*	1	–20	–3	1
McKinley (R)	1896*	–2	13	19	7
McKinley (R)**	1900	14	16	1	–19
T. Roosevelt (R)	1904	25	16	3	–33
Taft (R)	1908	37	14	–12	1
Wilson (D)	1912*	3	–14	–9	32
Wilson (D)	1916	3	–31	16	13
Harding (R)	1920*	–24	7	20	–3
Coolidge (R)	1924	19	23	5	26
Hoover (R)	1928	36	–15	–29	–47
F. Roosevelt (D)	1932*	–16	48	–2	39
F. Roosevelt (D)	1936	28	–34	13	0
F. Roosevelt (D)	1940	–12	–15	6	21
R. Roosevelt (D)**	1944	14	33	–10	–2
Truman (D)	1946	–2	11	20	15
Eisenhower (R)	1952*	7	–3	39	23
Eisenhowever (R)	1956	4	–13	33	11
Kennedy (D)**	1960*	–4	27	–13	18
Johnson (D)	1964	13	9	–11	17
Nixon (R)	1968*	12	–14	–1	10
Nixon (R)***	1972	12	–19	–32	32
Carter (D)	1976*	18	–10	2	11
Reagan (R)	1980*	26	–7	13	18
Reagan (R)	1984	0	26	20	–3
Bush (R)	1988	15	26	–6	16
Clinton (D)	1992*	12	7		
1904–1993 Totals		**224%**	**72%**	**65%**	**217%**
1832–1993 Totals		**262%**	**–3%**	**84%**	**295%**

*Party in power ousted   **Death in office   ***Resigned   D—Democrat, W—Whig, R—Republican

Source: *Stock Traders Almanac*, The Hirsch Organization, Inc.

Best Time to Buy Bonds

Buy taxable and tax-free bonds in the spring. An annual study by Technical Data Corp., Boston, shows that bond rates tend to rise in the springtime due to technical factors. So if you're thinking of investing in long-term bonds, keep some funds in reserve for that time of year.

According to Walter Frank, chief economist at IBC/Donoghue, Ashland, MA., tax-free money fund yields tend to move higher in April. There is usually a glut of note offerings this time of year. That coupled with selling pressures at tax time may push yields higher.

Gail Liberman, editor of *Bank Rate Monitor*, North Palm Beach, FL, notes that banks also raise CD rates during the heat of IRA and tax season. Most bankers don't want money moving out of the bank. In addition, there historically has been a lot of CD money that matures in October. So some banks may raise rates to keep the money from going elsewhere.

Points to Remember

- Stock and bond prices may move in cycles.
- There are noticeable trends that have emerged in the financial markets over the years.
- Investing based on trends and cycles can be risky. Things don't always happen at the exact same time as they did in the past.
- Trends and cycles, however, can help you make investment decisions.

Chapter 21

It Pays to Buy Funds with "Hot Hands"

There is a school of thought that says you should always invest in the best-performing funds. This is a trend-following strategy that should only be considered by venturesome mutual fund investors looking for growth.

The thinking goes like this: Funds with best current track records are on target with their stock selection. So you want to go along for the ride. When these funds start lagging behind, you sell and invest in other funds with the best current performance.

This may sound like a crap shoot. But a recent study by a Harvard University publication shows that mutual fund trend investing can be profitable.

Published in *The Journal of Finance* (Vol. 48, No. 1), the study gives some validity to the methods used by several mutual fund newsletter advisers that direct investors to funds with the best current performance trends.

The Mutual Fund Forecaster, NoLoad Fund X and *Moneyletter* all use some type of analysis that targets funds that should perform well over the current investment cycle (see Appendix).

The Harvard study was conducted by three professors who analyzed 165 growth-oriented no-load mutual funds available to investors over a 15-year period, 1974–1988.

They identify funds called "hot hands" because they have strong short-term performance. Only no-load funds were used because the strategy calls for frequent switching. The researchers looked at eight different performance groups. The best results were obtained by investing every quarter in the top performers based on the last four quarters.

The results of the study show investing in funds with the best one-year track record was profitable.

- For example, the funds with the best one-year past performance record earned 14.6 percent a year more than T-bills over the following two years.

- By contrast, if you invested in the funds with the worst previous one-year track record, the investment gained just 4.6 percent a year more than T-bills in the following two years.

The Harvard study authors say that if you actively managed a mutual fund portfolio by always investing in the best performing funds over the past 12 months, you should be able to outperform the market averages by 3 percent to 4 percent annually. By comparison, the average mutual funds usually trail the market indexes by 2 percent—the amount of their annual expenses. The Harvard professors concluded that the "hot hand" no-load growth funds outperformed similar funds over the past year and will continue to perform well over the next one to eight quarters. By contrast, funds with "icy hands" or funds that perform poorly continue to underperform over one to eight quarters.

Exhibit 21–1 One Year Return over T-bills Based on Hot or Icy Hand Funds

Strategy	% over T-bills	Comments
Icy Hands	4.6	Every quarter you invest in funds with the worst one-year track records
Hot Hands	14.6	Every quarter you invest in funds with the best one-year track record

Source: *Journal of Finance*

Other Studies

There are other studies that show you can't buy and hold funds based on long-term past performance. Bert Berry, publisher of *NoLoad Fund X*, a San Francisco-based mutual fund newsletter and money management service, found that investments based on five and 10-year track records don't work well.

For example, he looked at the 25 best performing funds based on 10-year performance results from Dec. 31, 1972 through Dec. 31, 1982. Then he looked at how these funds performed over the next 10 years from Dec. 31, 1982 through Dec. 31, 1992.

As you can see from Exhibit 21–2, just a few of the funds with the best 10-year track records outperformed the S&P 500 over the next 10 years.

For example, the VanEck International Investor gained 835.8 percent for 10 years ending in 1982. The next 10 years, the fund lost 7 percent, while the S&P 500 gained 347 percent.

The Evergreen Fund gained 513.5 percent for 10 years ending in 1982. But for 10 years ending in 1992, the fund gained 267.1 percent. By contrast the S&P 500 gained 347 percent.

Even investing based on five years' past performance didn't work. Exhibit 21-3 shows how the top 25 funds over five years ending in December, 1987 performed over the next five years ending in December, 1992. Most of the top funds with the best five-year track records underperformed the S&P 500 as measured by the Vanguard Index 500 Fund.

The Strong Total Return Fund, for example, gained 149.1 percent for five years ending in 1987. Over the next five years, the fund gained 48 percent. By contrast, the Vanguard Index 500 gained 106.5 percent.

How about the highly touted Vanguard Windsor Fund? The fund gained 142.2 percent for five years ending in 1987. Over the next five years the fund gained 87.3 percent and underperformed the Index 500 fund by 20 percentage points in total return.

Real World Performance

It is easier to conduct research on investment strategies than to actually invest. To adopt the Harvard Study's methods you need the time

Exhibit 21–2 Past Performance—No Indication of Future

	The 25 Best Performing Funds 12/31/72–12/31/82		And Then 12/31/82– 12/31/92
1.	VanEck Int'l Investors (Load)	835.8%	–7.0%
2.	Twentieth Century Select	631.3	277.5
3.	Twentieth Century Growth	547.4	355.2
4.	Evergreen Fund	513.5	267.1
5.	American Capital Comstock (L)	510.3	222.2
6.	Mutual Shares	496.2	391.7
7.	Fidelity Magellan (L)	453.0	502.2
8.	Pioneer II (L)	449.8	233.9
9.	Sequoia Fund	429.7	392.0
10.	Hartwell Leverage Fund	396.4	280.4
11.	American Capital Pace (L)	388.3	205.6
12.	Price OTC Fund	376.4	221.5
13.	Fidelity Destiny	345.9	443.3
14.	Fidelity Equity-Income	344.8	281.6
15.	American Capital Venture (L)	323.6	217.6
16.	Alliance Quasar	316.6	230.6
17.	American Capital Growth (L)	312.5	219.9
18.	Templeton Growth (L)	305.0	309.0
19.	American National Income (L)	304.3	228..0
20.	Value Line Leverage Growth	295.1	213.0
21.	Oppenheimer Equity Income (L)	284.3	281.2
22.	Value Line	279.4	209.6
23.	Neuberger Berman Partners	279.0	293.3
24.	Fortis Growth (L)	278.4	349.8
25.	Guardian Park Avenue (L)	272.4	400.8
	S&) 500 (Reinvested)	91.7	347.0

Source: *NoLoad Fund X*

and expertise to trade funds based on one-year track records. Don't forget, you have to pay taxes on your trades. You have to have the mutual fund data base to evaluate the fund performance. You also have to have the software so you can instruct the computer to tell you when to trade.

Exhibit 21-3 Is Long-Term Performance Predictive?

The Top 25 Equity Funds Five Years 12/82–12/87			Their Next Year's Record 1988		Their Next 5-Years' Record 12/87–12/92	
Rank	Name	5-Yr % Change	Rank	1-Yr % Change	Rank	5-Yr % Change
1	Putnam Emerg Gro	174.9%	404	16.1%	207	114.4%
2	Fidelity Magellan	152.9	132	22.8	106	138.1
3	Vanguard Hi Yld Stk	152.2	76	26.2	na	na
4	Pru-Bache Utility	150.5	133	22.8	279	104.3
5	Strong Total Return	149.1	435	15.6	1068	48.0
6	Phoenix Growth	148.1	1093	7.0	393	93.0
7	Mutual Qualified Inc	147.6	31	30.4	322	99.0
8	Mutual Shares	146.9	30	30.9	324	98.8
9	Dodge & Cox Stock	146.1	529	13.4	510	84.6
10	United Income	145.8	223	19.9	2335	109.8
11	Federated Stock Trust	142.6	606	12.7	611	75.0
12	Vanguard Windsor	142.2	52	28.7	478	87.3
13	New Perspective	139.3	770	10.4	631	73.5
14	Princor Cap Accum	137.2	528	13.9	615	74.7
15	Sequoia	135.2	725	11.1	243	109.2
16	Guardian Park Ave	134.6	193	20.8	216	113.5
17	Fidelity Destiny I	133.8	250	19.4	127	132.4
18	Phoenix Stock	133.5	1291	4.5	726	67.4
19	CGM Capital Dev	130.9	1390	–0.3	38	179.0
20	Phoenix Balanced	129.4	1343	2.9	596	85.4
21	Salomon Opportunity	128.0	154	21.7	490	86.4
22	Oppenheimer Eq Inc	127.7	515	14.0	725	67.4
23	MerLynch Basic Value	127.2	135	22.7	603	76.1
24	AIM Weingarten Eq	126.21	703	11.3	129	131.5
25	Pilgrim Magnacap	125.7	448	15.3	501	85.1
316	Vag S&P 500 Index	109.0	397	16.2	260	106.5

Source: *No Load Fund X*

Exhibit 21-4 Hot Hand Newsletter Total Gain for Period Ending July 1994

	3 yr%	5 yr%	8 yr%	10 yr%
NoLoad Fund X:				
Class 1. Most Speculative Growth	33.3	46.9	85.6	212
Class 2. Speculative Growth	38.7	47.2	79.8	184.3
Class 3. High Quality Growth	47.8	64.6	131.6	362.9
Class 4. Total Return	45.3	58.2	na	na
Wilshire 5000	33.9	61.6	118	286.9

Source: *Hulbert Financial Digest*

There are a few newsletters available that use the "hot hands" approach to invest in mutual funds. *NoLoad Fund X* comes closest to this approach because the service picks funds based on the best-weighted average performance over the past year. *Moneyletter,* an Ashland, MA-based publication also selects funds based on current trend performance. However, the newsletter makes those selections with an asset allocation model. So the investment may be split up between U.S. and overseas stock funds, bond funds and money funds. *Moneyletter* as well as *Mutual Fund Forecaster* also have programs that use market timing to switch between money funds and stock funds with the best performance trends. As you can see from Figure 21-4, although the tactics are successful, they are far from perfect.

Points to Remember

- Venturesome investors may profit by always investing in the fund the best one-year track records. Studies show the fund will continue to do well for about another 12 months.

- This is a trend-following strategy. So be prepared to make a number of trades during the year.

- There are several newsletters that will do the work for you.

Chapter 22

MoneyLetter's
Donoghue Signal

The Donoghue Signal is a market timing strategy that focuses on the relationship between stock prices and interest rates. You should consider using the signal, which shows when stocks are going up or down, if you have a long-term investment horizon and want to invest aggressively.

How does the system, which is reported in *MoneyLetter*, an Ashland, MA-based newsletter, time the market? First, by analyzing changes in interest rates and related economic trends.

A heavy emphasis is placed on the direction of interest rates in evaluating stock market trends. *MoneyLetter's* research has shown that interest rate trends are a major factor behind stock market behavior.

Exhibits 22–1 and 22–2, for example, show the relationship between interest rates and stock prices. When rates were at double-digit levels in the early 1980s, the S&P 500 languished at 120.

Why invest in stocks when you can earn almost 14 percent in a risk-free and liquid money fund or a bond? Fixed-income investments compete with stocks for investors' dollars. Historically, stocks have earned a premium of 6 percent more than the yield to maturity on bonds. Investors are then compensated for the risk of owning stocks because they get a much higher return than they would earn on bonds.

But when stocks begin to outperform fixed-income investments by a wide margin, the money flows back into equities and out of bonds.

Simply put: If you don't earn significantly more in stocks than you could earn in bonds, the smart money on Wall Street says it's not

Exhibit 22–1 S&P 500 versus Money Fund Yields

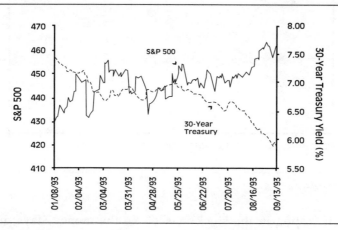

Source: *MoneyLetter*

Exhibit 22–2A S&P 500 versus Money Fund Yields

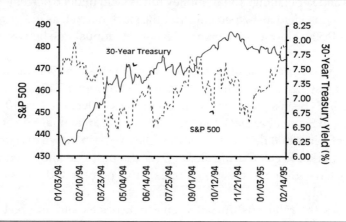

Source: *MoneyLetter*

Exhibit 22–2B S&P 500 versus Money Fund Yields

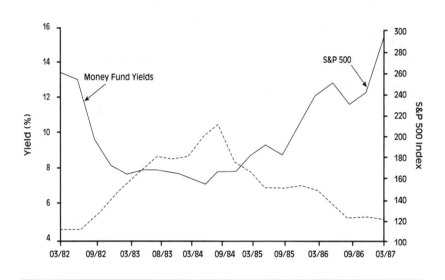

Source: *MoneyLetter*

worth investing in the stock market. So the money stays in cash and other fixed-income investments.

But look what happens when interest rates fall. By August 1982, stock prices shot up. Money fund rates dropped below 10 percent in the early 1980s and kept falling. Today, money funds yield under 6 percent. Long-term bonds yield just 7 percent. And the stock market, as measured by the S&P 500, grew at an average 16.8 percent annual rate between 1980 and 1990.

We've had a couple of corrections along the way. In 1987, the market gained just 5.26 percent. In 1990, the market dropped 3.12 percent. But overall, it's been a great time to invest in stocks. Over the past 10 years, ending in September 1993, the S&P 500 grew at an annual rate of 14.95 percent. Now that rates are the lowest they've been in two decades, the stock market keeps roaring along. Over the past one and three years, stocks have grown at an annual rate of 15.2 percent and 16.4 percent, respectively.

Does the relationship between stock prices and interest rates mean something? You bet ya!

How to Time the Markets

Money fund information is also is published each week in most newspapers, *The Wall Street Journal, Barron's,* and *USA Today.*

The Donoghue Signal analyzes the interest rate trend. The newsletter tracks it through a 25-week exponential moving average of Donoghue's 7-day uncompounded money fund yield. When interest rates, as measured by this moving average, trend down, stock prices generally rise. Conversely, when the rate trend rises, stock prices may drop.

Current Yield In Relation to the Trend

You want to be in stocks when interest rates are declining and expected to go lower. By contrast, if rates are expected to rise substantially, you want to be out of stocks and in money funds to protect your principal

Here is how to go about it. The strategy is reported monthly in *MoneyLetter:*

- Plot the 25-day moving average trend line against the actual 7-day yield and you get a strong picture of where rates are headed. When the 7-day yield breaks above the Donoghue Signal's trend line, it's a strong indication that rates are moving higher. By contrast, when the 7-day yield breaks below the moving average, it is a sign rates are headed lower and stock prices higher.

When to Sell

When the 7-day yield crosses above the trend line, switch out of your stock fund and invest in a money fund.

When to Buy

When the Donoghue Signal trend line is moving down and the actual 7-day yield breaks below the trend line, it's a strong signal that rates are moving lower. Extra confirmation: The average money fund maturity is getting longer.

**Exhibit 22–3 IBCDonoghue's Money Fund Averages ™
MFA (7-day yield) vs. The Donoghue Signal**

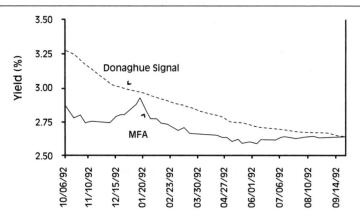

The Signal will change to a "sell" mode for stock funds when the MFA line crosses the Signal line. Current Status: BUY.

Date	Donoghue Signal	MFA	Average Maturity (*days*)
9/7/93	2.66	2.64	63
9/14/93	2.66	2.64	63

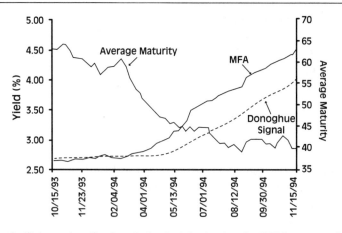

The Signal will change to a "buy" mode for stock funds when the MFA line crosses the Signal line by more than five basis points. Current Status: SELL as of 12/6/93.

Date	Donoghue Signal	MFA	Average Maturity (*days*)
11/08/94	3.93	4.41	40
11/15/94	3.97	4.50	40

MoneyLetter, published by IBC/Donoghue, 290 Eliot Street Box 9104, Ashland, MA 01721

The Proof Is in the Pudding

Since this system was launched in *MoneyLetter* several years ago, the track record has been good. Over the past four-and-three-quarters years, the Donoghue Signal has grown at an annual rate 13.5 percent, according to *MoneyLetter*.

Points to Remember

- You move in and out of stock funds based on the direction of interest rates.

- This is an aggressive market timing strategy that works well when a strong interest rate trend has emerged.

- You could get whipsawed if interest rates are volatile.

- You could switch out of a money fund and into bond funds because the rate trend is up, but your stock fund could do nothing. It may even decline in value. The reason: There are a lot of other factors besides interest rates that influence stock prices.

Chapter 23

Using Moving Averages to Switch Funds

If you asked a group of financial advisers how to make money on Wall Street, probably nine out of ten pros would say you have to buy low and sell high. However, if you asked them when is the right time to trade, most would say that no one can accurately catch the very bottom or top in the financial markets.

Although financial research has proven that no one can time the markets over the long haul with much success, there are several important indicators that can identify future market trends and enable investors to avoid large losses in the stock market or signal changes in investment strategies.

Trend indicators like the 39-week moving average and "relative strength" can help you decide whether to buy, sell, or change the asset mix of a portfolio.

Moving averages are one of the major market trend indicators in use today. The philosophy behind the moving average is that if the trend is moving higher, it could go higher. Conversely, if the trend is lower, there's a good change the market will go lower.

By averaging and plotting weekly prices, for example, for every successive 39-week period, you get an indication of whether the stock prices are gaining momentum or the trend line is deteriorating. When a stock's price breaks above its moving average, it's a confirmation of a trend and a buy signal. When a stock's price breaks below the moving average, it's a sell signal.

Relative strength also is a popular and widely used trend-following indicator that works well in conjunction with a moving average. Relative strength is simply a price or percentage change ratio of a mutual fund's price divided by, for example, the S&P 500.

When you plot the relative strength line you can compare mutual funds or mutual fund indexes and see which funds are performing best relative to the stock market. If a fund or fund group shows the best performance relative to the market it may be performing best under the current economic climate.

For example, if the relative strength line of balance funds shows a stronger and steeper positive trend compared with aggressive growth funds, this group of funds could outperform aggressive growth funds.

Relative strength leads the change in a moving average. So it's a strong buy signal if the relative strength line improves over time and some weeks later, the price of a fund or index breaks its moving average.

Stock market technicians say that when analyzing relative strength, investors should look for the following:

- A trend reversal, which is signaled if the relative strength of, for example, a mutual fund index to the market and the index price are both rising, but relative strength starts to decline.

  That trend reversal is confirmed, if the index price or moving average line later declines.

- Price strength, which occurs if prices are trending down and relative strength starts to improve, confirmed by moving average or index performance.

- There are cases in down markets when both the mutual fund and the stock market are in steep decline. As a result, you could see one group of funds showing stronger relative strength to the market than other funds. The fund is still losing money, though much less than other funds.

The experts say that making investment decisions based on relative strength and moving average is not a surefire way to profit in the stock market. However, if there are positive trends coupled with favorable economic and industry news, you have a benchmark to help asset-allocation decisions.

Douglas Fabian, publisher of *Fabian's Investment Resource,* Huntington Beach, CA, says that 39-week moving averages and trend indicators have been successful investment tools in recent years.

Over the past 14 years ending in June 1993, *Fabian's Investment Resource* was rated as one of the top five newsletters for risk-adjusted return, according to the *Hulbert Financial Digest,* an Alexandria, VA-based newsletter that tracks investment advisers' performance. In other words, based on the newsletter's investment, the recommendations got the best return with the least amount of risk compared with other investment advisory services.

According to the *Hulbert Digest,* based on market timing, Fabian's moving average market timing advice gained 232 percent, which represents a 12.75 annual rate of return. While the actual returns based on specific mutual fund investment moves into equity funds and out of money funds or vice versa registered gains of 10.75 percent annually.

Although fund switching based on the moving averages underperformed the buy and hold based on the Wilshire 5000, which gained a total of 287 percent during the 10-year period ending in June 1993, investing based on moving averages is as much a defense as it is an offense. When the moving average signals that the market trend is down, stock prices or mutual fund prices could go much lower. As a result, the signal tells you to get out of equity funds until the markets look better.

"Moving averages is a mechanical trend-following investment approach, " says Fabian. "If the trend is up you buy. If the trend is down you sell. As long as the current prices are above their moving averages, we want to be invested. When the prices fall below their moving averages, we want to invest in money funds."

Over the past 17 years, according to *Fabian's Investment Resource* newsletter, he's averaged about two trades a year—switching between a basket of stock funds and a money fund. The investment grew at a 16.16 percent annual compound rate of return.

Using the moving averages was successful in avoiding the October 19, 1987 stock market crash. Fabian's 39-week moving average signaled a sell on October 16, 1987. He moved into money funds and took a 19.56 percent gain with him.

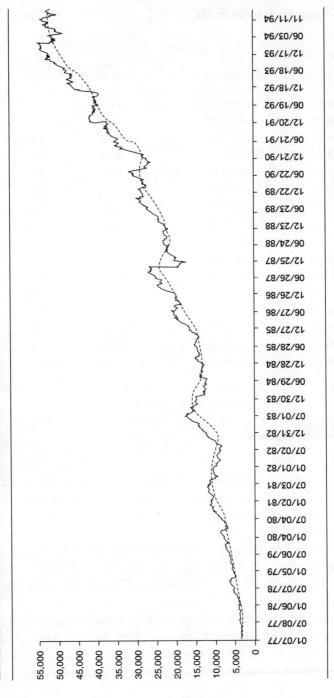

Exhibit 23–1 Fabian's Domestic Fund Composite, January 3, 1977–January 31, 1995

This chart tracks the week-ending prices and 39-week averages of the Domestic Fund Composite for a period spanning 17.75 years. When the composite's week-ending price crossed above its 39-week average, our plan generated a signal to buy domestc equity mutual funds; when it moved below its 39-week average, we issued a sell signal to money market funds.

Copyright 1995, Fabian Investment Resources

Exhibit 23–2 Moving Average Trades

	MFC PLAN		
Buy Dates	**Sell Dates**	**Stock Fund**	**Money Funds**
04/01/77	10/23/78	48.16	4.21
03/28/79	10/23/79	3.58	0.89
11/16/79	03/18/80	2.11	2.88
05/23/80	07/23/81	45.20	16.52
08/27/82	01/27/84	47.57	5.12
08/06/84	12/07/84	–6.72	0.94
01/17/85	09/12/86	32.05	0.44
10/30/86	10/16/87	19.56	3.16
04/11/88	04/15/88	–3.16	0.36
06/02/88	11/14/88	–1.13	0.45
12/06/88	01/23/90	23.44	0.90
03/19/90	03/22/90	–1.62	1.18
05/18/90	08/07/90	–4.25	3.55
01/25/91	08/24/92	33.99	0.56
11/06/92	03/31/94	20.39	1.02
08/30/94	Current	–0.26	N/A

Annualized Compounded Growth

For 17.42 Years . . . + 16.16%

Source: *Fabian's Investment Resource*

Moving averages, however, are fallible. Fabian got whipsawed in 1988. A whipsaw occurs when you move into the market on a buy signal, but the prices go lower. Or when you move out of a fund on a sell signal, but the fund moves higher.

He moved into the market on April 11, 1988 but got back out on April 15, 1988 and took a 3.16 percent loss. The same thing happened from June 2, 1988 to November 4, 1988. He took a 1.13 percent loss. There was a sell signal, but the market took a turn for the worst.

In 1990, a year in which the average stock fund lost 5.9 percent, Fabian cut his losses. From the period of March 19, 1990 through Aug. 7, 1990, he lost 5.9 percent. But he got back into stock funds in January 1991, and stayed fully invested until August 1992, to pick up a 34 percent gain.

Other data show that over five years that included the stock market crash of October 1987, the moving averages have worked well.

For example, a study published February 1988 in *Financial Planning Magazine,* by the author of this book, showed that using the 39-week moving average worked well in getting investors into stocks when the great bull market started in 1982. It also helped investors avoid the stock market crash of 1987.

Money was invested in the S&P 500 when the index price broke above the 39-week moving average. When it broke below the moving average it was invested in a money fund that yielded 6 percent.

The results of the study showed that from January 6, 1982 through October 30, 1987, you would have earned an annual compound rate of return of 19.88 percent by trading on the moving average without taxes or commissions being deducted from the return. Conversely, the buy and hold on the S&P 500 grew at an annual rate of 16.06 percent.

Using the moving average during that time frame got you into the bull market on August 25, 1982 and got you out of the market on October 16, 1987, the Friday before Black Monday on October 19 when the Dow lost 507 points.

In the interim, the moving average would have gotten you out of the market on February 1, 1984 and back in on August 1, 1984, and avoided a 6 percent decline on the S&P 500.

However, investors would have been whipsawed twice during the five-year period. In late September and early October 1985 and during the first two weeks of October 1986, investors would have cashed out of stocks only to find the market moving high. Subsequently, investors would have reentered the market at a higher price than their initial exit prices.

How to Invest Using Moving Averages

First you need to calculate and keep tabs on your fund's moving average. To calculate a 39-week moving average you simply take the average price of 39 weeks of a fund's net asset value. Each week you add in the new number and subtract out week number one.

That way you have a moving 39-week average. Then you compare the recent price to the moving average. If the price is above the average it's a buy sign. If the price is below the moving average it's a sell sign.

A quick way to estimate a 39 or 40 week moving average once per week is to:

- Take 95 percent of your mutual fund's net asset value for the previous week.
- Take 5 percent of this week's net asset value.
- Add the two together to get your moving average point.
- Plot those points against the weekly net asset values.
- If the weekly net asset value breaks above the moving average line, it's a buy signal.
- If the weekly net asset value breaks below the moving average line, it's a sell signal.

Fortunately, there are several software programs on the market that can calculate moving averages for you. For a complete listing of software programs, pick up a copy of *The Individual Investor's Guide to Computerized Investing,* published by the American Association of Individual Investors, Chicago, IL. For more information you can call them at 312-280-0170.

If you don't want to do it yourself, there are several mutual fund newsletters that make recommendations based on moving averages (see Appendix).

Second, once you have your buy or sell signal, you call your fund group. If it is a buy sign, you tell the fund representative to move the money out of your money fund and into your stock fund. If it's a sell signal, you offer instructions to move out of the stock fund and into the money fund.

Keep in mind that you will have to pay taxes on the trades if the money is not in a tax-deferred retirement account or variable annuity.

Using moving averages to invest in a mutual fund is not the secret to stock market success. Moving averages can add a level of comfort to your investment program because you may avoid large stock market losses. By contrast, if you jump out of your fund, you may get back in at a higher price than when you left to move into a money fund.

Some basic rules to use when interpreting moving averages:

- If the moving average flattens out following a previous decline, or is advancing and the price of the stock penetrates the average line on the upside, it's a major buy signal.

- If the price falls below the moving average price while the average line still is rising, this also is considered to be a buy sign.

- If a stock fund price is above the moving average line and is declining toward that line and fails to go through and starts to turn up again, this is a buy sign.

- If the moving average line flattens out following a previous rise, or is declining and the price of the stock penetrates that line on the downside, it's a major sell signal.

- If the stock fund rises above the moving average, while the average line still is falling, it's a sell signal.

- If the stock fund price is below the moving average and is advancing toward that line but fails to break above the line and turns down again, it's a sell signal.

- If the stock fund price advances too fast above an advancing moving average line, there is likely to be a move back toward the trend line.

There are dangers to using a moving average.

- In sideways or choppy markets, investors could get whipsawed—investing only to find the market falling or selling only to find the market improving.

- If the market is extremely volatile, investors may find themselves getting in at a higher price than the price at which they previously sold the fund. For that reason, the mutual fund investment adviser stressed that investors should keep an eye on other events and indicators.

- Relative strength can give a false signal. A fund could show strong relative strength, but nothing happens. You could have a risky fund showing strong relative strength but not showing a good risk-adjusted rate of return.

- You will pay taxes on your trades unless the money is invested in a tax-deferred plan like an IRA, 401(k) pension plan or variable annuity.

Points to Remember

- A moving average is a way to track the price trend of a fund.

- When a fund trends up, it is likely to continue.

- When the fund's trend is down, it is likely to go lower.

- You can get whipsawed when you use a moving average—sell only to find the fund go higher or buy only to find the fund go lower.

- You can avoid large losses by using a moving average because you get out when there is a possible down trend.

- You pay taxes on trades unless you invest in a retirement savings plan.

Chapter 24

Seasonality Investing

More aggressive investors can take advantage of seasonal trends and profit from mutual fund investing. Chapter 21 discusses several investment cycles that can tip you off when to invest in your mutual fund.

This chapter looks at investment patterns that frequently occur. Knowing when the pattern starts and ends can spell success for more venturesome mutual fund investors.

The Institute for Econometric Research, Ft. Lauderdale, FL, has found some seasonal patterns that you can take advantage of to trade stock funds. The seasonal patterns include:

- Above-average market returns on the last trading day and first four trading sessions of every month, a continuous five-trading-day span.

- Strong performance on the two trading sessions preceding each market holiday closing—i.e., the two trading days preceding the market closing for New Year's, Presidents' Day, Good Friday, Memorial Day, Independence Day, Labor Day, Thanksgiving, and Christmas.

Is this the secret to stock market success? No. But actual investment results have shown that it is profitable.

The research of Norm Fosback, president of the Institute for Econometric Research, shows that profits were made about two-thirds of the time by moving into stock funds at the beginning of a seasonal pattern and switching into a money fund at the end of the pattern. The average return per trade was less than one percent. In addition, seasonal mutual fund investing lost more than 3 percent in any single trade just five times in 12 years that an actual investment was made.

Where Can You Get Information about Seasonal Trends?

Advice about seasonality investing is published monthly in the Institute's highly respected newsletters, *Mutual Fund Forecaster* and *Market Logic* (see appendix).

Their advice has worked well over the years. According to the *Hulbert Financial Digest's* evaluation of market timing ability, or the ability to move between cash and an index of stock market performance, *Market Logic's* Seasonality timing tactic ranked second out of 15 strategies monitored over the past ten years ending December 31, 1993. For example, using the Seasonality indicator to move from cash into the Wilshire 5000 resulted in a 15.4 percent annual rate of return. By contrast, the Wilshire 5000 grew at a 14.9 percent annual rate.

Adjusted for risk, or how an investment performs per level of risk, the Seasonality trading tactic doubled the market's return over the past ten years.

How to Profit from Seasonality

There are two ways to profit from these seasonal patterns. The first is simply to buy common stock mutual funds or individual stocks near the beginning of the seasonal periods, then sell at the end of the favorable periods.

You buy a stock fund at the beginning of the first four trading days of the month and/or two days before a holiday.

You sell at the end of the fourth trading day of the month and/or sell at the end of the trading session before the holiday starts.

Fosback's research shows the seasonal patterns represent almost one-third of the annual trading that takes place on Wall Street. So investors that are in stock funds during the beginning of a seasonal pattern have a good chance of profiting from the trends.

If you have a computer, you can do it yourself. Or you can get advice from *Market Logic* and the *Mutual Fund Forecaster.*

How it Works with Mutual Funds

Based on the initial favorable historical results, Fosback actually invested in a common stock fund using the seasonality indicators on November 21, 1977. According to the Institute's Special Report, $5,000 was invested in the Indianapolis-based Unified mutual funds group. During the seasonally favorable periods, the investment was held in Unified Growth Fund. During the remaining days, the investment was transferred into Liquid Green Trust, a money fund which earns interest.

By year-end 1991, the $5,000 grew to $49,757, representing an 18 percent annual compound rate of return or a cumulative return of 895 percent.

During the same period, the Standard & Poor's 500 Index gained 709 percent, assuming reinvestment of dividends. As a result, the seasonally invested stock fund portfolio outperformed a continuously invested market portfolio while owning equities a mere 28 percent of the time. You get a better return with less risk.

The Institute's *Special Report* notes the seasonally traded mutual fund performance could have been higher. The Unified Growth Fund gained only 628 percent during the period. As a result the seasonally traded fund strategy had the disadvantage of using an equity investment whose own performance was marginally inferior to the market. But still, the seasonally traded portfolio beat the market.

For more information about using the seasonality system as a way to invest in mutual funds call The Institute of Econometric Research at (800) 422-9000.

There are drawbacks to this tactic. Some mutual fund families prohibit excessive fund switching. Also, be advised that you can underperform the market using this tactic. It's happened in the past. You may also lose money in any given year. So you have to use this tactic over the longer term.

Points to Remember

- Aggressive investors can use seasonality indicators to time the markets.

- Seasonality trading is based on idea that you can get good returns on the last trading day and first four trading sessions of every month, a continuous five-trading-day span.

- Seasonality also says you can get good returns by investing on two trading sessions preceding each market holiday closing—i.e., the two trading days preceding the market closings for New Year's, Presidents' Day, Good Friday, Memorial Day, Independence Day, Labor Day, Thanksgiving, and Christmas.

- You have to have the time and expertise to use this tactic.

- You may pay a lot of taxes on your trades since you make 17 round trip trades during the year.

Chapter 25

Bottom Fishing for Mutual Funds

You can't always rely on past performance when you invest in mutual funds. One important study shows that if you buy funds with the best 10-year track records, you will most likely be disappointed.

A better alternative if you are looking for profits is to bottom fish for funds—i.e., buy funds that have underperformed over the long term. These funds will likely gain ground.

Bottom fishing for mutual funds is only for venturesome investors who are will to take a chance on a poor-performing fund. Most bottom fishers buy low and want to sell high.

Why Bottom Fishing May Work

What is happening is known in statistical terms as the "regression to the mean." Over the long term, common stock investments tend to drift toward their historical average rate of return. Those that get hot tend to give back some of those fat gains. Those that underperform tend to gain back their losses.

Investing in a fund that has just been named the top performer of the year is a common practice. It is also not very productive, according to a study conducted by the Pioneer Group of Funds, Boston.

Top funds often slump badly the following year. Six of the last 20 annual winners actually lost money in 12 months after a banner year. U.S. Gold Shares was up 64.7 percent in 1989, but lost 34.2 percent in 1990. Oppenheimer Global Biotech Fund made 121 percent in 1991, but lost 22.9 percent the following year.

Even when a top performer does well, its results typically are far lower than in that winning year.

Pioneer calculates that an investment in the top-performing fund of the most recent year (1993), which then switched to the next year's top-performing fund, would have grown in the last 20 years from $10,000 to $139,602. That's a big increase, reflecting the strong stock market in most of those years.

But a similar investment that went into the conservatively managed Pioneer II Fund, a growth and income fund, and stayed there throughout would be worth $226,774, more than 60 percent more.

What you should know is that hot past performance is no guarantee of future results. You might be better off investing in funds that have hit rock bottom.

A study conducted by Dalbar Financial Services Inc, Boston, shows that an investor who purchased the 100 equity funds with the best 10-year track records at the end of 1992 wound up with lower returns in 1993 than investors who simultaneously had purchased the 100 funds with the worst 10-year track records.

The study showed that the 100 top long-term performing equity funds for the decade ending in 1992 actually underperformed the bottom 100 funds and the average equity fund. The top-performing funds gained 15.82 percent the next year while the bottom 100 funds rose 22.18 percent. The average equity fund rose 16.32 percent. Perhaps even more startling is that what happened in 1993 is not an anomaly, according to another segment of the Dalbar study.

The 100 funds with the worst long-term track records have outperformed-at least by a small margin—both the 100 funds with the best long-term track records and the average equity fund as a group since 1988.

The exhibit in this chapter shows that it's best to invest in funds that have lagged behind in the performance, rather than bet on the favorites.

Exhibit 25–1 Comparative Returns of Top 100 and Bottom 100 Equity Funds, 10 Year Average versus Next Year Actual %

	Average Return, 10-Year Historical				Actual 1-Year Return		
Period Ending	Top 100 Funds	Bottom 100 Fund	Average Equity Fund	Period Ending	Top 100 Funds	Bottom 100 Fund	Average Equity Fund
12/31/87	19.30	10.86	15.02	12/31/87	12.95	13.05	13.18
12/31/88	19.01	11.09	15.12	12/31/88	25.74	23.04	24.75
12/31/89	18.57	10.82	14.89	12/31/89	(6.17)	(9.02)	(6.39)
12/31/90	15.09	5.89	10.97	12/31/90	30.19	34.10	32.48
12/31/91	18.15	9.12	14.29	12/31/91	6.54	3.79	6.37
12/31/92	16.33	7.57	12.64	12/31/92	15.82	22.18	16.32
Average	17.74	9.23	13.82	Average	14.18	14.52	14.45

Source: DALBAR's *FundRATE Market Monitor.*

Here is what happened to the 100 funds with the best 10-year track records as of:

- 1987: Gained 12.95 percent in 1988 while funds with the worst 10-year track records gained 13.05 percent and the average equity fund rose 13.18 percent.

- 1988: Gained 25.74 percent in 1989 versus 23.04 percent for the 100 funds with the worst 10-year track record and 24.75 percent for the average equity fund.

- 1989: Lost 6.17 percent in 1990 versus a loss of 9.02 percent for the bottom 100 funds and a loss of 6.03 percent for the average equity fund.

- 1990: Gained 30.19 percent in 1991 versus 34.1 percent for the bottom 100 funds and 32.48 percent for the average equity fund.

- 1991: Gained 6.54 percent in 1992 versus 3.79 percent for the bottom 100 funds and 6.73 percent for the average equity fund.

If you look at the average performance of the top and bottom 100 funds in the year after they make the funds' hit parade list you'll see:

The bottom 100 funds rose an average 14.25 percent for each of the six years ended in 1993, while the average equity fund rose 14.45 percent and the top 100 funds rose 14.18 percent.

Other findings of the Dalbar study:

- The majority of funds with the best 10-year track records have declined in rank the following year. The study shows that only 34 percent of the funds with the best 10-year track record in 1992 appeared on the list of the top 100 funds in 1993.

- The performance of the average fund improved when the performance of the top funds declined. The average of all equity funds rose 3.5 percentage points while the top 100 declined .5 percentage points. In addition, 38 percent of 1992's top 100 funds improved in 1993 versus 48 percent of all funds.

- Even though the top 100 funds have not kept pace with the bottom 100 funds or even the average equity fund, it has not hurt their growth in assets. Assets of the 100 funds with the best long-term track records in 1992 grew by 34.6 percent in 1993 while the other funds gained only 29.6 percent in assets.

- Expense ratios increased on the funds that performed the best and declined on funds that performed worst. Of those top 100 funds that rose in the rankings, expense ratios rose 4 basis points, from 1.23 percent to 1.27 percent. Meanwhile, of those top 100 funds that fell in rank, expense ratios fell 1 basis point from .99 to .98 percent.

- Of the more than 2,000 equity funds that exist today, only 400 have a 10-year track record. What's more, of the 100 funds with the best 10-year track records as of 1987, only eight funds did better or as well over the next six years.

For example, Fidelity Magellan fund, which had the best average return for ten years ending in 1987, 30.90 percent, returned only 17.98 percent annually over the next six years. That's a decline of 12.92 percentage points.

The CGM Capital Development Fund was an exception. It posted the second best average return for the decade ending in 1987 (25.50 percent), but the fund kept pace with its average over the following six years.

A word to the wise. Sometimes you pass up some well-managed funds when you bottom fish. In fact, a fistful of funds outperformed their 10-year average rates of return, according to Dalbar. The AIM Constellation fund average return rose from 20.20 percent for 10 years ending in 1987 to 25.10 percent for the six years ending in 1993. Other funds that can boast about besting their average long-term returns include: Putnam Voyager, Acorn, Seligman Capital, Hartwell Emerging Growth, Kemper Growth, and Scudder Capital Growth.

Points to Remember

- When you bottom fish for funds, you invest in funds that have underperformed their peers and the market average.

- You hopefully profit when the funds rebound.

- Studies show bottom fishing can work.

- Long-term investors should stick with well-managed funds with good long-term track records.

- Bottom fishing is only for venturesome investors.

Chapter 26

Profiting from a Bear Market

Aggressive mutual fund investors take note. When your mutual fund tumbles, don't sell. Systematically buy more shares. Then you wait for the market to rebound and profit.

This is another buy-low-and-sell-high investment tactic that takes a strong stomach. Assuming you have invested in a well-managed stock fund and have a lot of faith in your fund's portfolio manager, you can take advantage of the pull back and profit over the longer term.

Statistics since World War II show that the average bear market can last between one and two years, give or take a few months. While the average bull market lasts 33 months, the average time it take the stock market to recover from its bear market losses is about 18 months.

So here is how to play the bear market for profits. This strategy, developed by Gerald Perritt, Ph.D., publisher of the *Mutual Fund Letter*, requires that you buy and hold during a bear market.

You may have to park your money in a money fund for 12 to 15 months before a bear market creates an attractive opportunity.

Strategy

Step 1. Invest one-third of your cash in mutual fund shares when the market or the fund moves down 10 percent.

Step 2. Invest half of your cash in more mutual fund shares during a serious bear market when the fund or market drops another 10 percent.

Step 3. Invest the remaining 17 percent of your cash over the six to eight months that an economic recession may last.

"As a result of this strategy, when prices begin their rise in a bull market you'll be able to take full advantage," Perritt stresses. "While the value of your stock portfolio will be lower during bear markets, the net cost of your investment is averaged downward as you buy at sale prices. The strategy is aggressive. However, many investors receive a less-than-adequate return not because they stayed with a bear market too long, but because they sold too early in a bull market! Therefore, hold your stocks during bull markets and reserve buying for bear markets."

Perritt's research shows there were 20 buying opportunities from 1950 through 1984 and several more over the past 10 years.

Lets look at some of the nasty bear markets.

Perritt notes that using this strategy, the bear market of 1969-70 would have signaled two successive buying opportunities (February 1970 and June 1970). The great bear of 1973-74 flashed three buying opportunities (December 1973, June 1974, and September 1974). In all other instances, stock price declines fell short of the 20 percent required to signal a second buying opportunity. The first buy signal since the market decline began on June 22, 1983, was flashed some 11 months later, in late May 1984.

Perritt suggests that you set up your own stock fund–money fund mix based on your tolerance for risk. Then you make the adjustments as the value of your investment declines. If you implement this bear market investment tactic, you should be prepared to invest for at least ten years. So those that are faint of heart should forget about it.

How did this tactic work during some nasty periods in stock market history? Here are Perritt's own words, as published in his book, *Dollars and Sense: Financial Wisdom in 101 Doses,* (published by Dow Jones Irwin, 1986).

> While this investment strategy is theoretically appealing, I decided to put it to the test using investment returns over the period January 1, 1950 to June 1, 1982. January 1950 was chosen as a starting point since this was in the middle of a bull market that began on June 15, 1948.

Thus, results are not biased either upward or downward by setting the beginning or ending of a bull market as the point of initial investment.

Here is how the study was conducted:

- Investments were apportioned between the Standard & Poor's 500 Index and one-month maturity Treasury bills. Since the S&P 500 Index was used, our simulated results reflected the returns from a common stock portfolio of average risk.

- A moderately aggressive posture was assumed initially. The initial "investment" of $10,000 was split 70%-30% in favor of common stocks.

- It was assumed that cash dividends paid by S&P 500 firms were placed in one-month Treasury bills on the first of each month and that interest on the Treasury bill investments was compounded monthly.

- Transaction costs or income tax in determining the end value of the investment portfolio were not included.

- The decision rule used to make stock purchases was: Buy on the first trading day of the month following each 10% decline in the value of the S&P 500 stock index.

- During these bear markets, one-third of available cash was invested after the first 10% decline in stock prices.

- One-half of the remaining cash balance was invested following the second successive decline in stock prices by at least 10%.

- All remaining cash was committed to the common stock portion of the portfolio when stock prices fell by another 10%.

- Stock purchases were made the first trading day of the appropriate month because this made calculation of dividends and interest income easier. In actual practice, such purchases should be made on the day following the signal of a buying opportunity.

The buy signal and the investment action taken are listed in Exhibit 26–1.

The results of this study show that if you have the patience to systematically invest in bear markets, you can profit over the long term. For example:

- The initial $7,000 investment in the Standard & Poor's Stock Index would have grown to $127,088 by July 1, 1982. In addition, the T-bill account would have contained $16,406.

Exhibit 26–1 Subsequent Purchase Opportunities*

Date	Action Required
September 1, 1953	Invest ⅓ of available cash in S&P 500
March 1, 1957	Invest ⅓ of available cash in S&P 500
October 1, 1957	Invest ⅓ of available cash in S&P 500
October 1, 1960	Invest ⅓ of available cash in S&P 500
June 1, 1962	Invest ⅓ of available cash in S&P 500
August 1, 1966	Invest ⅓ of available cash in S&P 500
February 1, 1970	Invest ⅓ of available cash in S&P 500
June 1, 1970	Invest ⅓ of available cash in S&P 500
December 1, 1971	Invest ⅓ of available cash in S&P 500
December 1, 1973	Invest ⅓ of available cash in S&P 500
June 1, 1974	Invest ⅓ of available cash in S&P 500
September 1, 1974	Invest balance of cash in S&P 500
October 1, 1975	Invest ⅓ of available cash in S&P 500
June 1, 1977	Invest ⅓ of available cash in S&P 500
February 1, 1978	Invest ⅓ of available cash in S&P 500
April 1, 1980	Invest ⅓ of available cash in S&P 500
September 1, 1961	Invest ⅓ of available cash in S&P 500
July 1, 1982	Invest ⅓ of available cash in S&P 500
June 1, 1984	Invest ⅓ of available cash in S&P 500

*Initial portfolio as of January 1, 1950, $7,000 in S&P 500 Stock Index; $3,000 in Treasury bill.

- Since a buying opportunity signal was flashed on July 11, 1982, implementation of the strategy would have resulted in $4,370 being invested in common stocks one month before the start of the most recent bull market. Thus, the equity portion of the overall portfolio would have grown to $196,034 by January 1, 1984.

Past performance is no indication of future results. But assuming you invest in a well managed equity fund that tracks the market average, you can expect to enhance your returns by systematically investing when your fund or the stock market heads south.

For this tactic to work, however, you should be prepared to invest for the long term. Start an IRA or 401(k) company pension, variable annuity or variable life insurance policy. Pick out a good stock fund or make up a diversified portfolio of U.S. and international stock and bond funds. Buy systematically when the funds decline in value. When you retire, you may have a pot of gold at the end of your rainbow if you've invested for 20 or 25 years.

Points to Remember

- Aggressive investors can buy low and sell high if they have a set of trading rules.

- You have to be a patient investor because a bear market can last as long as two years.

- You can use this bear market investment tactic with as many funds as you want.

- It works well with IRAs and 401(k) plans.

Chapter 27

Bond Fund Investment Strategies

If you're a fixed-income investor, you have to take steps to protect yourself against changing interest rates. If rates fall, you are investing your money at a lower rate. By contrast, a one percent rise in interest rates will trigger almost a 10 percent decline in the value of a long-term bond portfolio (see Exhibit 27-1).

The strategies discussed below can help you preserve your bond fund principal when interest rates change. They are designed for anyone, aggressive or conservative, who invests in bond funds.

Exhibit 27–1 Change In Value of 6 Percent Bond Assuming a $10,000 Investment If Interest Rates Move

U.S. Government Security	Up 1%	Down 1%	Duration
Money Fund	$0	$0	0
3-month T-Bill	24	+24	2.4
1 yr. T-Bill	–93	+94	9.4
5 yr. T-Note	–383	+401	4.0
10 yr. T-Note	–617	+672	6.7
30 yr. T-Bond	–940	+1,123	11.2

Immunize Yourself against Rising Interest Rates

Fortunately, there are several ways to reduce a bond or bond portfolio's sensitivity to interest rates.

"Immunizing" against interest rate risk is a popular way to reduce the volatility of a bond's price change due to changes in interest rates.

A bond or bond portfolio is immunized if its value at the end of the holding period is as great as it would have been had interest rates been constant while the securities were owned.

When you immunize a portfolio, you must first look at a bond's "duration." Duration measures how much a bond's price changes with 1 percent change in interest rates. The duration calculation measures the weighted average time to receipt of interest and principal. It factors coupon payments, or the income produced by the bond, as well as the eventual return of principal.

A bond's duration is always shorter than the bond's maturity. But the longer the duration of a bond, the greater the price change.

Immunization, best understood as duration matching, is the opposite of simply rolling over CDs. Over the last decade, CD investors have been reinvesting maturing CDs at lower and lower interest rates. As a result, those who need money for retirement have experienced a shortfall of funds.

You can avoid such losses by matching your investment with future liabilities, such as retirement income or college costs.

To do this, you first need to establish your investment's duration. Say a bond fund has a duration of 5. That means if interest rates rise 1 percent the value of the portfolio will decline 5 percent. If interest rates rise 1 percent, the bond fund will gain about 5 percent.

A portfolio of bonds is immunized from interest rate risk if the duration of the portfolio is equal to the holding period. That way, the cash flow from the bond and change in a bond's price due to interest-rate fluctuations reduce the portfolio's volatility.

Presently 30-year Treasury bonds have a duration of about 9. A duration of 9 means a 9 percent price change for every 1 percent change in interest rates. A 5-year T-note, by contrast, is less than half as volatile with a duration of about 4.

That's a lot of technical talk. The most important point about immunization is that you want the value of your bond fund or portfolio bonds to be worth a specific amount of money to meet future financial commitments.

A Simple Way to Use Bond Immunization to Help You Save

You can use immunization to save for a child's future college education or for your retirement.

It works this way.

Assume money is needed for a child's future college education in 7 years:

- The investor buys an individual bond or a professionally managed bond fund with a duration of seven years. The single bond matures in ten years. The bond fund's portfolio has an average maturity of about ten years.

- If interest rates decline by the time the child is ready for college, the capital gain on the bond fund with a ten-year average maturity or bond fund sold in the seventh year will more than offset the lost income from reinvesting the bond proceeds at lower rates.

- By contrast, if interest rates rise, reinvesting the income at higher rates will offset the decline in the market value of the ten-year bond or bond fund sold in the seventh year.

There is no free lunch, however, with immunization. Buying a single bond and reducing its volatility to interest rates is a lot easier than immunizing a whole portfolio of bonds for several reasons.

First, if you own a portfolio of bonds for a specific time frame, you have to rebalance the portfolio annually so that the duration each year matches the new time frame.

Second, the portfolio must be rebalanced when there is a substantial change in interest rates. Duration declines when interest rates rise. When interest rates drop, however, duration increases. As a result, rebalancing brings the duration back in line with the holding period.

Third, the investor must avoid purchasing bonds with short call protection, which allows the bond to be redeemed early by the issuer. A bond that's called in early will change the duration of the portfolio.

Fourth, a seller who is rebalancing a portfolio may not get the right price for the bonds due to liquidity problems in the corporate bond market.

Keeping It Simple and Avoiding Headaches

One way to avoid these problems is to buy zero coupon Treasury bonds or zero coupon Treasury bond funds. Zero coupon Treasury bonds sell at a large discount to face value. At maturity, you collect your principal, plus all the accrued interest. Since you collect face value at maturity, you don't have to worry about investing your interest income at lower rates if interest rates decline.

"The maturity and the duration are the same," says James Benham, president of the Benham Group of Funds, Palo Alto, CA. Since you collect both principal and interest at maturity, there is no reinvestment risk. The investor can lock into a rate and know exactly how much money he or she will have at maturity."

Laddering Maturities

Laddering maturities is another safe way to boost your income over certificates of deposit and other money market instruments. A laddered portfolio is a portfolio of bonds maturing at various times, usually in consecutive years. The portfolio earns more than money market rates. In addition, maturing bonds annually have the chance to be rolled over at high rates. Today, a high-quality corporate bond laddered portfolio would yield about 7 percent or more.

You can also ladder your bond fund maturities. You keep a certain percent of your investment in a money fund, short-term bond fund, intermediate-term bond fund and longer-term bond fund. Use municipal bond funds if you are a high-tax-bracket investor.

Watch the Yield Curve

Watch the yield curve. James Benham of the Benham Group also recommends that you keep an eye on bond yields in relation to their terms. Then you invest based on the shape of the yield curve. For example:

- A positive sloping yield curve. This exists when long-term rates are higher than short-term rates by more than 200 to 250 basis points. Today there is a 400 basis-point difference between long and short-term rates. Under these conditions, Benham suggests investing in the five-year maturity range. This is the point in the yield curve with the best risk-return trade-off.

- An inverted yield curve. This exists when short-term rates are higher than long-term rates. An inverted yield curve existed in the 1980s when short-term rates yielded 16 percent compared with 14 percent in long-term bonds. The curve also inverted in June 1989 when short-term rates traded at 100 basis points more than long-term rates. An inverted yield curve suggests that investors should buy longer-term bonds and profit when interest rates decline later on.

- A humped yield curve. This exists when intermediate-term rates are higher than both short- and long-term rates. Investments should be made at the hump, the highest spot in the yield curve. It is considered the safest place on the maturity spectrum.

- A flat yield curve. This exists when there are only slight differences among short-, intermediate-, and long-term rates. Investors should keep up with economic and monetary developments. If the Fed tightens money supply or inflation heats up, investors should invest short-term because interest rates will rise. By contrast, loose monetary policy favors the long bond.

At the time of this writing, the yield curve had flattened. Short-term rates rose and long-term bond rates dropped about 25 basis points from their highs of over 8 percent (see Exhibit 27–1). Short-term rates rose because the Federal Reserve tightened up the discount rate, or the rate the Federal Reserve banks uses when they loan money to banks. Long-term rates have come down because lately the bond market doesn't think inflation is a problem with the economy possibly slowing down in the near future.

When the yield curve flattens it is a signal the economy is slowing. As a result, those that invest in intermediate or long-term bond funds or bonds may benefit when interest rates decline and bond prices fall. But be careful. If short-term rates are still high and long-term rates have not really dropped, it might be a good idea to invest in money funds and bonds or bond funds that sport average maturities of 1 to 10 years. That way you are protected in case interest rates rise a little more.

Exhibit 27–2 Yield Curves

Positive Yield Curve

This is the "normal" yield curve. The interest rates on short-term issues are lower than rates on long-term bonds.

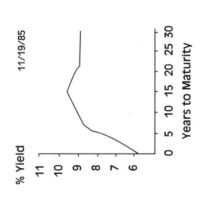

% Yield   11/19/85

Years to Maturity

Risk and Reward:
This is the "normal" risk/reward trade-off. The more market risk (i.e., price fluctuation, and potential purchasing power erosion due to inflation) you're willing to take, the higher your potential reward (return on your investment).

Negative Yield Curve

In this unusual, inverted configuration, short-term issues yield more than long-term issues.

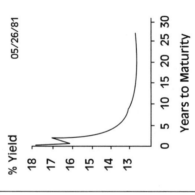

% Yield   05/26/81

Years to Maturity

Risk and Reward:
The highest returns are available in short-term securities, which also carry less market risk than long-term securities.

Flat Yield Curve:

In this configuration, there is little difference between the yields of short- and long-term issues.

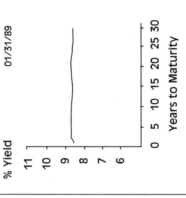

% Yield   01/31/89

Years to Maturity

Risk and Reward:
Your return is nearly the same short-term as long-term, so you can invest short-term and enjoy high returns.

Buy and Hold Bond Funds for the Long Haul

John Bogle, chairman of the Vanguard Group of Funds, says that if you are a long-term bond fund investor, don't worry about temporary declines in the market value of your fund.

He says you have to look at the total return on your investment over the long-haul of ten years or more. Total return is the return on a fund that looks at the gain or loss in the price of the fund with dividends and capital gains reinvested.

Over the shorter-term, Bogle says that the loss of principal due to rising interest rates "overwhelms" the income return from the bonds a mutual fund owns.

But over the longer term, less principal is lost due to higher interest rates usually available on longer-term maturities. Since you are reinvesting the interest income in new shares, you're in effect dollar cost averaging so that over the longer term, your buy-and-hold strategy will pay for itself. But for buying and holding to work, you need a reasonable yield spread over the long term between T-bills and T-bonds. It should be at least 1.2 percent (120 basis points).

For example, Bogle says a 25-year Treasury bond would provide a one-year total return of –10 percent if interest rates rose by 200 basis points and a return of 31 percent on a commensurate rate decline; however, after five years the range of respective rates of return narrows to 6 percent and 11 percent. After 11 years the gap is in fact eliminated, and the interest rate rise then turns to the bondholder's advantage. At maturity, the average rate of return would be 9.2 percent in a rising rate environment and 7.0 percent in a declining rate environment.

Perhaps the obvious long-term value to investors of higher rates versus lower rates is dramatic (see Exhibit 27–2).

As the exhibit shows, a $10,000 investment in a 25-year Treasury bond would have a value (including interest) of just $9,000 one year later following the 2 percent rate increase, and a value of $13,000 following the 2 percent rate decline. Then the values begin to converge, crossing in the 11th year. After 25 years, when the bond ultimately matures, the $10,000 investment is worth nearly $94,000 in the rising rate environment and just $55,000 in the declining rate environment—a 60 percent difference in value!

"This reversal is, in a sense, a reaffirmation of the centuries-old aphorism that it's an ill wind (indeed) that blows no good," says Bogle. "The reason is that higher yields, while they have a negative short-term impact on prices, have a positive long-term impact on returns since interest payments are reinvested at higher (i.e., more attractive) rates."

Rules of Thumb

Keep in mind the following rules of thumb when you invest in bond funds.

- Long-term bonds are for investing, not saving. Any signs that inflation will pick up, fueled by increased spending by the administration, is likely to force up interest rates. In 1994, for example, long-term rates increased almost 2 percent sending some bond funds down more than 10 percent for the year. If rates fall, then you will likely see more capital appreciation in long-term bond funds.

- "Barbell" your investment mix if you think rates may come down, but you are not sure. If you keep part of your money in a money fund and part in a longer-term bond fund, you can pick up some extra total return on your investment if interest rates fall. But in the event they do not, your money fund position reduces your losses when the value of your long-term bond fund drops. Since a larger percentage of your investment is in money funds, you benefit when interest rates rise.

- Ladder your bond fund investments over several years if you think interest rates will decline. It is a safer way to profit.

- Reinvest your bond fund dividends if you don't need the income. You will get a higher total return when interest rates decline and bond fund prices rise.

- If you want to play it safe, stick with money funds and short-term bond funds with average maturities of under three years. You earn higher than money market yields, and lose 75 percent less than a long-term bond fund when interest rates fall.

Chapter 28

Easy-to-Use
Bond Timing Strategy

Here's a simple strategy to help you avert large losses in your bond fund.

Paul Merriman, mutual fund portfolio manger and publisher of *Fund Exchange,* Seattle, WA, says you don't need a computer to keep tabs on trends in the bond market either.

Over the past year bond fund investors have headed for the exits as short-term interest rates rose more than 3 percent and long-term rates 2 percent. They redeemed billions of dollars and reinvested the money in CDs or money funds.

But when should they get back in?

Merriman suggests this simple strategy for nervous investors who want to get out of their bond funds when rates rise, invest in money funds and re-enter when the interest rate trend is declining.

So pick out a bond fund and get a pen or pencil and a notebook. Here's how to start, according to Merriman.

When to Buy

- Record the price of your bond fund daily.

- Keep track of the lowest price you have recorded.

- When the fund reaches 2.5 percent above that low, consider that you have received a "buy" signal—and invest in the fund. Now you are "in" the market, hoping the upward price trend continues.

When to Sell

- Continue recording the fund's price daily.

- Make note of each new high price.

- When the fund price drops to 97.5 percent of its highest price since you bought, you have a "sell" signal. Move your money into a money market fund.

When to Re-Enter

- Buy back into your bond fund when it reaches 102.5 percent of the lowest price since you last sold.

Be sure to adjust for month-end dividend distributions and year-end capital gain distribution. For example, if your bond fund has declined 2 percent since you purchased it, a month-end distribution of one-half of one percent will trigger a sell order unless you adjust for the distribution. The easiest way to keep track of the distributions is to deduct the dividend from the most recent high price and watch for the 2.5 percent decline from that adjusted price.

"This is a very simple system, and you can easily see that it doesn't take any forecasting ability," Merriman stresses. "It simply tries to identify existing price trends and either rides them up or sits them out. Like all market timing systems, this will produce some losing trades. You'll sometimes buy at a higher price than your last sale, and sometimes you'll be on the sidelines when the market is going up.

"If you're human," he adds, "there will be times you will want to second-guess the system. But if you follow it without question over a period of years, you'll likely improve your return and reduce your risk."

Best Types of Bond Funds to Use

Use no-load long-term bond funds with average maturities greater than ten years. These funds show a greater change in price when interest rates change. You need that kind of volatility to catch the trends. The type of funds to consider include high-yield bond funds as well as U.S. and international corporate and government bond funds.

You don't want to do this with a short-term bond fund because you may wait forever for a buy or sell signal. Also, make sure you can transfer your money in and out of your chosen bond fund without a penalty.

Merriman's research based on actual fund prices from 1987 through 1993 shows that this simple market timing system improved the return on the Vanguard High Yield Bond Fund and the T. Rowe Price International Bond Fund. It also reduced the funds' volatility by about 40 percent, based on the number of winning and losing periods during the time the study was conducted.

The results of the study show that the investor who used this simple timing tactic, for example, exceeded the earnings of one who bought and held the fund by more than $3,000. What's more, this timing reduced the number of losing periods.

Exhibit 28–1 Comparative Results of Buy-and-Hold versus Market Timing on Vanguard High Yield Bond Fund and T. Rowe Price International Bond Fund for the Period December 31, 1986 through December 31, 1993

	Vanguard High Yield Bond Fund	Same with Timing	Price International Bond Fund	Same with Timing
Annual Compound Rate of Return	10.0%	12.3%	10.8%	12.4%
$10,000 Grew to:	$19,490	$22,530	$20,480	$22,720
Losing Quarters	6	2	10	7
Worst Four Consecutive Quarters	–9.3%	6.0%	–6.9%	3.1

Source: *Fund Exchange*

Points to Remember

- You can avoid large losses if you get out of your bond fund when interest rates look like they may rise.

- The best buying opportunities exist near the bottom of the bond market when interest rates are high.

- You sell when your fund's net asset value drops to 97.5 percent of its highest price since you bought it.

- You buy when your fund reaches 2.5 percent above the lowest point since you have owned it.

- Buy back into your bond fund when it reaches 102.5 percent of the lowest price since you last sold.

Chapter 29

Strategy Mutual Funds

There are a number of funds that have specific investment strategies to meet your needs. This makes it easy because the fund manager does the manuevering for you. So if you have a tax problem or want to hedge against a stock market correction, here a few funds that may be just what you need.

Get the Ball Rolling

The easiest way: Cut investment expenses and you will save. Buy no-load funds instead of load funds. Load funds, on average, charge 5 percent front-end or 5 percent back-end loads that drop to zero after five years. Also watch out for 12b-1 sales distribution fees. That's an annual charge, ranging from 1 percent to .25 percent, which pays for marketing expenses.

Invest $10,000 in a no-load fund that earns 7 percent annually for ten years and the money grows to $19,671. By contrast, invest the same money and pay a 5 percent load: The money grows to $18,688. You made $983 less with the load fund.

Steve Savage, editor of the *Value Line Mutual Fund Survey*, also says to "watch those fund expense ratios." The expense ratio is the total amount deducted from your fund's earnings every year, excluding any front-end charge. The average stock fund has an expense ratio of 1.4 percent. The average bond fund sports a ratio of about .75 percent.

Savage says that when a stock fund's expense ratio is significantly above average, a fund's total return suffers.

"Funds with the highest expense rankings, charging an average of 2.25 percent performed significantly worse than funds with lower expenses," stresses Savage.

On the bond fund side, high expenses take a big bite out of the returns of investments with a fixed stream of income.

Specialized Managed Mutual Funds

Looking for a low-risk way to invest in the stock market? Some financial advisers recommend the Gateway Index Plus Fund. It is designed to lose less money in down markets than other stock funds. What's more, it still performs well enough on the upside to merit attention. Over the past 15 years, the fund grew at an annual rate of 10.32 percent.

Morningstar rates it as a low-risk stock fund. Its report says that it's an excellent fund that provides a return in line with the overall market with 60 percent less risk.

The Gateway Index Plus Fund invests in stocks like GE, Exxon and AT&T. Peter Thayer, fund manager, uses conservative tactics to buffer any significant downside risk.

The results of his strategy have been excellent. In the first half of this year the fund was up 1.6 percent even though the S&P 500 lost money. Over the past five years, the fund gained 10 percent annually. It underperformed the S&P 500, but it is 60 percent less risky.

This fund achieves its low volatility rating by selling its upside appreciation potential and buying downside protection. Thayer starts with his portfolio of S&P 100 stocks. These stocks also provide high-dividend returns.

To reduce the volatility of the fund, Thayer sells call options against his underlying stock positions. The buyer of the call option has the ability to buy a stock in the future at a present price. If the stock goes up, Thayer profits since he can buy the stock at a below-market price.

At times when the market could drop 10 percent or more, Thayer will buy put options. Puts gain in value when the stock market declines. The added protection from puts, combined with call premiums and dividends, supports the stability of the fund.

"We stay fully invested in all 100 blue chip stocks that make up the S&P 100 index," says Thayer. "We always sell index call options on the entire portfolio. We collect 10 percent a year in income on the options in exchange for stock market profits. We keep the dividends. Realistically though, the best the fund could do in any year would be a 15 percent gain."

Thayer says he hasn't resorted to buying put options. Nevertheless, he sees continuing market volatility. Over the next ten years, he expects the stock market to grow at a 7 percent annual return—far below its historical average of 10 percent.

With ordinary income taxed as high in 1994 as 42.5 percent at just the federal tax level and the maximum long-term capital gains tax still at 28 percent, savvy investors will want to convert ordinary income into long-term capital gains whenever they can.

One answer for heavily taxed investors lies in the Permanent Portfolio Family of Funds. Using a little known but well established accounting practice, two of this family's funds can turn most of their ordinary income into long-term capital gains for tax purposes.

The Treasury Bill Portfolio, which yields close to 4 percent, is a typical money fund except for two factors. First, it does not declare daily dividends. It retains its daily investment income, which permits the price of the shares in the fund to rise from day to day. The rise in share price is equal to the investment income that has been retained. Then, once a year, usually in December or January, the fund pays out, as per-share dividends, only the minimum amount required for the fund itself to avoid income tax.

This special accounting technique minimizes taxes. If an investor buys and holds, then little is paid on the interest income to the taxman.

If you have invested for longer than one year and redeem shares, your gain is a long-term capital gain. So it is taxed at 28 percent, rather than as income, which is taxed at much higher rates.

The Versatile Bond Portfolio, which yields 5.34 percent, is a sister fund that works the same way. The fund invests in investment grade rated bonds with maturities of two years or less. Year-to-date ending in July 1994, the fund returned 1.3 percent. By contrast, the average corporate bond fund declined 2.7 percent.

"Both funds are useful in different ways," says Terry Coxon, president of the Permanent Portfolio Family of Funds. "Either investment compounds faster with tax-deferral. You have more spendable cash when you take redemptions rather than receive interest income. Or you can let your assets grow and step up the basis of the assets for your heirs."

Coxon says he plays it safe with both funds. Neither fund invests in derivatives. The money is invested strictly in T-bills and currently sports an average maturity of 75 days. The bond fund buys and holds T-bills and notes to maturity.

"Money fund investors will benefit from the rise in short-term rates," says Coxon. "The yield curve will flatten and long-term rates come down. The Versatile Bond Fund's average maturity is just one year. So those that accumulate shares will benefit from higher yields, although there will be a little price fluctuation in the fund."

If you want high after-tax income, consider the Fidelity Spartan Bond Strategies Fund. The fund, which yields 5.5 percent, is designed to maximize after-tax returns from fixed-income investments. Unlike most bond funds, which invest exclusively in either taxable or tax-exempt bonds, the Spartan Bond Strategies Fund will invest in either sector based on which bond market is expected to deliver the greatest after-tax returns. The fund invests in intermediate and long-term bonds, and emphasizes total returns over yield.

Currently, George Fischer, fund manager, is 80 percent invested in investment grade rated municipal bonds and 20 percent in corporate bonds with an average maturity of 13 years.

Although the fund is down 4 percent this year, he expects that municipal bonds will outperform corporate bonds when interest rates decline. His strategy is to accumulate underpriced municipal bonds.

"I've slimmed the fund down to the bonds I like best, those with the best value,' says Fischer. "Twenty-five percent of the portfolio is invested in New York state and California bonds. "I've been buying them on weakness because they have good value. You could see significant gains when they turn around."

Tax swapping, says Fischer, is one of the major strategies he uses to maximize after-tax returns. He sells a bond below its cost basis to take a loss. He then buys another bond that gives him essentially the same investment performance of the first bond. But for tax purposes he has realized a loss.

"I have frequently use this tax strategy during this period of rising rates and falling bond prices," says Fischer. "The tax loss carried forward will enable me to take gains on bonds in the future and not distribute them."

On the equity side, the Vanguard Group has developed an innovative solution for tax-conscious mutual fund investors the Vanguard Tax-Managed Fund. The new fund offers the first series of no-load mutual fund portfolios specifically designed to minimize the impact of taxes on investment returns.

Assets in the series now total more than $60 million. The fund consists of three portfolios: Growth and Income, a fund which is highly correlated to the S&P 500; Capital Appreciation, which tracks the Russell 1000 index; and Balanced, which tracks a combination of the S&P 500 and a bond market index. All employ various techniques to reduce taxes.

Each of the funds will track their respective markets. But they are not pure index funds. Since the focus is tax reduction, there will be differences in the returns of the funds compared with the market averages. Over the long term, he says the new funds should show much higher after-tax returns than the market averages.

The reason: The fund manager will sell securities that have the highest cost basis to minimize realized capital gains. The manager also may sell securities at a loss to offset any capital gains. The fund invests in low-dividend yield stocks or tax-exempt bonds. In addition, the portfolio turnover in the funds is low in order to keep capital gains distributions to a minimum.

The funds primarily invest in growth stocks because growth companies have lower dividend yields. As an anchor to the portfolios, the five largest holdings in both the Growth and Growth and Income Fund include AT&T, GE, Exxon, Coke and Phillip Morris. However, the majority of companies owned have earnings which are expected to grow 20 percent annually.

Expenses are low and low dividend yielding growth stocks help tax reduction and enhance returns. Otherwise, taxes along with high costs represent a bad combination that can reduce long-term equity fund returns by as much as 44 percent.

Reducing Your Capital Gains Taxes Builds Wealth

You might want to sell mutual fund shares at a loss so you can write them off on your income taxes. But if the fund is a good long-term investment, you might want to buy it back later. To qualify for a tax write-off, however, you have to stay clear of a wash sale. You can't repurchase your stock for 31 calendar days after you sell it. You can't be a front-runner either. You can't buy more stock in the same firm up to 30 days before the planned tax-loss sale. Otherwise, the IRS won't let you write off the loss on your income taxes.

The IRS allows you to write off up to $3,000 in net capital losses in a year. The rest can be carried forward into next year.

Here are several ways to work around the wash sale rules.

- Sell the fund shares at a loss, wait 31 days and buy it back. The sale at a loss can occur at the close of trading on the last business day of the year. The advantage: Your realize the loss and can re-invest in your favorite fund. The disadvantage: The fund's price could rise in 31 days and you would have to invest at a higher price than when you sold.

- Buy and then sell. Buy the same amount of mutual fund shares you already own, wait at least 31 days to avoid the wash sale rule, and then sell the original holding. You use this tactic until the end of November, so you can sell at the end of the year. The advantage: You get the tax-loss and still own the fund. The disadvantage: You own more shares and could be subject to greater losses if the market tumbles.

Swap Funds

You can swap funds as a way to avoid the wash sale rule. Sell your fund and invest in a similar fund that sells at about the same price. You can take the capital loss on your taxes and still have an investment that fits your needs.

You want to make sure the funds are comparable, otherwise you could be taking on more risk than you anticipated. Then you roll out of one fund and into another.

Here is how it works:

Say you invested $10,000 in the Putnam High Yield Tax Free Fund at $14.73 and own 678.72 shares. The fund's net asset value drops to $14.10 by the end of June. Your $10,000 is now worth $9,570. Then you sell the fund for a $430 loss. Next you reinvest the $9,570 in the T. Rowe Price Tax Free High Yield fund. You now own 823.58 shares at a net asset value of $11.62. As a result, you have realized a loss, but you still own a tax-free high yield investment.

Loss Carry Forward Funds

Take advantage of loss carry forwards available to certain stock funds. Until 1993 some international stock funds have performed poorly. Many overseas funds lost money because the dollar strengthened against securities owned in foreign currencies. Many international stock funds took losses when they sold their stocks in dollar terms. As a result, in 1994 many of the funds had capital loss carry forwards.

In 1994 the average bond and municipal bond fund lost more than 5 percent when interest rates shot up over 2 percent from their lows at the beginning of that year. Many of these funds also had loss carry forwards.

Now the funds can tax shelter their capital gains against those losses. This is an additional and very real advantage to investors enjoying this year's very attractive returns. Funds with losses in one year can carry those losses over into the next year. As a result, if you invest in a fund with loss carry forwards, the capital gains earned by the fund will be offset by the capital losses. So you don't pay capital gains taxes on fund distributions.

It works this way:

Say for example your international fund has a loss carry forward that amounts to $1.50 a share. That is $1.50 a share in losses that you can offset against this year's profits. Suppose you buy the fund this year and the fund profits from trading securities worldwide to the tune of $1.50 a share: You are the lucky one. You don't have to pay taxes on the capital gains since you had a buck and a half of loss-carry forwards. So if you had 1,000 shares of the fund, you avoided paying $1,500 in capital gains distributions to Uncle Sam. Next year, however, if the fund profits, you may have to pay taxes on your capital gains distributions.

Kylelane Percell, editor of the *Morningstar 5 Star Investor*, thinks investing in funds with capital losses is a smart move.

Several funds with large loss carry forwards, according to Morningstar, include Fidelity Global Bond Fund, Fidelity New Markets Fund, T. Rowe Price High Yield, and MFS High Income Fund. "Investors who buy a fund when it has a tax loss carry forward on its books can tax advantage of this tax benefit without suffering the lost that makes it possible," says Percell. Right now many funds have generous capital loss carry forwards.

Tax Sensitive Funds

Check out the Morningstar tax analysis on each stock fund before investing. In August 1993, *Morningstar Mutual Funds* initiated an intriguing and valuable tax analysis service which we will be watching closely.

Morningstar Mutual Funds calculates two tax-sensitivity statistics:

Percent of PreTax Return, i.e., the percentage of the funds' total return (dividends plus realized and unrealized capital gains) that was left after the maximum federal (but not state) income taxes calculated at the tax rates in effect at the time. The closer the number is to 100 percent, the better.

Noting that "those funds that have paid the fewest recent capital gains are likely to be those sitting on the greatest future taxable gains," Morningstar calculates a second statistic:

Estimated current tax liability as defined as "The maximum percentage of a fund's current assets that might be paid out as a taxable (realized) gain were the fund to liquidate all its holdings today (a highly unlikely event)."

The percentage is not actually the tax liability but the unrealized capital gains remaining in the fund's price per share. For example, a fund with a 33 percent estimated tax liability would have a cost basis of its portfolio on average equivalent to 67 percent of the current market value. The actual maximum possible capital gains tax liability would, of course, be only 28 percent of the 33 percent or 9.2 percent of the net asset value.

There will always be a number of no-load stock funds with unrealized capital gains. So check the Morningstar reports. Try and stay clear of funds with more than 25 percent unrealized appreciation in net asset value. If you own the fund, it doesn't mean you should sell it. Just be careful and monitor the fund's activity.

Avoid Buying Funds at the End of the Year

If you plan on investing in a mutual fund, do it before the end of the year. Otherwise, you will pay taxes when a fund distributes capital gains in December.

Burton Berry, publisher of *NoLoad Fund X,* says it's best to wait until after a fund's ex-dividend date to buy fund shares to avoid taxes. The ex-dividend date is the date on which the value of the income or capital gain distribution is deducted from the price per share.

Here is an example of the problem Berry says you face if you buy a stock fund right before it goes ex-dividend:

- On January 1, 1993, Fund A, which pays dividends and capital gains annually at year end, is offered at $9 a share. The fund portfolio appreciates $1 from stocks that were sold during the year. The fund also had net dividend earnings over the year, after all fund expenses, of 50 cents per share.

- As 1993 comes to a close, the net asset value of the fund grew to $11.50 from $9 due to $1 in gains and 50 cents from net income.

- The law requires that the fund distribute by year end its realized gains of $1 and its net earnings of 50 cents for a total of $1.50 per share.

- On December 30, 1993 the fund goes ex-dividend for $1.50. As a result, the closing price of the fund on that day declines by $1.50. from $11.50 to $10. If you look at the mutual fund table in the newspaper, you will see an "x" listed by the fund that day, indicating the fund went ex-dividend.

- You will either receive a check from the fund for $1.50 a share or you will have the money reinvested in new fund shares. Regardless of what you do, you owe taxes on the entire $1.50. So if you own 100 shares of fund A, you owe Uncle Sam tax on $150.

Berry says that before you invest, check when the fund distributes income and gains. You could buy Fund A for $10 a share if you buy after the ex-dividend date. You don't have to worry about paying taxes until year-end 1994. Those with retirement savings accounts don't have to worry about fund dividends and capital gains distributions. Your money grows tax-deferred in variable annuities, IRAs, Keoghs, SEP Plans and

401(k) company pension plans. Should investors take dividends in cash or reinvest the money in new fund shares? If you don't need the income to live on, reinvest the distributions.

"With reinvested dividends, you get the benefit of compounding," says Berry. "At 10 percent compounding annually, money doubles in seven years, triples in slightly less than 15 years. Add growth from market appreciation and some real miracles occur. Conversely, reinvested dividends and gains are subject to market risk along with original principal." Berry recently self-published an excellent book titled *Loaded Questions on No Load Funds.* For more information about the book and his newsletter write: DAL Investment Company, 235 Montgomery St., Suite 662, San Francisco, CA 94104.

Points to Remember

- There are specialized funds to meet specific investment needs.

- Be aware of tax strategies when you invest.

- There are stock funds on the market that minimize capital gains distributions. So you pay little in the way of taxes.

- Invest in funds that have lost money recently. If they are well managed investments you benefit. The fund carries losses over into the next year for tax purposes. So any gains the fund earns from the sale of securities are written off against profits. That way you will not pay tax on capital gains distributions.

Chapter 30

Systematic Withdrawals from Mutual Funds

Now that you've got all this money from investing in mutual funds, how do you take it out? There are several ways to pay yourself a pension out of your well-managed stock funds. The first part of this chapter covers what is called systematic withdrawals from after-tax dollars you have invested in a mutual fund.

In the second half of the chapter, you will read about making withdrawals from your pre-tax investments in IRA or company pension plans. Also covered are withdrawals from deferred annuities that enable you to invest tax-deferred until you take payments when you retire.

With a systematic withdrawal plan, you take regular payments from your fund. The money comes out of three parts of the fund—your principal, dividends and capital gains.

Keep in mind that since your money isn't in a retirement savings account, you will pay taxes on the trades when shares are redeemed and the money is sent to you.

You can have the fund send you a check every month. Or you can have the money directly deposited into your checking account or money market mutual fund.

If you have money deposited into your checking account, be sure to get an interest-bearing NOW account. Have the money deposited at the beginning of every month. That way you will earn interest on the deposited money in the checking account.

Experts say that you should take no more than 6 percent annually out of your stock fund. The reason: Stocks have historically grown at an annual rate of 10 percent over the last six decades. There are years, however, when stocks have lost money. So you don't want to take too much out of the fund or you will deplete your capital too soon. At six percent, you still can expect your principal to grow 4 percent if you have at least ten years or more to withdraw the money. Six percent gives you some room. However, you can always adjust your payout. Depending on your financial condition, you can take a lower payout in years when the fund is performing poorly. By contrast, in good years you can withdraw more than 6 percent.

You should look at your life expectancy to help determine how much to withdraw from your stock fund.

For example:

- At age 60, a male is expected to live 18 years. A female should live 23 years.

- At age 65, a male is expected to live 14 years. A female should live 19 years.

- At age 70, a male is expected to live 12 years. A female should live 16 years.

- At age 75, a male is expected to live nine years. A female should live 12 years.

How long will your money last if you take out 6 percent and your investment grows at the follow rate of return:

- At a 4 percent annual return the money will last 28 years.

- At a 5 percent annual return the money will last 36 years.

- At a 6 percent annual return and above the money will last indefinitely.

How Systematic Withdrawal Works

Let's assume you put a $100,000 lump sum into the T. Rowe Price Growth Fund at year-end 1973. Also assume you withdrew $500 a month (6 percent annually) from the fund for your retirement.

Exhibit 30-1 shows you year-by-year how much of your income comes from the fund's dividends and principal. It also shows that even though you take money out, you have the fund's capital gains reinvested in new shares. The capital gains are the profits the fund made on stocks which were sold.

Over 20 years ending in December 1993, you withdrew $120,000 from your investment. You paid yourself $6,000 a year from your $100,000 kitty. But by year-end, the total value of your investment was still $158,767.

Your savings still grew because the investment grew at an annual compound rate of return of 7.55 percent.

You Have to Withdraw over a Long Term

To make systematic withdrawal work, however, you have to take money out over at least ten years. Otherwise, a few poor performing years could deplete your principal.

Look what happened in 1974, when the stock market declined almost 25 percent! In December, 1973 our investor invested $100,000 into the fund. Now look at the total value column in table for December 31, 1974. Our investor withdrew $6,000, but the total value of the investment dropped to $60,567.

Now that's a whopping decline in the value of your principal. Hopefully, history will not repeat itself in the same manner in years to come.

As you can see our retiree continued to take withdrawals and the market value of the savings kitty continued to increase in value. By year-end 1986, the total value of the investment increased to $103,961. Our investor took out a total of $78,000 from the fund.

Bingo: we now hit 1987, the year of the stock market crash. In the third quarter of 1987, the average growth fund lost 20 percent in value. For the year the funds were now just a few percent.

In 1987, the table shows that the total value of the fund dropped to $102,378, including the withdrawal. In subsequent years, the fund gained in value as the bull market in stocks progressed.

Exhibit 30–1 T. Rowe Price Growth Stock Fund

Systematic Withdrawal Plan
Dividends and Capital Gains Reinvested
Monthly Withdrawals of $500.00 (6.0% Annually) Beginning 1/31/74

	Amounts Withdrawn			
Date	From Income Dividends	From Principal	Annual Total	Cumulative Total
12/31/73	0	0	0	0
12/31/76	1804	4196	6000	6000
12/31/75	1043	5947	6000	12000
12/31/76	1761	4239	6000	18000
12/31/77	1636	4366	6000	24000
12/31/78	1882	4118	6000	30000
12/31/79	2134	3866	6000	36000
12/31/80	2556	3444	6000	42000
12/31/81	2913	3087	6000	48000
12/31/82	3011	2989	6000	54000
12/31/83	2716	3284	6000	60000
12/31/84	1883	4117	6000	66000
12/31/85	1724	4276	6000	72000
12/31/86	1915	4085	6000	78000
12/31/87	3851	2149	6000	84000
12/31/88	2176	3824	6000	90000
12/31/89	2281	3719	6000	96000
12/31/90	3071	2929	6000	102000
12/31/91	1801	4199	6000	108000
12/31/92	1299	4701	6000	114000
12/31/93	1035	4965	6000	120000
Totals	42491	77509	120000	120000

Average Annual Total Return for this Illustration: 7.55% (Annual Compounding)

Source: T. Rowe Price

Systematic Withdrawals from Mutual Funds

Date: 12/31/73   Shares Purchased: 8,396.306
Initial Investment: $100,000   Net Asset Value per Share: $11.9100
Offering Price: $11.9100   Initial Net Asset Value: $100,000
Sales Charge Included: 0.00%

Value of Remaining Shares

Annual Cap Gain Distrib'n	Remaining Original Shares	Capital GAin Shares	Total Value	Shares Held
0	100,00	0	100000	8936
1935	60567	1354	61921	8094
0	75908	1804	77712	7626
0	79666	1993	81659	7252
0	67944	1814	69758	6806
0	69634	1968	71602	6439
0	71223	2127	73350	6102
0	85631	2669	88300	5855
259	69190	2484	71674	5635
496	73075	3358	76433	5432
0	75930	3630	79560	5231
2354	66328	5683	72011	5071
3246	79080	11360	90440	5038
21661	71366	32595	103961	6130
16446	58917	43461	102378	7174
1768	56311	46100	102411	7039
10599	59449	62478	121927	7494
3071	51154	59563	110717	7527
4467	60478	80389	140867	7513
7652	55496	87679	143175	7673
7317	55501	103266	158767	7775
71270	55501	103266	158767	7775

The Best Type of Funds
for Systematic Withdrawals

You want to invest in well-managed growth or growth and income or equity income funds. This example uses a growth fund to show how you could withdraw 6 percent a year and still see your capital grow over the longer term.

Growth and income or equity income funds also are good candidates. The funds tend to pay higher yields because they invest in well-seasoned blue chip companies that pay high dividend yields. At the time of this writing, the typical growth and income fund sported a dividend yield of 4 percent. So with a growth and income fund, you are likely to see more of your monthly income come from the dividends compared with a growth fund.

You will take out less of your principal from a high-yielding stock fund. The trade-off: You may not get the growth of capital over the years that you would receive from a growth fund.

Withdrawals from IRA and 401(k) Plans

When you must live off your retirement savings, plus your Social Security and other assets, it's important to set up a diversified portfolio with a mix of common stock and fixed income funds. A diversified portfolio will give you the best possible return with the least amount of risk based on your risk level.

Once you have a diversified portfolio, you can take systematic withdrawals from your funds, based on IRS payout rates for retirement savings plans.

Why is it important to diversify? In late 1994 and early 1995 many retirees who invested only in bonds or income funds saw the market value of their investments decline as much as 10 percent.

Many parents or grandparents experienced the dreaded double whammy. Already out of the work force, they must withdraw from their retirement accounts when the poorly performing stock and bond markets have driven down the value of their investments. Now they are worried their principal won't last.

"Don't sell your income funds," stresses Elizabeth Sorrells, senior vice president at Colonial Investment Services, Boston. Sorrells says her phones have been ringing from retirees who mistakenly invested their retirement savings in only a bond or income fund. They now are finding out the hard way, she says, that bonds can be riskier than stocks.

Instead of selling, "restructure your portfolio and diversify into other types of mutual funds," is Sorrells' suggestion.

As a rule of thumb, the older you are the more you should be concerned with preservation of principal. But those who recently have retired may well live into their 90s, and need to make certain their money will hold out.

The newly retired, Sorrells says, should consider investing in a balanced fund that maintains about a 50-50 stock-bond mix. Those who are at least 70 always should have about 30 percent in a conservative stock fund, such as an equity income fund that invests in blue chip high-dividend-yielding stocks.

These funds, she says, are a low-risk way to earn higher yields and still participate in the long-term growth of the stock market. That growth comes in handy whenever the financial markets rebound.

What if you are losing money? Cuyler Findaly, chairman of the AARP Investment Program, Boston, says that the first step, even for those in their 70s and 80s who have suffered losses, is not to worry.

"Given the short-term volatility of stocks, there may be periods when the value of your principal declines, perhaps by 15 percent or more in a year, Findaly says. "But by letting your money work for you over time, having part of your investment in stock funds historically has provided a return that will enable you to say ahead of inflation and taxes."

Depending on your age and risk tolerance, there are several ways you can diversify your retirement savings' mutual fund portfolio. According to T. Rowe Price, a Baltimore-based mutual fund company, here are several ways you can invest and take payouts from your IRA and other retirement savings plans.

- Portfolio I. Safety. The elderly should play it safe. Stick with income investments.

- Portfolio II. Income. This is a portfolio designed for the newly retired or those in their early 80s. The breakdown:

  1. 40 percent of assets are invested for income.

  2. 35 percent of assets are invested for safety. The investment options include checking and savings accounts, money funds,

T-bills, short-term CDs and short-term notes maturing in less than two years.

3. 25 percent of assets are invested for growth to help maintain your purchasing power. The investments include common stock, stock funds, variable annuities, precious metals funds, and real estate stock funds.

- Portfolio III. Moderate risk. This portfolio is designed for younger retirees who can afford to invest for 10 to 15 years. The investment mix may be more volatile, but the portfolio provided more inflation protection than the other portfolios mentioned above.

  1. 20 percent of assets are invested for safety. The investment options include checking and savings accounts, money funds, T-bills, short-term CDs and short-term notes maturing in less than two years.

  2. 40 percent is invested for income.

     Your investment options: Long-term CDs, Treasury notes and bonds, municipal bonds, bond funds, unit investment trusts, and annuities.

  3. 40 percent of assets are invested for growth. The investments include common stock, stock funds, variable annuities, precious metals funds and real estate stock funds.

How have these portfolios performed over the past 20 years? Remember what's happened in the past is no indication of what will happen in future. What you can learn, however, is how these portfolios reacted. You will notice that the safe portfolios lost less money in down markets. The more aggressive portfolio lost more money on the downside and gained more on the upside.

For example, Portfolio I with minimal risk grew at an annual rate of 7.5 percent over the past 20 years ending in December of 1993. After inflation, the fund earned just 1.6 percent. The best year was 14.7 percent; the worst year was 2.9 percent. There were no years of negative returns.

By contrast, Portfolio III, with modest risk, grew at an 11.6 percent annual rate over the same time. After inflation, the portfolio gained 4.5

Exhibit 30–2 Model Retirement Portfolios

Portfolio I: Minimal Risk

Safety
100%

Portfolio II: Low Risk

Growth
25%

Income
40%

Safety
35%

Portfolio III: Moderate Risk

Income
40%

Growth
40%

Safety
20%

Portfolio IV: High Risk

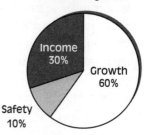

Income
30%

Growth
60%

Safety
10%

Performance of Retirement Portfolios*
20 Years Ending December 31, 1993

| | Asset Mix | | | Average annualized Returns* | | | | |
	Growth	Income	Safety	Nominal Return	Real Return**	Best Year (nominal return)	Worst Year	Number of Years with Negative Total Return
Portfolio								
I. Minimal Risk	0%	0%	100%	7.5%	1.6%	14.7%	2.9%	0
II. Low Risk	25	40	35	10.4	4.5	20.7	–4.0	2
III. Moderate Risk	40	40	20	11.3	5.4	24.9	–9.3	2
IV. High Risk	60	30	10	12.1	6.2	29.1	–15.6	3

*Based on actual performance for the 20 years ending December 31, 1993, of stocks (85% Wilshire 500 and 15% Europe, Australia, Far East (EAFE) Index), 30-day Treasury bills, and bonds (Lehman Brothers Aggregate Bond Index from January 1976–'93 and Lehman Brothers Government/ Corporate Bond Index from 1974–'75).

Past performance does not guarantee future results.

Figures include changes in principal value and reinvested dividends and assume the same asset mix is maintained eac h year. Ths exhibit is for illustrative purposes only and is not representative of the performance of any T. Rowe Price fund.

**Based on an inflation rate of 5.9% for the 20-year period ended 12/31/93.

Sources: T. Rowe Price Associates; data supplied by Lehman Brothers, Wilshire Associates, and Ibbotson Associates.

percent. The best year was 24.9 percent; the worst year was –9.3 percent. There were two years out of 20 when the portfolio lost money.

What kind of payments do you receive from these different kinds of portfolios? Withdrawals were made at the beginning of the year and increased annually based on inflation. Assuming a $150,000 investment on December 31, 1978, here is what would have been withdrawn every year for 14 years from the portfolios.

As you can see our retiree took total withdrawals of $239,823 over the 15 years. However, because of the explosive growth in the stock market during that time and declining interest rates that raised the value of bonds, the moderate risk portfolio still was worth a total of $276,524. By contrast, the minimal risk portfolio was worth just $75,990.

The lesson to be learned from this exhibit: Don't expect to invest based on the portfolio's returns today and expect to earn the same amount of money. The illustration covers a record-breaking period in the stock market. All you can assume is that the more you invest in common stock funds over the longer term, the more growth you will likely to see. But be prepared to see the value of your investment decline in bad years.

Stretching Out Your Retirement Pay

Besides restructuring your investments, there are a couple ways to stretch out your mandatory IRA or 401(k) company pension payouts over several more years.

You are required to withdraw all your money based on life expectancy. But there are at least three ways to do this, and your mutual fund company can help crunch the numbers.

- Term Certain. The first way is to base it on your life expectancy at retirement. If you have 20 years to live, you would take out one-twentieth or 5 percent of the money in the first year. In year 20, however, you would withdraw the entire balance remaining.

- Recalculation. You can recalculate your life expectancy annually to stretch out your payments over several more years. If you do this, your annual income will be less, but you'll be able to take the payments over a longer period of as much as five years.

- You also can base your payout on a joint life expectancy using either the term certain or recalculation method. For example, at age 71 with no beneficiary, your life expectancy would be 15.3 years. The first required distribution on a $100,000 investment would be $6,536 in taxable dollars. But if you designate your 62- year-old spouse as beneficiary, the joint life expectancy increases to 24.7 years and the distribution drops to $4,049.

There are limits, however, to naming younger beneficiaries. The IRS sets a maximum age spread of ten years between the retiree and the non-spouse. In addition, if you use the recalculation method based on a joint life expectancy and one spouse dies, future distributions are based on the surviving spouse's single life expectancy.

Another way to extend your income is to move your 401(k) investment into a variable annuity via a direct transfer. With an IRA or 401(k) plan you must begin receiving your pension at age 70½. But with most annuities, you needn't take withdrawals until you are 80 to 85.

In addition, since variable annuities are insurance products, your principal is protected. Variable annuity death benefit guarantees insure that when you die, your heirs will receive your principal or market value, whichever is higher. Remember, though, that the death benefit guarantee is only as strong as the insurance company behind it.

Points to Remember

- With systematic withdrawal you take money out of your mutual funds every month.

- You can withdraw a percentage of assets or a specific amount of shares.

- Systematic withdraws work best with balance funds or growth and income funds because you still get capital appreciation on the money that is in your account.

- You can withdraw money out of your IRA based on your life or joint life expectancy.

- Preservation of principal is important when you retire, but you also need some growth so that your money preserves its purchasing power.

Chapter 31

Systematic Withdrawals from Variable Life Insurance

In addition to getting income protection for your family when you die, you can use a variable life insurance policy as a tax-free source of money when you retire.

The earnings on a life insurance cash value policy are not taxed. In addition, you can borrow against the cash value in your policy every year as a source of tax-free income. Of course, your death benefits are reduced by the amount of loans outstanding.

Here's how you could set up a universal life insurance policy to give you tax-free retirement income:

A male, age 40, who was a non-smoker would make premium payments of $5,000 a year for 19 years and receive $500,000 of death benefit coverage. Assume our 40-year-old diversified his cash value mutual fund investments so that 70 percent went into stock funds and 30 percent was invested in bond funds. Also assume that the cash value fund investment grew at a modest 7.5 percent internal rate of return—that's the return made after fees, commissions, and other charges have been deducted from the policy. The money would grow to $220,715 by the time the 40-year-old was 60 years of age.

At age 60, the policyholder could borrow $16,024 a year against the cash value over the next 35 years. At age 95, there would not be much in the way of death benefits. Death benefits are reduced by the policy loans and accumulated loan interest. But at age 80, the policyholder still would have $215,000 in death benefits.

Although universal life insurance can be a source of tax-free income during retirement, there are the following drawbacks:

1. The insurance industry is on shaky ground due to junk bond and real estate investment losses. To protect against this, you should only do business with insurance companies that carry top ratings from firms such as A.M. Best, Standard & Poor's, Moody's, and Duff and Phelps.

2. Always look at an illustration with a guaranteed low rate. There's no guarantee the interest rate in the life insurance illustration will be used to calculate your cash value over the years. If interest rates stay low over the next ten years, a 7 percent rate of return could be an overestimated rate. Most insurance companies guarantee they will pay you 4.5 percent. If you earn that rate, you won't be getting those fat retirement checks.

   At 4.5 percent over 19 years, our 40 year-old would have only $145,317 of cash value to tap. That's over $75,000 less than the policyholder expected. If he or she took money out at the same rate, only $6,536 would be withdrawn annually.

3. If your payment schedule violates the tax laws, your loans might be considered taxable income. By law you must make a minimum lump-sum payment or required level premium payments for the first seven years of the policy life. Otherwise, you would have to pay income tax on the amount that is in excess of the premiums paid into the policy.

Life insurance is supposed to be used to protect your family over the longer term. If you are not around, money will be needed to support the family and help pay the bills. Your surviving spouse may need income to live on and raise the kids. Your children may need money to pay for their future college education. Then there is the mortgage, the car payment, other debts, burial expenses and taxes that must be paid.

Exhibit 31–1 Annual Withdrawals from $100,000 Cash Value Life Insurance Policy

% Withdrawn Annually	Annual Withdrawals
4%	$7,458
5	8,024
6	8,718
7	9,439

So the experts say you should not be using life insurance as a sole way to fund your retirement.

But say you have lived a long, happy and prosperous life: You have accumulated wealth over the years and don't really need the life insurance any more. Then you can borrow against the cash value and have an extra source of retirement funds.

Let's assume that you want to tap the $100,000 of cash value in your life insurance policy over the next 20 years. The figure above shows you how much you could take out of a life insurance policy over 20 years.

Don't forget, you plan to take the entire $100,000 out of the policy. So at the end of 20 years, you will have very little cash value left in the policy.

In addition, the death benefits will be reduced by the amount of the policy loan and accumulated debt interest outstanding when you die. So you will have little in the life insurance coverage for your loved ones when you die.

Points to Remember

- Life insurance is income protection for your loved ones.
- The cash values grow tax free.
- Provided you don't need the insurance protection, withdraw money or take out a policy loan as a extra source of retirement income.
- Your death benefits are reduced by the amount of money taken out of the policy or the amount of the policy loans, plus accrued interest.
- Assume that your investments grow at a conservative rate of return.

Chapter 32

Variable Annuity Investment Strategies

If you are a conservative investor, but still want the growth that comes along with investing in common stock mutual funds, consider this tactic for your retirement savings.

Invest in a variable annuity. It's a tax-deferred investment, so right away you are saving money. By the way, you also can use the strategies in this chapter in your retirement savings plan.

When you invest in a deferred variable annuity, you have a contract with an insurance company. You make lump sum or regular payments into an annuity. Then you can invest in a wide variety of mutual funds including both U.S. and international equity funds or bond funds, as well as money funds and a fixed-rate account.

When you retire, you can take a lump sum distribution and pay taxes on your accumulated earnings, or you can receive monthly payments from the insurance company for your lifetime. You also can set up the annuity so that your beneficiaries receive the balance in your account when you die.

Variable annuities have another added attraction. Insurance coverage in the form of a death benefit guarantee. When you die, the insurance company agrees to pay your heirs the principal or market value, whichever is higher.

Just like with any mutual fund family, you can switch your variable annuity among investments as market conditions or your needs change.

What's attractive about investing in variable annuities is that your money grows tax-free until you are required by the insurance company to take payments at age 80 to 85.

Of course, if you take money out of the account before age 59½, you have to pay the IRS a 10 percent fine, plus income tax on the earnings. In addition, you may owe the insurance company a back-end surrender charge.

You Don't Pay Taxes on Your Dividends

Tax-deferral of your stock fund dividends is important. The above-average returns that investors enjoyed during the 1980s are a thing of the past, but expectations of those high returns persist into the 1990s.

Unfortunately, history doesn't always repeat itself in the same manner. Stocks gained a whopping 16 percent annually during the decade of the 1980s. You doubled your money every 4½ years.

In the 1990s, the return on stocks is likely to be closer to their historical long-term average of 10 percent, rather than 16 percent.

That's why stock dividends are paramount. According to Ibbotson Associates, Chicago, the income from dividends has accounted for 47 percent of the historical total return on common stocks. That trend will likely continue.

Boosting Your Total Return

Total return is a calculation that includes reinvestment of fund distribution, such as dividends and capital gains, and the price appreciation of the fund net asset value.

Lets say that the Stock Fund for Lifetime gained 10 percent annually over the past ten years. Almost half of its return was due to the reinvestment of dividends into new shares.

How does the IRS tax these dividends? Depending on your tax bracket, you will pay Uncle Sam between 15 and 39.6 percent in federal income taxes on those dividends. For most of us, Uncle Sam takes about $1/3$, substantially dropping the after tax return on our investment.

On the other hand, say you invest $2,500 a year in a diversified portfolio of variable annuity stock and bond funds and the money grows at 8 percent, tax deferred, for 20 years.

In this case your savings kitty will grow to $123,557. If you had to pay taxes on the earnings and were in just the 28 percent tax bracket, the investment would be worth $68,248.

As you can see, investing in a tax-deferred variable makes a lot of sense. Your investment is worth much more than it would have been worth assuming you paid taxes on your dividend income.

Of course, you will eventually have to pay taxes on your annuity when you begin taking distributions. But you will still pay tax only on the earnings, not the principal when you withdraw money each year.

The rest of your money will continue to grow tax deferred. This means you are earning money on the money that would have been used to pay taxes.

A Safe Way to Invest in Stock Funds

Although the tax savings makes variable annuities an attractive way to invest in common stock mutual funds, you still face investment risk. If the stock market goes into a correction, the chances are your fund will also decline in value. You could also lose money if your fund manager picks the wrong stocks or if a rise in interest rates causes stocks to look less attractive.

Historically, stocks have grown at an annual rate of 10 percent a year. But it has not been a steady rise. Stock returns have varied considerably. Sixty-eight percent of the time stock returns have ranged from -11 percent to +31 percent. So, when you invest in stock funds you can experience some rough weather along the way to building your wealth.

Fortunately there is a way to invest in stock funds, defer federal income taxes on your earnings and lower your investment risks.

MetLife has a variable annuity called the "Preference Plus Account" that has a nifty way to invest in stock funds without worrying about losing your shirt in a crash. They call this investment strategy the "Equity Generator". This tactic, along with their other investment strategies are designed to simplify investing while limiting risk.

If you have always invested in traditional guaranteed savings account, you've never lost any money and you've always received a guaranteed return. The trade-off for that guarantee might have been a return that left you wanting more, especially as interest rates declined to record lows and the stock market hit record highs. However, concern for the safety of your money may have kept you from exploring other investment choices.

Here is a way around that problem.

Strategy 1. The Equity Generator. You put your money in the Fixed Interest Account of MetLife's Preference Plus, where it earns a guaranteed rate and is protected against investment risk. As your interest accrues, an amount equal to it is swept, each quarter, into the Stock Index Portfolio. This portfolio is managed to mirror the return on the S&P 500. Your principal remains in the Fixed Interest Account, guaranteed by Met. With the amount that is swept each quarter, you dollar cost average into the Stock Index Portfolio where you have the potential for higher rewards. (This strategy is also available with the Aggressive Growth Portfolio.)

Strategy 2. The Equalizer. You start with equal amounts in the Fixed Interest Account and the Stock Index Portfolio. At the end of each quarter, the accounts are put back into balance. This means if the Stock Index Portfolio outperforms the Fixed Interest Account (FIA), money is transferred from the Stock Index Portfolio to the FIA. By contrast, if the Fixed Interest Account outperforms the Stock Index Portfolio, money is transferred into the Stock Index Portfolio.

This tactic helps you to buy low and sell high and dollar cost average your investment over the long term.

The stock market may have historically outperformed fixed interest investment, but many people cannot tolerate the roller coaster ride along the way. The highs may be higher, but the lows are lower. If you can't stomach the volatility of the stock market using these variable annuity tactics might be right for you.

The following exhibits illustrate the importance of picking an investment that fits your degree of risk tolerance as well as your performance expectations.

The first exhibit (Exhibit 32–1) compares the volatility of two $10,000 deposits—one in a fixed interest account and the other in the stock index fund. As you can see from the graph, there is no loss of principal with the fixed rate account—just a steady climb. The stock index fund is

Exhibit 32–1

Fixed Interest Account & Stock Index Division

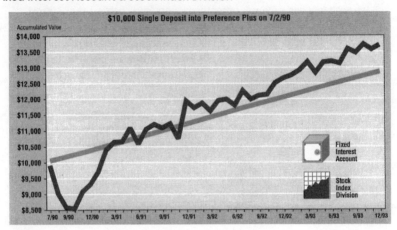

Four Risk & Return Strategies

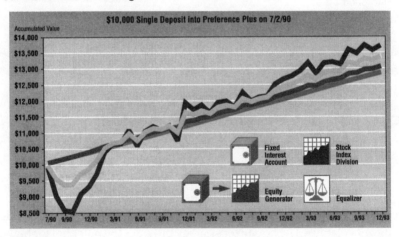

Source: MetLife

a different story. Although it ended up higher, the drop that came two months into the investment might have been too drastic for some investors to tolerate.

The next exhibit (Exhibit 32–2) shows the middle ground that can be achieved from the Equity Generator or the Equalizer.

Exhibit 32–2 Preference Plus® Performance

Changes in Accumulation Unit Values (1)

(after all fees and expenses other than withdrawal charges) as of 7/31/94

Division	Year to Date	Past 12 Months	Year Ending 1993	Year Ending 1992	Year Ending 1991
Income	−2.94%	−0.79%	9.94%	5.61%	15.94%
Inception 7/2/90					
Diversified	−2.90	1.48	11.42	8.09	23.42
Inception 7.2/90					
Stock Index	−0.73	3.66	8.21	6.11	28.11
Inception 7/2/90					
Growth	−3.12	3.25	12.98	10.25	31.41
Inception 7/2/90					
Aggressive Growth	−9.93	1.31	21.09	9.00	64.39
Inception 7/2/90					
International Stk	10.82	20.76	46.07	−11.31	−
Inception 7/1/91					
Strategy					
Equity Generator[SM] (4)	2.65	4.50	5.27	5.67	8.15
Agg. Eq. Generator[SM] (4)	2.52	4.19	5.52	6.08	9.04
Equalizer[SM] (4)	0.97	4.13	6.73	5.84	17.75
Agg. Equalizer[SM] (4)	−3.74	3.15	13.02	7.67	34.87

Source: MetLife

When the Equity Generator is used, the return can beat the fixed interest rate account alone without risking any principal or adding significant volatility. The Equalizer strategy provides the potential for higher return while at the same time helping to minimize the downside risk of the stock index fund.

The figures illustrate how you diversify for different risk and return strategies using just two funding choices in the variable annuity.

Although past performance cannot in any way guarantee future results, here is how the investment tactics performed in MetLife's variable annuity. The results show that the strategies performed as expected. What

Past 3 Years	Inception to Date	Past 3 Years (ann.) (2)	Inception to Date Ann. (2)	Hypothetical Annualized (3)	Accum. Unit Value
24.55%	39.55%	7.59%	8.31%	9.74%	$13.85
				6/2/83	
30.86	37.40	9.37	8.09	8.66	13.74
				7/25/86	
23.17	36.10	7.19	7.84	–	13.61
34.98	36.60	10.51	7.94	10.57	13.66
				6/24/83	
50.37	62.40	14.55	12.61	14.93	16.24
				4/29/88	
47.96	52.40	13.94	14.63	–	15.24
20.44	34.03	6.39	7.44	–	–
20.92	373.74	6.54	8.16	–	–
22.04	35.70	6.86	7.77	–	–
35.96	51.62	10.78	10.73	–	–

you may earn in the future will depend on the performance of the stock and bond markets and the variable annuity portfolio options.

- From July 2, 1990, when the variable annuity was started to July 31, 1994 the Equity Generator gained 4.5 percent over the past 12 months and 20.44 percent annually over the past three years.

- From July 2, 1990 to July 31, 1994, the Equalizer gained 4.13 percent over the past 12 months and 22.04 percent annually over the past three yeas.

You would have made more money investing directly in the stock fund or aggressive stock funs in the variable annuity. But you faced greater downside risk. As you can see from the figure over the past 12 months both the Equity Generator and Equalizer strategies outperformed a 100 stack in the stock index, growth or aggressive growth portfolios.

A Word about Historical Performance

Dollar cost averaging is the keystone of retirement savings investment success. In addition to the benefits of regular investing, dollar cost averaging has flexibility. By reinvesting your bond fund income or income fund dividends in a stock fund, you are putting your profits to work with little risk.

For example, this tactic performed well during a 15-year period from 1967 through 1982. That included the disastrous stock market crashes of 1973 and 1974, when the S&P 500 lost nearly 40 percent of its value.

When the stock market hit bottom in 1974, many investors registered big losses of 50 percent or more. Look at what happened in 1983: Using the average bond fund and the average stock fund and switching bond fund interest into the stock fund was profitable.

The bond interest income bought more stock fund shares at lower prices. So when the market recovered, the investor reaped attractive profits from this dollar cost averaging tactic. Those who used this strategy lost just 8 percent when the market tanked in 1974.

Over the entire 15-year period, a $10,000 initial investment grew to $34,136 by year-end 1982. That represents an annual return of 8.53 percent.

Our hypothetical investor didn't score a touchdown with this tactic. However, it is a low-risk way for him or her to build wealth and avoid being ravaged by a stock market crash.

The subsequent bull market(s) enhanced the value of these shares, so that by year-end 1982, the shares purchased with the dividends were worth almost two-and-one-half times the original bond fund purchase. This is truly a painless way to buy into the stock market. For the entire period, the average annual return was 15 percent; since the market bottom in 1974, the average return has exceeded 25 percent annually. That was a lot better than the inflation rate.

Either salting annual stock fund profits into a fixed income fund or kicking more dollars into the stock fund in down years takes more guts than having your bond fund interest reinvested in a stock fund over the long term. Over the short term, if the stock fund is down, you will add more money into the account. However, you also are dollar cost averaging your investment.

You have to be prepared to go against the wind with this dollar cost averaging tactic. Short term, your investment may decline. But over the long haul, you'll profit.

Points to Remember

- Conservative retirement savings investors can reinvest the interest income from their bond funds into their stock funds. That way they dollar cost average into the stock market for long-term growth.

- Retirement investors can sweep stock fund profits into bond funds. That way they are sure to take profits. They also can sweep bond fund profits into their stock fund after their stock fund has underperformed.

- Low-risk retirement savings and investment tactics will not outperform a 100 percent investment in a stock fund. However, your investment is less risky.

Chapter 33

Variable Life Insurance

When you own a variable life insurance policy, you have to manage the mutual funds in your cash value account, the same as you would if you invested directly in a fund. You can use dollar cost averaging, asset allocation and even some market timing if you like.

The kicker with variable life insurance is that your life insurance premiums buys term insurance and the rest is invested in your choice of stock and bond funds in the cash value account.

Because it is life insurance, the cash value grows tax-free. And you can access the cash whenever you want by borrowing against the cash value. You don't have to repay the policy loan. However, your death benefits are reduced by the amount of the outstanding loans.

Meanwhile, your money is protected against an insurance company default because the investment portion of your payment goes into a separate account at a custodian bank that also acts as the trustee. Creditors of an insurance company cannot lay claim to your money. The account is under your name—just as if it were a passbook savings account.

Be advised though, the IRS places limits on the amount you can pay into your policy without paying income tax on withdrawals or loans from your policy.

There are two types of variable life insurance to pick from. The old style policies require you to pay level annual premium over the years. Then you invest the cash value in the underlying mutual funds.

The newer polices are called variable universal life insurance. With this kind of policy you can vary your premium payment over the years as long as you meet minimum funding requirements over the first seven years you own the policy.

You have two options when you buy a fixed premium or universal variable policy.

Option A

Premium payments can decrease or increase within allowable limits, but the death benefit coverage remains the same.

If you use option A, your cash value and your death benefits add up to give you a level amount of death benefits. If you have a $100,000 policy that has accumulated $50,000 in cash value, your beneficiaries would collect a death benefit that's half a return of their cash value and half pure insurance.

But suppose you don't die, and you keep on paying your premiums. At age 95, the cash value in the policy will equal the death benefits. Before that time, there must be a gap between the cash value and the death benefits. In certain circumstances, your death benefits can increase above the face amount of the policy. This occurs if the cash values grow more quickly than expected due to high returns. An adjustment must be made based on IRS rules.

Option A policies may have one exception under which death benefits can increase. As long as you have enough cash value to pay for the cost, you can buy additional insurance. However, if you try to boost your level of death benefits too high, the insurance company may ask you to take a medical exam to prove that you are in good health and can qualify for the extra coverage.

Option B

Your death benefits increase or decrease with the growth of your cash value.

If you pay higher premiums and the cash value grows at a high rate of interest, your death benefits will increase. Conversely, if your cash value earns less money or you reduce your premium payments, the death benefits will decrease. The death benefits cannot go lower than the face amount of the policy.

How do I decide between option A and option B?

If higher cash value is your goal, then option A is the answer. Option B is better if you want your insurance coverage to increase over the years.

Universal Variable Gives You Greater Flexibility

Ben Baldwin, CLU, CFP, and ChFC, president of Baldwin Financial Systems, Northbrook, IL, favors the universal version of variable life insurance. You can vary your annual premium payments as your lifestyle or financial situation changes. The built-in flexibility is a plus. But Baldwin advises policyholders to invest a regular amount every year.

Along with traditional ways to invest in your variable life insurance mutual funds, Baldwin suggests two other strategies.

I. Profits can be taken out of stocks and locked up in a fixed rate account with annual investment options offered by many variable life insurance policies. The rapid accumulation of funds enables policyholders to have an extra source of retirement income or to pay for a child's college education.

Policyholders can also take advantage of the current tax laws and borrow against the cash value of their policy without having to worry about paying taxes on the money. If they owned an annuity or retirement savings account and took money or used it as collateral for a loan before that age, they would pay a 10 percent fine and ordinary income tax on the withdrawal.

You will have to keep an eye on your accounts if you want to take profits. The easiest way is to set up a simple rule that says whenever you have a 10, 20, or 30 percent profit, you will switch the gains into the fixed rate account. Or you can go one step further and use the constant dollar method of investing that was talked about in Chapter 11 of this book. In that case your stock fund would always be rebalanced, for example, to have $X at the end of the year. So you must take profits when the fund is up and invest more when the fund is down.

II. Along with the traditional way of dollar cost averaging into a variable insurance policy's mutual funds, Ben Baldwin, president of Baldwin Financial Systems, Northbrook, IL, offers another way to maximize the return. He suggests investing part of the cash value in a universal variable's fixed-rate account to cover the cost of the insurance. The rest is invested in a stock fund.

"When you use the interest to pay your life insurance costs, you never pay income taxes on it, Baldwin says. "Then you can maximize the capital appreciation of the cash value."

Your life insurance agent or financial planner will help you work out the details based on your specific needs. Let's keep it simple and assume the fixed rate account yields 5 percent. So for every $100 of insurance expenses, you must invest $2,000 in a fixed rate account.

Baldwin, author of the *New Life Insurance Investment Advisor* (Probus Books), offers the example of a 35-year-old nonsmoking male, who buys a $500,000 variable universal life insurance policy. The policy is set up so that a $5,000 annual premium is paid until age 65.

Over the premium-paying years of the policy's life, $1,000 of the $5,000 is invested in the fixed-rate account. The annual earnings will then cover the cost of the insurance.

The rest, $4,000 per year, is invested in a stock fund over the next 30 years until age 65.

Over the life of the policy, with 20 percent invested in the fixed rate account and 80 percent invested in the stock fund, it is assumed the investment grows at 8.96 percent annually.

Of course actual investment results and insurance company charges may differ. The cost of the insurance and other charges are subject to change. So the policy's returns may be more or less than in this hypothetical example.

Baldwin says that the life insurance illustration shows that our 35-year-old paid annual premiums of $5,000 for 30 years. During the first 15 years of the policy, the policyholder would pay a back-end surrender charge. After 15 years, there is no back-end exit charge.

Over 30 years, our insured paid $150,000 in premiums. The policy account value and the cash surrender value at age 65 is illustrated to be worth a whopping $557,543.

The death benefit at age 65 is $1,057,543. The coverage grew as the underlying investment portfolio grew.

By the time the 35 year-old policyholder is ready to retire, Baldwin says money can be taken out in the form of a policy loan or withdrawn for extra retirement income. What's more, the income from a policy loan is not taxed. Nor is the amount withdrawn taxable up to the $150,000 amount our 35-year-old invested.

What's more, when you use the interest to pay your life insurance costs, you never have to pay income taxes on it.

Be advised that this is just a hypothetical example. Actual investment results and insurance company charges may be different. Your returns may be more or less than what is shown in the hypothetical example. The cost of insurance and other charges are subject to change. As a result, everything will be different than what is shown in the example.

This is important for you to remember when viewing any life insurance policy.

What's also important:

You can diversify your universal variable life insurance investments.

You can take profits without paying capital gains taxes, or in most cases without paying transaction costs. This may be the most important and significant savings investors will realize over the life of the policy.

You can vary your premium depending on your economic circumstances.

You can used the fixed rate account as a parking place for your mutual fund profits.

You can put money in the fixed rate account. The earnings in the account will cover the cost of the life insurance. The rest of the money can be invested free of charge. But keep in mind that all mutual fund investors pay a fund management fee that averages about one half of one percent. This is also true with mutual funds in a life insurance policy.

This is not a book about life insurance.

You can get the same riders and options with variable life as you can get with whole life, too. Here's a list:

- Waiver of premium. You don't have to pay premiums if you become disabled.

- Accidental death benefits.

- Term insurance on other family members.

- Cost-of-living increase in coverage.

- Survivor options (insurance pays death benefit when the surviving spouse dies).

- Living benefits. You can use the insurance proceeds to pay medical expenses if you are terminally ill.

Chapter 34

Immediate Annuitization

If you are looking for alternative sources of retirement income, here are couple of often overlooked ways to manage your money.

An annuity will provide you with lifetime income to help supplement your other sources of retirement pay.

Annuitization is a variation to the systematic withdrawal from your mutual funds during retirement.

An immediate annuity is a contract with an insurance company. In return for a lump sum investment, the insurer promises to pay you an annual income for as long as you live.

When you withdraw money from your IRA or an after-tax investment, you could outlive your investments. Or you may be strapped with poor performing investments and have to dip into your principal.

There are two kinds of immediate annuities. With the fixed-rate immediate annuity, the insurance company pays you a fixed monthly income based on the amount of your investment, your age and the type of payout option.

With variable immediate annuities, the monthly payout is based on the performance of your underlying mutual fund investments.

To understand how variable annuitization works, it is important to see how fixed annuitization works because some contracts offer both.

Fixed-Rate Immediate Annuities for the Safety-Minded Saver

People living on a fixed income know all about interest rate risk. Every year or two they roll over their CDs at lower and lower interest rates. And if they have cashed out their CDs and invested in bond funds, the market value of their shares declined due to rising interest rates.

Immediate annuities may be a solution to the CD rollover problems. The big advantage of immediate annuities over CDs: You know you'll get a monthly check from your annuity for as long as you live. In addition, you can pass on the proceeds to your loved ones when you die. With one of the most common contracts, called "10 year certain and life," monthly checks keep coming for a minimum of ten years. If the annuitant dies before the 10-year period is up, the checks are sent to a designated beneficiary until the ten years are up.

The big drawback that merits serious consideration: You are giving up an asset to the insurance company which agrees to pay you income for your lifetime. For example, if you die after the 10-year period stipulated in the insurance contract, the insurance company keeps the balance of the assets in the account.

But there are other advantages to investing in immediate annuities if you are a safety conscious saver. For example:

- Tax advantages. You only pay taxes on part of the monthly income you receive from an annuity. Depending on your contract, you would pay taxes on about 33 percent to 40 percent of your monthly check. For example, if you receive $400 a month from your annuity, you pay the taxman only $130. Assuming your are in the 28 percent tax bracket, you owe Uncle Sam about $36 a month.

- Favorable monthly income compared with CDs. Insurance companies are annuitizing or basing their annuity payments (which include both principal and interest) on current interest rates.

Today's payouts from some of the strongest insurance companies stack up favorably against CDs.

For example, assume a 70 year-old widow has locked $50,000 into a 5 percent five-year CD at the local bank: She would earn $2,500 in annual interest income from the CD. Assuming she is in the 28 percent tax bracket, she earns $1,800 in after-tax income.

By contrast, if she bought a $50,000 immediate annuity with a 10-year period certain, she would get a check for about $385 a month or $4,620 a year for as long as she lives.

The taxable part of her monthly annuity income is $143, and she owes Uncle Sam $40 a month. After taxes, she earns $103 from the annuity investment earnings or $1,236 a year. The total after-tax income, which includes principal and interest income, from the annuity is $345 month or $4,140 a year.

Remember that with an annuity, part of your money is considered a return of principal and the other part is considered taxable earnings.

Insurance companies base their payouts on their pool of people with annuities, the annuitants' life expectancies and the earnings on their investment portfolio. So you can't directly compare a CD return, which is a debt obligation, with an immediate annuity.

You would get less after-tax income from the taxable portion of the annuity compared with the income from a five-year CD. However, you get the annuity income for a lifetime. By contrast, you may not earn the same interest income from the 5 percent CD when it matures in 1999. You might roll the money over at more or less than 5 percent depending on what rates are five years from now. And if you took principal from your CD, you would deplete your funds in just a few years.

There is no free lunch, however, with an immediate annuity. Drawbacks:

- You can't surrender an immediate annuity contract.

- You earn a net rate of return on your annuity. The insurance company may earn 8 percent on its investments but pay you 6 percent. The 2 percent represents their profits.

  But with interest rates on the rise, you might be able to get higher income from a U.S. Treasury bond or investment grade corporate bond.

- If the insurance company is financially weak today, it could be gone tomorrow. You may not get all of your money when an insurance company goes bankrupt. By contrast, your CDs are federally insured for $100,000 in the event a bank or thrift fails.

What can you expect to earn today from an immediate annuity? The amount of monthly income you receive can vary from company to company by more than $100 a month on a $100,000 immediate annuity. According to A.M. Best, a 70-year-old male would receive between $750 and $850 a month with a "life and 10-year certain" plan. A 70-year-old female would collect between $650 and $750 a month with a "life and 10-year certain" plan. A joint and survivor policy would pay between $630 and $730 per month.

If you are interested in an immediate annuity, shop around. Stick with the safest insurance companies rated at least A+ by A.M. Best or B+ by Weiss Research and double A claims paying by Standard & Poor's and Moody's.

Variable Income Annuity

Putting a chunk of your retirement money into an immediate annuity might make sense if you want some guaranteed income.

The big problem with fixed-rate immediate annuities is that the fixed income does not keep pace with inflation. If you are in your 60s or 70s that could be a problem. Someone age 65 has a 25 percent change of living to age 90.

Just say you receive $1,000 a month from your immediate annuity for 15 years and inflation grows at 3 percent: In 15 years your today's annuity dollar will buy just 64 cents of groceries.

So if you have just retired, it might make sense to put some of your money in a variable income annuity (VIA). The money may be invested in a common stock fund so that your payouts will grow as your investment returns grow and keep pace with the rate of inflation.

Andrea Bloch, a financial planner with Fidelity Investments Life Insurance Company, says that "the easiest way to think of a variable immediate annuity is as a self-directed retirement plan."

When you own a variable income annuity, you make your own investment decisions. You can invest in a wide range of common stock and bond mutual funds. Sometimes a fixed-rate option is also included in the contract.

What's the benefit of investing in mutual funds compared with a sure thing like a fixed-rate immediate annuity?

Growth. Common stocks historically have paid higher rates of return if held for the long term (see Chapter 1).

One major benefit of a VIA: It provides you with an income that can increase over time based on fund performance.

Bloch says that when you buy a VIA, you choose an assumed interest rate, which is a "benchmark return."

The "benchmark return" is used as an estimate of the first income payment. A typical benchmark is 5 percent.

Should a person earn exactly the benchmark, income will remain the same.

If the fund's performance is greater than 5 percent, the income will increase.

"Over time, monthly income can double, triple or even quadruple," says Bloch. "On the other hand, there is the risk that the income will go down if the fund's performance falls short of the benchmark return."

Exhibit 34-1 illustrates this concept. Since it is impossible to predict future returns, we can look at historical returns to provide insight into both income potential and volatility.

The straight dotted line assumes that a $50,000 fixed income annuity was purchased in 1974. This annuity was guaranteed to pay $375 a month as long as the person lived.

The solid line depicts a $50,000 purchase into a VIA using an S&P 500 index fund, which would have provided only $330 in the first month. However, 20 years later, the income from the variable annuity would be over $1,000 a month. By contrast, the fixed annuity still pays $375.

No one knows what the future will bring. The chart, however, shows you the monthly income from the VIA in both good times and bad. As you can see from the chart, from 1974 through 1980, you earned more from the fixed annuity than the VIA.

If we ever have another one of those periods, you could expect your VIAs to underpay the fixed annuity.

The lesson to be learned. If you are in your mid-70s and 80s, you might be better off with a fixed annuity or just a small position in a VIA. If you are in your early 60s and have just retired, time is on your side. You can invest in a VIA. If you have a few underperforming

Exhibit 34–1 Monthly Annuity Income

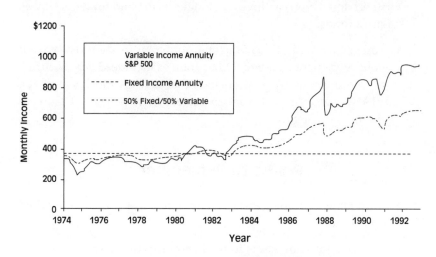

This example is hypothetical and your own results will vary.
Example assumes a 65-year-old person purchased a $50,000 income
annuity with a 10-year guarantee period. The variable income
annuity assumes a 5% benchmark was chosen. The numbers
assume the S&P 500 annuity portfolio had the same return as the
S&P 500 Index with the annuity charge and management fee
(1.28%) deducted from the results.

Source: Fidelity Investments Life Insurance Company

years, you have time for the stock market to recoup its losses and then
profit.

Bloch says that it might be a good idea to get a combination fixed
and variable income annuity for a couple of reasons.

- You will reduce the volatility of your income stream by diversifying.

- A combination fixed and VIA will give you more cash flow
  (monthly income) than a fixed annuity.

- You have investment flexibility. You can switch among different
  kinds of mutual funds as investment conditions change. Using
  market timing or just plain old common sense, you can move out

of stock funds when a bear market looms on the horizon. Or when interest rates rise, you can invest in a money fund. When rates trend down, you can invest in longer-term bond funds as well as stock funds.

- You get diversification of income. Your annuity should be part of your retirement nest-egg. Other sources include: Social Security, an IRA or company pension and other savings. Bloch says that a VIA should represent from 25 percent to 40 percent of your retirement nest egg.

Points to Remember

- Immediate annuities can be an alternative source of income when you retire.

- You give up your assets to the insurance company in return for lifetime income. You collect even if you live to be 200!

- You can get a fixed-rate payout from an immediate annuity.

- You can get a variable payout based on the performance of the underlying stock and bond funds.

- A fixed payout is a sure thing. But your income might fail to keep pace with inflation.

- With a variable payout, you can collect more if your stock and/ or bond funds have performed well. Your payouts may be more likely to keep pace with inflation.

- Stick with financially strong insurance companies.

Chapter 35

Other Annuity Strategies for Seniors and Juniors

Combination Annuities

If you are about to retire and want monthly income plus a tax deferred investment, you might consider buying a split funded or combination annuity. That means you buy an immediate annuity and a deferred annuity at the same time. You get income from the immediate annuity for a set period of time, say five or ten years. After the funds from the immediate annuity are depleted, payments come from the cash that has accumulated in the deferred annuity.

A split-funded annuity is for conservative investors who want to preserve their principal. You get income from the annuity and at the end of the term, you still have your initial investment which has been growing tax-deferred.

This type of annuity can be advantageous because it avoids this problem: Say you have $100,000 to invest and want monthly income. Here's what would happen if you put the entire $100,000 in an immediate annuity that pays you income for 10 years: (1) All the money would be used up over time; (2) you would have to pay income tax on that part of your immediate annuity payment that represents investment earnings;

273

and (3) you are also locked into the insurance company's rate for ten years. If rates rise, you lose potential income.

Here is how the split-funded annuity would work:

Judy, age 68, decided to do a split fund annuity. Her financial planner explained how she could get current income and a tax deferred investment at the same time. She invested $100,000.

Judy put $68,058 in a deferred variable annuity that paid 8 percent annual interest for five years. At the end of five years, the money will have grown to $100,000.

The remaining $31,942 was put into a five-year immediate annuity. At current rates, she receives $633 in income each month for five years. Only $99 a month—or 16 percent of that amount—is taxed. The rest is considered principal.

At the end of the five-year period, there is no money left in the immediate annuity. However, Judy still has $100,000; the $68,058 in the deferred annuity and $31,942 in tax deferred interest income.

A word to the wise. A combination annuity is not a magical way to invest. Inflation will erode the purchasing power of your second annuity. Even though you have the same dollar amount at the end of that time, you will have less purchasing power. You may be able to earn more after-tax interest income from a corporate bond fund or tax-free municipal bond fund.

Tax Reduction Strategy

If you purchased a deferred annuity before August 14, 1982, you don't have to pay income tax on cash withdrawals. They are treated as a return of principal. After that date, withdrawals are taxable if your investment has registered gains over the years.

So those lucky enough to have purchased deferred annuities before that magic date can put their accumulated cash to work free of charge.

- Most insurers let you withdraw 10 percent of your principal annually without having to pay a back-end surrender charge. In addition, if you are 59 1/2 years of age or older, you can withdraw money from your annuity without paying a 10 percent fine to the IRS.

- Then every year, invest the money you've withdrawn from your annuity into a stock fund for capital appreciation. Conservative investors can invest in a balanced fund or growth and income fund. More venturesome should consider a growth fund.

The benefits:

- Your investment grows tax-deferred in your annuity.

- The money taken out of the annuity is invested for growth, assuming you can invest for at least ten years.

- After ten years the tax-deferred gain in the annuity should replace your principal that you withdrew. What's more, you have dollar cost averaged into a growth stock fund for more than ten years.

You've created a new pool of money in the annuity from your original investment at the expense of good old Uncle Sam!

The drawback: This tactic assumes that you have made good mutual fund investments inside and outside of your annuity. If the stock funds underperform, this tactic could wind up as a mediocre performer.

There are a couple of other strategies you can use with your life insurance products that are worth mentioning. For example:

Buy Term Insurance and Invest the Difference

Buy term insurance and invest the difference in a mutual fund or annuity. This tactic enables you to purchase low-cost term insurance and invest the difference in premiums that you would pay for a cash value policy into a mutual fund or low-cost variable annuity.

A 40-year-old would pay an average of $277 per year for a 10-year level term policy that was renewed after the first 10 years. By contrast, annual whole life policy premiums would run about $1,500. But life insurance is a high-cost product. You pay mortality and expense charges and other fees. So that almost 3 percent may be taken out annually, in addition to commission.

As a result, pay $250 for the term coverage and invest $1,223 in a no-load mutual fund. To avoid taxes, put the mutual fund in your IRA or variable annuity.

You save whopping insurance commissions which can be as high as 100 percent of your first year's premium, plus the high cost of life insurance coverage.

Be advised. This tactic isn't for everyone. Historically, whole life insurance polices paid about 5 to 8 percent on cash values. That's tax free. So even after all the fees in commissions, you have to do some fancy investing to beat those returns.

If you buy term and invest the difference, you have to take on more risk to beat the tax-free returns on whole life insurance. You also have to have the discipline to invest the difference year in and year out, through rain and shine!

Life Insurance Policy Loans

Borrow against the cash value of your life insurance policy and invest in a growth stock fund or bond fund if you need income. You don't pay taxes on life insurance policy loans. The loan rate since the net interest cost is just 2 percent—your cash value earns 6 percent and the loan rate is 8 percent. What's more you don't have to pay back the policy loan. Be advised. Your death benefits are reduced by the amount of the loan outstanding. So if you need the coverage, don't play with the cash values.

Paying for Your Insurance Coverage

Use your bond fund or income stock fund dividends to pay for your life insurance coverage. This works well if you need additional term insurance coverage. Assuming you qualify for the insurance coverage that will cost you an average of $250 a year over 20 years—$175 in annual premiums over the first 10 years and $310 in annual premiums over the next 10 years.

Let's assume to be on the safe side your bond fund or income fund yields 6 percent and you plan to fund the insurance based on $310 in annual premiums. All you need to invest in the income-producing investment is about $5,200. That will give you the annual income you need to pay for your life insurance premiums.

Be advised. You are giving up some of your mutual fund returns to invest in term life insurance. So you don't have use of the money.

Term coverage usually ends at around age 70 to 75, it is not permanent coverage.

In addition, insurance companies have the right to raise premiums. When you buy term you should be shown the guaranteed rates they can charge as well as the current premium rate. If there is a death increase among insurance company policyholders, you could end up paying more for your coverage.

Points to Remember

- If you want monthly income, plus the ability to keep your principal intact, do a split-funded annuity.

- Those who purchased an annuity before 1982 can take out their principal without being taxed and invest in a well-managed stock fund. Meanwhile, the earnings in the annuity will grow to replace the principal you have withdrawn.

- You can get a loan from your life insurance policy tax-free and invest in a mutual fund for growth.

- Those who want to save money on their life insurance can buy term and invest the difference in mutual funds wrapped in an IRA or variable annuities

Chapter 36

Buying Mutual Funds on Margin

Buying mutual funds on margin should only be done by the most so-phisticated investor. It is a high-risk investment tactic that can lead to whopping gains or big losses.

You need to have an account with a discount stockbroker with a no transaction fee mutual fund program to buy funds on margin.

When you borrow on margin, you are using your stocks and bonds and other securities in the account as collateral. You can borrow up to 50 percent of the market value of your stocks, 70 percent of the market value of your corporate bonds and 90 percent of your government bonds for a loan. If the market value of your investments declines to prescribed limits, you will have to ante up more cash as collateral.

If you have a brokerage firm account, you can borrow at rates rang-ing from 6.5 percent to 8.5 percent.

In addition to getting a low-rate loan, there are other advantages to margin loans. For example:

- There are no set-up fees for a margin loan.

- You can tap the cash whenever you want.

- You can repay the loan in a lump sum or keep a running balance.

- Investment interest expense is tax deductible up to your net investment income.

But there are some big drawbacks to borrowing on margin. For example:

- A margin loan is a variable-rate loan which is pegged to the broker loan rate, which may be 1/4 percent to 1/2 percent below the prime rate. So if rates rise, you'll pay more loan interest.

- You also could be subject to a margin call. If the equity value or the value of the stock you own minus the amount you borrowed drops below 30 percent of the total market value of your securities, you will get a call from your broker the next day asking you to cough up enough money to bring the equity to total loan value back up to at least 30 percent. If you don't, your stockbroker will sell your stock and use the money to pay off part of your loan. You must pay back the rest of the principal and interest on the loan out of your pocket.

It works this way. The market value of your stock is $20,000 because you bought 1,000 shares of Widget Growth Fund at $20 a share. You need to borrow $10,000, so you put up half of the value of your stock as collateral in a margin loan. Your equity or market value less the loan is $10,000. The margin equals 50 percent—your equity, $10,000, divided by the market value of your stocks, or $20,000.

Say your fund's price drops to $14.28 per share due to bad news about the company's quarterly earnings report. The market value of your collateral is now worth $14,280. Your equity is worth $14,280 less the $10,000 loan or just $4,286. Now your margin stands at 30 percent or $4,286 divided by $14,280.

The 30 percent mark is where you can get into trouble. If the margin drops below 30 percent, you will get a margin call on the next business day. You will have to bring your margin level back up to 30 percent.

Say your fund hits $13 per share. Your margin level is now 23 percent or $3,000 divided by $13,000. To bring the margin back up to the 30 percent, you have to kick in an extra $3,900 (30 percent of $13,000).

The Advantages

Margin gives you what is called leverage. It works this way. Imagine that you borrow $10,000 to invest in a growth stock fund and the fund goes up $3,000 after six months. You sell for a $3,000 profit and pay back your loan, plus six months' interest. Your net profit is $2,045. Not bad for not putting any money up.

The Disadvantages

But the pendulum can swing the other way. Say the mutual fund lost 30 percent: You sell the fund for $7,000. You lost $3,000 on your investment and owe your broker $10,000 plus loan interest.

In the words of the immortal P.T. Barnum, "There is a sucker born every minute." Buying mutual funds on margin is a strategy that should be avoided.

Selling Mutual Funds Short

This is a margin tactic used to profit from a decline. Or it can be used as a hedge against losses. But be advised that selling a mutual fund short is also long on risk.

Boston-based Fidelity Investments and discount broker Jack White & Co. will let customers sell specific funds short. It is primarily done by speculators with sector funds—funds that invest in one specific industry.

Here is how it works:

Short selling is a form of betting against the house. The investor bets that the net asset value of such funds as Fidelity Select American Gold, Select Energy or Select Financial Services will go down. If the price decline occurs, the investor wins. If the price goes up instead, the investor loses.

In its actual mechanics, shorting is complicated. If you think a fund is in for a big decline, you arrange with your broker to borrow fund shares (margin) from another investor. The borrowed fund shares are then sold. The cash from the sale is held as collateral against the borrowed shares.

Later you purchase the same number of fund shares in the open market and use them to replace the borrowed shares. The broker returns your cash used as collateral less the cost of the repurchased shares.

Your profit—or loss—is the price received on the sale of the fund less the purchase price.

For example, say you sold the fund shares for $10. Then you bought shares at $7. Your profit is $3 per share.

Selling short can also be used as a hedge. Say you think a fund has a longer-term potential, but you want to protect yourself over the short-term. You could short the fund you already own. If the fund goes down in value, you have temporarily protected yourself.

You can also sell short against the box. Say you want to lock into a long-term capital gain, but you have to wait for a few days after the first of the new year to qualify: You must own a security for a year to qualify for the lower long-term capital gains tax.

So you sell short the stock you own. Then you unwind the position after the investment qualifies for a long-term capital gain status. That way if the underlying investment declined in value, you've profited from the short sale and hedged your bet.

A Word to the Wise

Most stockbrokers will recommend placing a stop-loss order on any investment that is shorted. This order instructs a broker to buy an equivalent amount of stock at a price somewhat higher than the price at which the stock was shorted. How much higher depends on the amount of risk you are willing to accept and the volatility of your stock fund. Moreover, a stop-loss order should be adjusted downward as the price of the stock fund falls to protect any profits that might have already been made. A stop loss order affords a modest degree of safety. But it does not protect against sudden price swings, which could hurdle over the price of the stop loss order.

Points to Remember

- You borrow money from your broker when you buy on margin.
- This should only be done by the most sophisticated investors.

- You can win big or lose big when you buy on margin.

- If you win, you pay back your loan and keep your profits.

- If you lose, you pay back your loan and lose money on the investment.

- You can borrow on margin from just a few discount brokers.

Chapter 37

Feeling Bearish?
Hedge Your Bets

Put Options on the Market

Want to protect your gains on $15,000 to $30,000 in mutual funds because you think there might be a stock market crash? You can hedge by taking out a "put" on the S&P 100 stock option index.

An option gives you the right to buy or sell a stock or index futures contract at an agreed-upon price. In the case of a put option, you have the right to sell at a set price at a specific time. So if the stock market drops to that specified price, you profit from the decline.

The stock index option lasts for a term of one month and can be purchased three months in advance. In addition, your losses are limited to the amount you paid for the option or what is known as the "premium."

It goes without saying that the older a bull market gets and the higher stocks rise, the greater the chance of a stock market correction. No one knows for sure when a correction will occur or how steep it will be. If we knew that we would all be millionaires and write books about "The Secrets of Stock Market Success."

Here is how it could work. You hedge your bets by taking out a put option, assuming you own a diversified stock fund that essentially tracks the stock market averages.

- If you buy a S&P 100 (OEX) put option, you have the right to sell about $31,000 worth of the S&P 100 stock indexes at any time until expiration date.

  For example, you could hypothetically buy a September put at a strike price of 310 for $600. If the S&P 100 drops to 280 at expiration, the put would be worth $3,000.

- If you are looking to protect yourself from a 5 percent decline in the value of your stock fund, you could buy at a strike price of 295. The September option would cost you $162.50 and would be worth $1,500 if the S&P drops to 280.

This tactic of buying S&P 100 index put options to offset losses in your common stock fund holdings should only be used by sophisticated investors who have options trading experience. Options are volatile investments that are traded mostly by institutional investors who use program trading to hedge or profit from changes in the market.

However, if the stock market drops and you've hedged your mutual fund holdings with a put option on the market, you will cover your losses.

What if things go the wrong way? If the stock market goes higher, your losses on the options are limited to your initial investment. So you will most likely offset your losses on the put options with the gains in the stock funds you own.

Futures Contracts on the Market

If you have a sizable sum, six figures, invest in equity funds, and are concerned about a crash, you have another hedging option. Again, this tactic is only for savvy investors.

You can short the S&P 500 Index futures contract. Stock index futures are quoted in terms of the actual S&P 500 index.

The futures which have a face value of 500 times the S&P 500 index, move in tandem with the market. In addition, unlike other types of futures contracts, you don't have to take delivery of the securities when the contract expires.

A hedge works this way: Say you own a portfolio of mutual funds worth $1.1 million. Assume the S&P futures contract is at 108.85.

The market looks like it could dive. So you short the S&P 500 futures index to protect your portfolio.

Each futures contract has a value of $54,425 or 500 x 108.85. So you sell 10 contracts. Three months later your portfolio value drops $82,860 to $1,017,174.

But your short position covered most of the decline in your equity fund portfolio.

Only for the Pros

Using put options and short futures contracts are not for the faint at heart. They should only be used by highly sophisticated investors or their professional money managers. You have to have the time and expertise to watch the markets, so you can close out your trades. That way you can hedge your investments.

Less Sophisticated Investors Hedge with Zero Coupon Bonds

The average mutual fund investor has less risky and complex options he or she can use to trim losses. A number of tactics were discussed earlier in the book, such as dollar cost averaging and numerous forms of portfolio rebalancing (see Chapters 10 and 16).

Another option that's frequently overlooked: You can invest in zero coupon Treasury bonds that will mature to a value equal to the principal you invested in mutual funds.

Zero coupon Treasury bonds sell at a discount to face value. When the bonds mature, you collect both principal and accumulated interest.

At current zero coupon bond rates, you could invest $221 and collect $1,000 in 20 years.

So say you had $100,000 invested in a growth stock fund, but you wanted to be sure that years down the road you had your principal:

You could invest $22,100 today in a 20-year zero coupon Treasury Bond and collect $100,000.

Of course there are problems with this tactic. First, in twenty years the purchasing power of the $100,000 will be less than it is today due to inflation. Second, it is highly unlikely that you will lose money in a well managed stock fund if you own it for twenty years.

Nevertheless, if you can sleep at night knowing you've covered your backside for catastrophe, then it's worth it. Consider the zero coupon bond as part of your portfolio. Over the long haul, you will probably be counting your profits in the stock fund, as well as the bond.

Chapter 38

Some Mutual Funds Go on Sale

Buying Closed-End Funds at a Discount

Some of the hottest sales in town are in the closed-end mutual fund market. Most of the time you can find some well-managed stock or bond funds for 80 to 90 cents on the dollar.

Buy recommendations pop up when closed-end fund stock prices pull back due to rising interest rates or sluggish economic growth here or abroad.

In 1990, diversified closed-end stock funds were selling at bargain prices following the recession. In 1992, bad news about the Japanese, Latin American and European stock markets created buying opportunities. When interest rates rose in 1994, bond and municipal bond funds were cheap.

How Closed-End Funds Work

Closed-end funds are a different kind mutual fund organism. The funds sell a fixed number of shares which are traded on the stock exchange. Unlike open-end funds, there is no cash moving in and out of the managed portfolio. When you invest in a closed-end mutual fund, you are essentially buying stock in a company that manages a portfolio of securities.

Investors have two stock prices to contend with when they invest in a closed-end fund—the price of the shares which are traded on the exchange and the net asset value (N.A.V.) of the portfolio of securities managed by the fund. As a result, when the stock price trades at a substantial discount to the net asset value, the fund is considered an attractive investment.

There are several kind of closed-end funds on the market, such as diversified U.S. stock funds, U.S. bond and municipal bond funds, diversified international stock funds and single country stock funds.

You can check closed-end fund share prices and their discounts in *The Wall Street Journal* or *Barron's* each week.

Historically, closed-end stock and bond funds tend to drift to discounts to net asset value for a couple of reasons. After the initial offering of the fund, stockbrokers don't push the funds and the stock price drops because of lack of investor interests. Thomas Herzfeld of Herzfeld Advisors, Miami, FL, notes that two years ago, a number of new single country overseas fund stock prices were bid up to 102 percent of their net asset values. Fueling the momentum was strong investor interest in overseas economies. But that didn't last long. There was a sell-off and single country funds sold at 12 percent discount to net asset value.

Closed-end fund discounts also change with the investment cycle. During the initial phases of a bull market, Herzfeld says, the discounts to N.A.V. are great. For example, after the October 1987 stock market crash, the average discount on closed-end stock funds stood at 16 percent. As the bull market rebounded during the middle stage, the discounts narrowed to 7 percent of net asset value and investors who sold earned 20 percent. At this writing, however, the average equity fund traded at just a 3 percent discount to N.A.V.

Seth Anderson, finance professor at the University of North Florida, Jacksonville, and author of *Closed-End Investment Companies: Issues and Answers*, published by Klewur Academic Publishers, Boston, also says the drift in closed-end fund share prices from premium to discount reflects the 7 percent mark-up by brokers on new offerings.

"After about 10 weeks, closed-end funds originally sold at premiums moved to discounts," Anderson says. "In part, it reflects the mark-up."

Discounts Create Buying Opportunities

The discounts make closed-end fund investing attractive because closed-end funds historically have outperformed open-end funds. Investors can buy a dollar's worth of solid-performing assets for less than a dollar.

For example, over the past ten years ending in June 1992, the net asset value of closed-end funds outperformed the net asset value of open-end funds by a wide margin. According to Morningstar, Inc. data, closed-end equity funds grew at an annual rate of 16.98 percent over the past ten years. By contrast, open-end equity funds grew at a 14.83 percent annual rate.

Closed-end bond funds also outpace open-end bond funds. Over the same period, closed-end bond funds grew at an annual rate of 14.04 percent, compared with 12.58 percent for open-end bond funds.

Catherine Gillis, editor of *Morningstar Closed-End Funds*, Chicago, cites two reasons for closed-end funds' superior performance to open-end funds. First, the funds stay fully invested compared with open-end funds which must hold cash to meet shareholder redemptions. The added risk of a full investment position enhances the return over the longer term. In addition, the discounts have a leveraging effect on portfolio performance similar to that of price-to-earnings ratios that are expanding.

Closed-End Fund Trading Strategy

You buy closed-end funds at a discount to their net asset values and wait for the discounts to narrow. The shrinking of the discounts, experts say, is what makes closed-end fund investing attractive.

"If you can buy a stock or bond fund at a 20 percent discount, do it," says Anderson of the University of North Florida. "I would own at least five funds. When the discounts shrink, you can register some profitable returns."

Anderson says his research, published in the fall 1986 issue of the *Journal of Portfolio Management*, shows that buying funds at a discount and holding the investments for a the long term can be profitable. Buying either closed-end stock or bond funds at 20 percent discount and selling when the discount to N.A.V. narrows to 10 percent, resulted in a 15 percent annual compound rate of return from 1965 through 1985.

Conversely, Anderson found that if you bought new offering funds during the mid-80s, you would have lost 10 percent as the funds drifted from a premium to discount because brokers stopped pushing the funds.

Anderson's research study examines eight different closed-end fund trading strategies. Each tactic was based on buying closed-end funds at a specific discount to their net asset values. The funds were sold when the discounts narrowed from 15 percent to 0 percent.

The study assumed $100,000 was invested proportionately among funds selling at discounts to their net asset values. Anderson used the weekly stock price, net asset value, and distribution data for 17 diversified and specialized closed-end funds over three periods: July 1965 to December 1969, January 1970 to December 1976, and January 1977 to August 1984.

When a fund's discount narrowed to the required amount, it was sold. Then a new fund was purchased based on the trading strategy requirements.

The study shows that all eight trading strategies outperformed the buy and hold on the S&P 500. The best-performing strategy, recorded over the three periods: Buy funds at a 20 percent discount and sell them when the discount narrows to 15 percent.

The results of this study, in Exhibit 38–1, demonstrate that the inefficiencies of the market for closed-end fund shares do indeed offer potential for profit.

Closed-end funds shouldn't be overlooked when putting together a mutual fund portfolio. However, due to the complex nature of this type of mutual fund, analysts say you have to shop for the best deals.

"First, stick with funds that have consistent long-term track records of performing as well as or better than the S&P 500," Anderson says. " Avoid funds with management fees above 75 basis points. Buy funds that trade at least 2,000 plus shares a day. Otherwise, you could get burned if someone sells a large block of a thinly-traded stocks."

There are several sources of information available on closed-end funds.

- Morningstar, Inc., Chicago (800/8765005) publishes *Closed-end Funds*, a monthly report that sells for $195 per year.

- Thomas J. Herzfeld Advisors Inc., Miami, (305/2711900) publishes an annual encyclopedia on closed-end funds for $140. Herzfeld Advisors also publishes a monthly newsletter which includes performance and portfolio holdings.

Exhibit 38–1 Study Results of Eight Trading Strategies

Buy at Discount from net Asset Value of:	Sell when Discount Narrows to:	Average Performance		
		July 1965 to Dec. 1969	Jan. 1969 to Dec. 1976	Jan. 1977 to Aug. 1984
5%	0%	114%	105%	260%
10	5	129	110	262
15	10	147	104	334
20	10	136	83	387
20	15	135	126	448
25	10	171	61	404
25	15	123	86	387
30	15	49	98	344
Buy and Hold (No Trading)		86	51	273
Standard & Poor's 500 Index		24	49	126

Source: *The Journal of Portfolio Management,* Seth Anderson, Fall 1986.

- International Publishing Corporation, Chicago, publishes *The Complete Guide To Closed-End Funds* by Frank Cappiello. The guide sells for $24.95.

- For a free report on closed-end funds call the Institute of Econometric Research, Ft. Lauderdale, Fl, (800/4229000).

- *The Value Line Investment Survey,* available at most public libraries, reports on a dozen closed-end funds.

- Two excellent books on closed-end funds include: *The Investors' Guide To Closed-End Funds,* published by McGraw Hill and available from Herzfeld Advisors; and *Closed-End Investment Companies: Issues and Answers,* by Seth Anderson and Jeffrey Born, published by Klewur Academic Publishers, Boston, MA.

Points to Remember

- Closed-end funds trade on the stock exchange.

- Closed-end funds have two prices—the stock price traded on the exchange and the net asset value of the portfolio the fund manages.

- You can profit by investing when the stock's price is less than the net asset value of the fund. You sell when the price difference shrinks.

- Trading closed-end funds is for speculative mutual fund investors.

Chapter 39

Dow Theory

Whether you are a conservative or highly aggressive investor, you can use the Dow Theory to estimate when the market is going into or out of a bull market.

This is not a sure fire way to make profits. But it's important to note that the Dow Theory called the stock market crashes of 1929 and 1987. It has also called a number of major bull markets in this century, including the great bull market of the 1980s.

The Dow Theory holds that stock prices represent current expectations about future business conditions. If stock prices are rising, it means investors are optimistic about the economy and business profitability. By contrast, when stock prices fall, investors are pessimistic.

It's more complicated than that. In 1885 Charles H. Dow, founder of *The Wall Street Journal,* began publishing the average price of 14 stocks meant to represent the direction of the whole market. A couple of years later he came up with the Dow Jones Industrial Average and what is today called the Dow Jones Transportation Average.

The Dow Theory looks at the trends in both averages. Dow said there are three trends in the market:

Trend 1. The most important trend is called primary market trend. This trend can last a few months to a few years.

Trend 2. This is secondary trend that moves in the opposite direction from the primary trend. This trend can last a few weeks to a few months. You may see several secondary trends occur during the period of a primary trend.

Typically a secondary reaction retraces 33 percent to 66 percent of the movement of the primary trend since the end of the last secondary reaction.

Trend 3. This is day-to-day changes in stock prices. But Mr. Dow was not concerned with the day-to-day movement in stock prices.

Reading a Bullish Trend

1. You see stock prices rally and break above their previous high marks. According to the theory, successive rallies of the averages penetrate previous highs

2. Rallies are followed by declines. But stock prices fail to fall below their previous lows.

3. The trend is confirmed when the Industrial and Transportation Averages both change direction. This should happen within 30 days. If it happens in just a few days, it is a stronger signal that there may be a trend change.

Reading a Bearish Trend

1. Stock prices fail to go above their previous highs.

2. When stock prices fall they go below their previous lows.

3. The trend is confirmed when Industrial and Transportation Averages both change direction. This should happen within 30 days. If it happens in just a few days, it is a stronger signal that there may be a trend change.

Spotting a Change in Market Direction

When the Dow Jones Industrial Average and the Dow Jones Transportation Average go in opposite directions, it's an indication that there may be a change in the direction of the trend in the stock market.

Exhibit 39–1 Dow Jones Averages

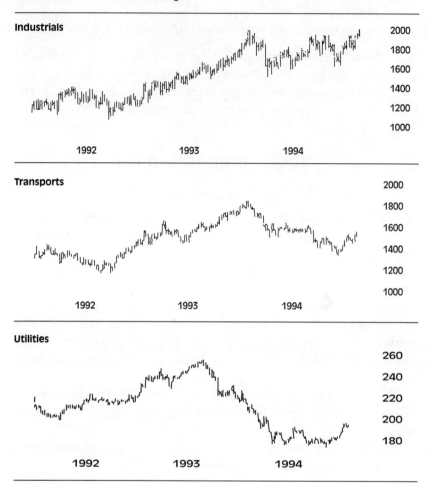

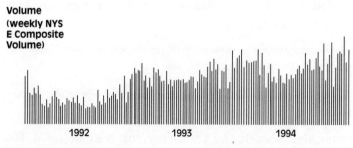

Source: *Dow Theory Forcasts*

1. There is a secondary reaction. Stock prices will fall, in the case of a bull market, and then go back up again. Or stock prices will rise, in the case of a bear market, only to go back down again.

2. Next there will be change in the primary trend. The price trend in the Dow Jones Industrial Average may change following a secondary reaction. But for this to occur, the Dow Jones Transportation Average has to go in the same direction.

Other Indicators Help Too

Volume

Technical analysts say that when you use the Dow Theory you should also look at the volume (the number of shares traded on the New York Stock Exchange).

Volume is the amount of money that is traded each day on the stock exchanges. It is an indication of the supply and demand for stocks.

The Dow theory says that during a bull market, volume increases with price advances and declines with price declines. In a major bear market it is the reverse. When the stock price trend is down, volume increases on price declines. Volume fizzles out, however, when stock prices rally.

Volume also has a habit of declining in advance of a major drop in stock prices. But it shoots back up in advance of a major stock market rally.

Needless to say, volume and changes in stock price go hand in hand. For example, here is what to look for:

- A increase in volume coupled with an upward move in stock prices is a good signal.

- But a volume increase when stock prices move lower is a bad signal.

- If volume decreases during a price drop, this is a good signal. The supply of stocks has declined.

- If volume decreases during a price rise, this is a bad signal. The demand for stocks is declining.

Advances versus Declines

The number of stocks advancing versus the number of stocks declining is a measure of breadth. It works this way:

1. You want to see a wide number of stocks advancing rather than declining.

2. If the advance/decline ratio is strong, it is a confirmation that the stock price trends is up.

3. When there are more declines than advances, it indicates the trend is down.

New Highs and New Lows

Watching the number of stocks that hit new highs or new lows may further confirm the changes in stock price trends based on the Dow Theory. It works this way:

1. If more stocks are reaching new highs compared to stock hitting new lows, it means the price trend is up.

2. When there are more new lows than highs, it indicates the trend is down.

Drawbacks

There is no free lunch. One of the major criticisms of Dow theory is that its signals can get you in and out of the markets too late—sometimes 20 to 25 percent after a peak or trough in the average has occurred.

One measure that has traditionally helped investors avoid entering the markets too late is the dividend yield of the Dow Jones Industrial Average. It works this way:

1. When the yield on the Industrial Average has fallen to 3 percent or below, history indicates that stock prices are far overvalued and a bear market is looming on the horizon.

2. A yield of 6 percent indicates that stock prices have hit bottom and a bull market looms on the horizon.

How the Dow Theory Has Performed

Charles Carlson, CFA and editor of the *Dow Theory Forecast* looked at the return on the S&P 500 as proxy for the return on the average common stock mutual fund. Buy and sell investment decisions were based, however, on anticipating changes in price trends on the Dow Jones Industrial and Dow Jones Transportation Averages. Carlson assumed the following to test the results of how the Dow Theory works as a mutual fund investment strategy.

- A $10,000 initial investment into a buy and hold on the S&P 500 versus a $10,000 investment using the Dow Theory to move between a stock fund and a money fund.

- The study was based on returns from August 20, 1982 through March 14, 1995.

- When he was out of stocks, he assumed the money earned 5 percent in a money fund.

- He did not reinvest dividends.

- The calculations did not take into account commissions and annual management fees.

The results of his study show that Dow Theory strategy outperformed the buy and hold tactic over the past 13 years.

A $10,000 investment grew to $43,600 based on the buy and hold.

By using the Dow Theory, the $10,000 investment grew to $55,700.

Exhibit 39–2 shows when the Dow Theory call the major trends in the market. The arrows pointing up indicate buy signals. The arrows pointing down indicate sell signals.

As you can see the Dow Theory got investors into the great bull market of the 1980s. Carlson called a buy on August 20, 1982.

The Dow Theory told investors to sell stocks on October 16, 1987, just three days before the Dow Jones Industrial Average plunged 500 points or 20 percent in value on October 19, 1987.

On December 7, 1987, the Dow Theory said to get back into stocks.

We held onto our stock fund until January 26, 1990, when we sold.

We reentered our stock fund on January 18, 1991 and have stayed put.

Exhibit 39–2 S&P 55 Index

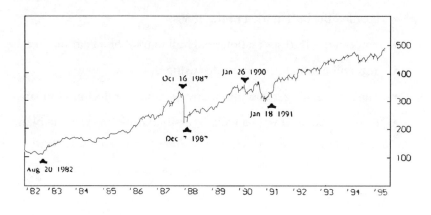

Source: *Dow Theory Forecast*

You May Need Help Reading the Tea Leaves

The Dow Theory can help you make investment decisions. However, it is not for the novice. It takes years of experience to execute trades based on the trends espoused by this system. Fortunately, there are a couple of newsletters that will show you what to do.

The *Dow Theory Forecast* (210/931-6480) advises investors whether to buy, sell or hold. The fund also recommends mutual funds. Over the past ten years the funds growth stock picks have grown at an annual rate of 12.8 percent.

The *Dow Theory Letters* (619/454-0481) also provides market timing advice based on the Dow Theory. This is one of the oldest investment newsletters in the business. Based on market timing or switching between stocks and cash, the newsletter registered a 11.3 percent annual return over the past 10 years.

Points to Remember

- Subscribe to a newsletter to follow the advice.

- The Dow Theory can help you spot long-term trends.

- It was successful in calling the stock market crash in 1929. It also called the bear markets in 1973–74 and 1987.

- It called the bull market of the 1980s.

- You can use it to spot a potential bull market or a bear market.

- You will not make many trades using the Dow Theory.

- The advice can get you into many advances or declines too late.

- It should be used with a well diversified investment game plan.

Chapter 40

Market Timing Mutual Funds

If you don't have the time to time the markets, you might consider investing in a fund that does it for you.

But don't expect to get rich quick by investing in a market timing mutual fund.

Mutual funds that use signals to move in and out of stocks and T-bills have failed to outperform the S&P 500 over the past several years.

Over five years, the S&P 500 Fund, a proxy for the market, gained 8.7 percent annually. The fistful of market timing funds did not do as well as a buy and hold on the market.

That is not to say these funds are bad deals. What they offer investors is asset protection, as well as upside potential. The portfolio managers who use market timing will get you out of stocks when the market looks like it is going lower. Maybe the market will not take a dive. But you are out and safe.

On the upside, you might get back into stocks at a higher price then when you exited. However if the trend is up, you are likely to profit.

There are several market timing funds to pick from. Some move in and out of individual stocks. Others buy mutual funds and switch between the funds and cash. They all have different systems that gauge the trends and the financial markets and tell when to move in and out of stocks. Most systems, however, are highly correlated to stock price, economic and interest rate trends.

There are several well-managed timing funds available. Here are a few that provide investors with low-risk returns in the equity markets, according to Morningstar.

Market Timing Growth Funds

- The Zweig Strategy A Fund (800/444-2706) invests in undervalued blue chip stocks with good earnings growth rates. The fund times the markets using strategies designed by Martin Zweig, a well-known Wall Street money manager. The fund goal is capital appreciation; however, it focuses on risk reduction. Market timing is based on models that look at economic indicators, cash flow and stock price momentum.

Morningstar Inc. reports that over the past three years, the fund has earned one of the lowest-risk ratings among growth stock funds. The fund moved heavily into cash in 1993 and remained in that position in 1994. As a result, the fund gained 1.14 percent in 1994, while the average growth fund lost 2 percent.

At the time of this writing, the fund was 60 percent in cash and 40 percent in stocks. Largest holdings include Micron Technology, Signet Banking, Citicorp, National Semiconductor and McDonnell Douglas.

The fund carries a 5.5 percent front-end load. The minimum initial and subsequent investments are $1,000.

For the period ending in 1994, the fund annually gained 1.14 percent over one year, 7.8 percent over three years and 8.6 percent over five years.

- Merriman Capital Appreciation Fund (800/423-4893). This is a no-load fund of funds. It invests in other growth stock mutual funds based on a proprietary market timing system developed by Paul Merriman, fund manager. Merriman looks at a number of technical, economic and fundamental indicators before he makes a move into stock funds. He says the system is highly correlated to the signals given by a 40-week moving average.

No-load funds are selected based on their current trends. Funds that have shown the strongest relative strength—performance that is better than their peers—are selected.

The fund carries a low-risk rating by the *Value Line Mutual Fund Survey*. And over the past five years, it has grown at an annual rate of 6.6 percent.

The fund is designed to reduce market risk. It invests in both U.S. and international stock funds as well as cash. In 1994, the fund lost no money it gained zero percent. By contrast, the average growth fund lost 2 percent.

At the time of this writing, the fund was about 70 percent in cash and 30 percent in stock funds.

The fund is no-load. The minimum and subsequent investment minimums are $1,000 and $100 respectively.

- Rightime Fund (800/242-1421). This is a no-load market timing fund that invests for growth and income in other mutual funds. The fund manager uses quantitative methods to determine if he should invest in stock funds or cash. The fund also can sell short in the futures market. The fund was in cash before the stock market crash of October 1987 and the plunge in 1990. In 1994, the fund was about 70 percent in cash. Now the fund is just 24 percent in cash.

Morningstar gives the fund a low-risk rating.

The fund gained almost 1 percent in 1994. By contrast, the average growth and income fund lost 2.1 percent. Over the past three years, the fund has grown at 4.3 and 8.3 percent annual rates, respectively.

The minimum initial investment is $2,000. Subsequent investments must be at least $100.

- Flex-funds Muirfield (800/325-3539) is a no-load fund that uses market timing and diversifies its investment among different types of mutual funds. The fund is classified as an asset-allocation fund.

The fund manager uses technical analysis—the evaluation of stock price movements and trends—to determine his stake in the stock market. In 1994, the fund was 100 percent in cash and gained 2.7 percent. By contrast, the average asset-allocation fund lost 3.2 percent.

This year the fund is about 40 percent invested in large and small company growth stock funds. The rest is invested in cash.

The minimum initial investment is $2,500. Subsequent investments must be at least $100.

Points to Remember

- Market timing funds analyze the trends in the financial markets and switch between stocks and cash.

- Some funds invest in individual stocks. Other funds invest in mutual funds.

- Market timing funds have been rated as low-risk funds by Morningstar.

- Don't expect to hit a home run with a market timing fund.

Appendix

Sources of Information

Mutual Fund Newsletters

Cabot's Mutual Fund Navigator
P.O. Box 3044
Salem, MA 01970
Focus: Market timing

The Chartist Mutual Fund Timer
P.O. Box 758
Seal Beach, CA 90740
Focus: Market timing

Dow Theory Forecasts
7412 Calumet Ave
Hammond, IN 46324
Focus: Overall market trends, plus mutual fund picks.

Fabians' Investment Resource
P.O. Box 2538
Huntington Beach, CA 92647
Focus: Market timing

Fidelity Insight
Mutual Fund Investors Association,
P.O. Box 9135
Wellesley Hills, MA 02181
Focus: News, education, and investment advice about Fidelity
Investments's funds

Fund Exchange
1200 Westlake Ave. N. Suite 700
Seattle, WA 98109
Focus: Market timing

Growth Fund Guide
Growth Fund Research Building
Box 6600
Rapid City, SD 57709
Focus: Long-term investment strategies and market timing

Hulbert Financial Digest
316 Commerce St.
Alexandria, VA 22314
Focus: Tracks the perfromance of newsletter recommendations

Income & Safety
The Institute for Econometric Research
2200 SW 10th Street
Deerfield Beach, FL 33442
Focus: Money fund and bond fund recommendations

InvesTech Mutual Fund Advisor
2472 Birch Glen
Whitefish, MT 59937
Focus: Market timing

MoneyLetter
290 Eliot St., P.O. Box 91004
Ashland, MA 01721

Mutual Fund Forecaster
The Institute for Econometric Research
2200 SW 10th Street
Deerfield Beach, FL 33442
Focus: Mutual fund forecasts and recomendations

Mutual Fund Investing
7811 Montrose Rd.
Potomac, MD 20854
Focus: Outook, advice, and market timing

Mutual Fund Letter
Investment Information Services, Inc.
680 North Lake Shore Dr., Suite 2038
Chicago, IL 60611

Mutual Fund Monthly
525 B Street
San Diego, CA 92101
Focus: Long term investment advice, model portfolios and education

Mutual Fund Strategist
P.O. Box 446
Burlington, VT 05402
Focus: Market timing

No Load Fund Analyst
300 Montgomery St., Suite 621
San Francisco, CA 94104
Focus: Long-term investing

No Load Fund Investor
P.O. Box 318
Irvington-on-Hudson, NY 10533
Focus: Long-term investing

No Load Fund X
235 Montgomery St., Suite 662
San Francisco, CA 94104
Focus: Best performing funds to buy

Personal Finance
1101 King Street, Suite 400
Alexandria, VA 22314
Focus: Personal finance and mutual fund advice

Sector Funds Newsletter
P.O. Box 270048
San Diego, CA 92198
Focus: Market timing with sector funds

Stockmarket Cycles
P.O. Box 6873
Santa Rosa, CA 95406
Focus: Market timing with mutual fund advice

Mutual Fund Performance Reports

CDA/Wiesenberger
1355 Piccard Drive
Rockville, MD 20850

Donoghue's Mutual Fund Almanac
290 Eliot St., P.O. Box 91004
Ashland, MA 01721

Handbook for No Load Investors
P.O. Box 318
Irvington-on-Hudson, NY 10533

Individual Investor's Guide to Low Load Mutual Funds
American Association of Individual Investors
625 North Michigan Ave.
Chicago, IL 60611

Lipper Analytical Services
74 Trinity Place
New York, NY 10006

Micropal
Investment Company Data
2600 72nd Street
DesMoines, IA 50322

Morningstar Mutual Funds
53 West Jackson Street, Suite 352
Chicago, IL 60604

Mutual Fund Encyclopedia
Investment Information Services, Inc.
680 North Lake Shore Dr., Suite 2038
Chicago, IL 60611

Value Line Mutual Fund Survey
711 Third Ave.
New York, NY 10017

Books

Anderson, Seth C., *Closed-End Investment Companies: Issues & Answers*, 1992, 160 pp.

Bogle, Kluwer, John C. *Bogle on Mutual Funds: New Perspectives for the Intelligent Investor.* Irwin Professional Publishing, 1993, 320 pp.

Boroson, Warren. *Keys to Investing in Mutual Funds.* 2nd ed. (Business Keys Ser.) Barron, 1991, 160 pp.

———*Mutual Fund Switch Strategies & Timing Tactics.* (Investor's Self-Teaching Seminar Ser.) Probus Publishing Co., 1991. 250 pp.

———*The Ultimate Mutual Fund Guide: Seventeen Experts Pick the 46 Top Funds You Should Own.* Probus Publishing Co. 1991, 235 pp.

Bouquet, Frank L. *Do-It-Yourself Mutual Fund Book*, 4th ed. (Illus.) Systems Co. 1990, 105 pp.

Brouwer, Kurt. *Kurt Brouwer's Guide to Mutual Funds: How to Invest with the Pros.* Wiley, 1990, 300 pp.

Christensen, Donald. *Surviving the Coming Mutual Fund Crisis 1994.* Little. 240 pp.

Clements, Jonathan. *Funding Your Future: The Only Guide to Mutual Funds You'll Ever Need.* Warner Books, 1993, 238 pp.

Coleman, David H. & Coleman, Aaron H., *How to Select Top-Performing Mutual Fund Investments.* International Information Associations, 1993, 205 pp.

Daugherty, Greg & Consumer Reports Books Editors. *The Consumer Reports Mutual Funds Book: Minimize Risk, Maximize Returns,* St. Martin's Press, 1994, 230 pp.

Donoghue, William E. & Tilling, Thomas. William E., *Donoghue's No-Load Mutual Fund Guide,* Bantam, 1985. 356 pp.

Dorf, Richard C., *The New Mutual Fund Investment Advisor: Everything You Need to Know about Investing in No-Loads,* Probus Publishing Co., 1991, 210 pp.

Fosback, Norman G., *Mutual Fund Buyer's Guide: Performing Ratings, Five Year Projections, Safety Ratings,* Probus Publishing Co., 1995, 450 pp.

Harvey, Louis S., *How to Save Smart: A Quick Simple Guide to Using Mutual Funds.* Dalbar Publishing, 1989. 105 pp.

Haslem, John A., *The Investor's Guide to Mutual Funds.* (Illus). Prentice Hall, 1988, 304 pp.

Hirsch, Michael, *The Mutual Fund Wealth Builder. A Mutual Fund Strategy That Won't Let You Down No Matter What the Market is Doing,* Harper Business Books, 1992. 224 pp.

Jacobs, Sheldon, *Sheldon Jacobs' Guide to Successful No-Load Fund Investing.* Irwin Professional Publishing, 1995.

Keller, Howard, *Right Mix: How to Pick Mutual Funds for Your Portfolio.* McGraw, 1993.

Lavine, Alan, *Getting Started in Mutual Funds,* Wiley, 1994, 216 pp.

Littauer, Stephen, *How to Buy Mutual Funds the Smart Way.* Dearborn Financial Publishing, 1995, 225 pp.

Merriman, Paul, *Investing for a Lifetime: Paul Merriman's Guide to Mutual Fund Strategies,* Irwin Professional Publishing, 1991, 291 pp.

Rugg, Donald D., *New Strategies for Mutual Fund Investing.* Irwin Professional Publishing., 1988, 300 pp.

Schabacker, Jay & Ross, Marjory, *Jay Schabacker's Winning in Mutual Funds,* AMACOM, 1994, 240 pp.

Taylor, John H., *Building Wealth with Mutual Funds,* Windsor, 1993, 210 pp.

Upton Robert C., Jr., *Mutual Funds Explained: The Basics & Beyond,* Probus Publishing Company, 1991, 150 pp.

Vujovich, Dian, *Straight Talk about Mutual Funds.* McGraw, 1995, 238 pp.

800 Directory of No Load Mutual Fund Families

AARP Funds   800/253-2277

Acorn Funds   800/922-6979

ASM Fund   800/445-2763

Aetena Mutual Funds   800—238-6263

Babson Funds   800/422-2766

The Benham Group   800/4-SAFETY

Berger Funds   800/329-0200

The Boston Company   800/225-5267

Bull and Bear Group   800/847-4200

Cadwell Funds   800/338-9477

Century Shares Trust   800/321-1928

Charles Schwab & Co. Inc.   800/435-4000

Dreyfus Corporation   800/782-6620

Eclipse Financial Asset Trust   800/872-2710

Eclipse Funds   800/872-2710

Evergreen Funds   800/235-0064

Fidelity Investments   800/523-1919

Founders Funds   800/525-2440

Fund Trust Funds   800/638-1896

Gabelli Funds   800/422-3554

Ivesco Funds Group   800/525-8085

Janus Group of Mutual Funds   800/525-8983

Jones & Babson, Inc   800/422-2766

The Kaufman Fund   800/666-6151

Lexington Group of Investment Companies   800/526-0057

Loomis Sayles Funds   800/633-3330

The Montgomery Funds   800/572-FUND

Neuberger & Berman Funds   800/877-9700

The Oakmarket Funds   800/625-6275

PBHG Funds   800/809-8008

SAFCO Mutual Funds   800/426-6730

Scudder Stevens & Clark   800/225-2470

Stratton Mutual Funds   800/634-5726

Strong Funds   800/999-2780

T. Rowe Price Associates   800/638-5660

Twentieth Century Mutual Funds   800/634-4113

USAA Investment Management Company   800/531-4327

Untied Services Funds   800/873-8637

Value Line Funds   800/223-0818

The Vanguard Group   800/662-2738

Glossary

Advance versus decline. The number of stocks going up versus the number going down. A way to spot price trends.

Adviser. An Investment professional hired by a mutual fund company to provide investment advice and management.

Annuitization. Taking fixed or variable payments from an immediate annuity.

Asset allocation. A systematic way of splitting up investments among different assets to get the best returns with the least amount of risk.

Automatic investment program. Many fund groups will electronically debit your checking account and automatically invest the money in the fund of your choice. Some funds have contractual plans and you agree to invest a regular amount for a specific time period.

Bond barbell. A bond investment strategy where you keep your investments at the short end and the long end, with nothing in between.

Bond fund. A mutual fund that invests in fixed income securities. Bond funds are distinguished by the type of securities (government or corporate, domestic or foreign) in the portfolio, the average maturity of securities and the credit quality of the issuer.

Bond ladder. Investing in bonds that mature in successive years.

Bottom fishing. Investing in underperforming mutual funds that are expected to rebound.

Broker dealer. The company that buys and sells fund shares to investors. Underwriters sell funds to broker dealers who in turn sell fund shares to investors.

Capital appreciation. The profit one makes on his or her investment. The increase in the value of the fund shares over time.

Capital gain. The profit a fund manager makes when he or she sells securities in the portfolio. The capital gain can also be the profit the shareholder realize when fund shares are sold. When a fund realizes capital gains, the gains are distributed to the shareholders of the fund either in cash or reinvestment of new shares.

Constant dollar investing. An investment strategy that requires rebalancing your stock fund periodically to a fixed dollar value.

Constant ratio investing. An investment strategy that requires keep a fixed percentage of your investment in different kinds of mutual funds. For example, a constant ratio of 1 means you keep 50 percent in stock funds and 50 percent in bond funds.

Contingent deferred sales charge. A back end redemption charge that declines over time. After a specified number of years the contingent deferred sales charge declines to zero. Then you can sell fund shares without paying a back end load.

Custodian bank. A bank responsible for custody of fund shares. Shareholders investments are kept in a separate account with a custodian.

Diversification. Splitting up your investments among different types of mutual funds to reduce risk. Mutual funds also diversify by holding a large number of issues in a wide variety of industries. That way bad news about a specific company will not hurt the overall performance of a fund.

Dividends. Mutual funds distribute short-term profits, stock dividends or interest income to shareholders in the form of cash or more shares.

Dollar cost averaging. Making regular investments in a fund. You always stay fully invested and buy more shares when a fund's price declines. Over time the average cost of your investment will hopefully be more than the current market price when you sell. Dollar cost averaging takes on many forms. By rebalancing a portfolio based on a constant dollar or constant ratio investment plan, you use a sophisticated form of dollar cost averaging.

Double Percentage Adjustment (DPA). DPA is a trend-following strategy that has you invest more when the fund is rising and selling more when the fund is declining.

Dow Theory. Developed by Charles Dow, this trading technique spots major trends in the stock market.

Duration. A number that tells you the percent gain or loss your bond or bond fund will experience if interest rates rise or fall 1 percent.

Diversification. Spreading your risk of losing by investing a number of assets.

Immediate annuity. An insurance product that pays you income for your lifetime.

Immunization. When your duration matches your holding period.

Indicator. A specific measure that is used to time the markets. Indicators can be economic or financial measures or trendlines.

Investment company. This is another name for a mutual fund company.

Investment objective. This is a description of a fund's investment plan. Funds that invest for growth look for capital appreciation. Some funds invest for both growth and income. Other funds invest in stocks for income. Other funds preserve capital by investing in both stocks and bonds. Fixed income funds invest for safety, liquidity, or yield.

Load. A sales charge that ranges from 8 1/2 percent to 2 percent. You may pay a front end load or a back end load on some funds.

Management fee. The fee a fund pays to its investment advisor.

Market timing. Using measures to tell you when to buy and sell mutual funds and switch into money funds.

Margin investing. You borrow against the value of your securities and invest in mutual funds.

Moving average. A market timing indicator that looks at the average price of a fund plotted over time. If the current fund price is above the moving average, it is an indication the fund could go higher. By contrast if the price is below the moving average, it is an indication the price could go lower.

Net Asset Value (NAV). This is the price of the fund per share net of fund expenses. Funds with sales loads have two share prices—the offering price which reflects NAV plus sales charges and the redemption price which is the NAV the broker charges to buy back the shares.

No load mutual fund. A fund free of sales charges.

Option. You can buy or sell (put) a fix amount of a security at a specified price within a specified time. Mutual fund investors can use S&P 100 options to hedge their mutual fund portfolio.

Portfolio rebalancing. A conservative investment strategy that requires keeping the same percentage mix of funds for a specific time period. After one year, for example, the investor would have to rebalance the portfolio to maintain the same mix of funds.

Prospectus. The legal document which investors are required to read before they invest. The prospectus lists important investment information about investment objectives, risks, fees and management of the fund. Upon request, a "statement of addition information" will be sent to prospective investors. This document provides investors with more detailed information about the fund, its risks and investment objectives.

Relative strength. How a fund performs in relation to another fund, group of funds or the market.

Retirement savings plans. If you have earned income you can put money into a Individual Retirement Account (IRA) or a company pension plan to save for your retirement. Most people can make tax deductible contributions to an IRA. If you have Keogh or 401(k) plans at work, you can also make tax deductible contributions.

Risks. Stock and bond mutual fund investors may face a number of risks including market risk, non-market risk, interest rate risk, credit risk, foreign currency risk and political risk.

Sales distribution fee. This is also know as a 12b-1 charge. This annual fee ranges from .25 percent to 1 percent of total assets in the fund. The money is used to pay for promotion and distribution of fund shares.

Security and Exchange Commission. The U.S. government agency that regulates mutual fund or investment companies under the Investment Company Act of 1940.

Short selling. A way to profit from a decline in the stock or bond market. You borrow securities from your broker and sell them to another investor. Then you buy them back at a lower price than your sale price. You can short stocks, bonds, mutual funds and stock futures.

Split funded annuity. A term for splitting an investment between a deferred and fixed annuity.

Systematic withdrawals. A fixed percentage of fund assets are paid out to investors who primarily want additional income. A retiree, for example, may have 4 percent of a fund paid out to him or her every year to supplement retirement income.

Tax free mutual funds Funds that invest in municipal bonds. Shareholders don't pay federal income taxes on municipal bond interest income. Investors in single state municipal bond funds don't pay local, state or federal taxes on the interest income from a municipal bond fund.

Transfer agent. A company hired by the mutual fund to keep shareholder account records.

Trustee. A person or organization that holds property for you when you sign a trust agreement. For example, when you have an IRA with a mutual fund group, the investment company acts as your trustee.

Value added gain. The extra return of your investment versus a benchmark.

Value averaging. A method of dollar cost averaging the requires an investor to always ensure that the fund will grow by a specific amount during a specific period of time. For example, every six months the fund investment should grow by $500. If the value increases by more than that, the investor takes excess profits and invests them in a money fund. By contrast, if the investment is down, the investor has to invest more money to keep the value rising.

Value ratio. A conservative investment tactic that requires you to become more conservative when the stock market is overvalued based on the price to dividend ratio. By contrast, when the market is undervalue, you become more aggressive.

Variable annuities. A tax-deferred insurance product that lets you invest in mutual funds.

Variable life insurance. Life insurance that lets you invest the cash value in mutual funds.

Volume. The amount of money changing hands on the stock exchange. It indicates supply and demand.

Whipsaw. A market timing term when you invest only to find your investment declining. Or when you sell only to find the market value of the investment increasing.

Yield curve. A chart that show you the yield of bonds ranging from three months to three years in maturity.

Index